SHELL SHOCKED

SHELL SHOCKED

My Life with the Turtles, Flo & Eddie, and Frank Zappa, etc. . . .

Howard Kaylan
with Jeff Tamarkin

An Imprint of Hal Leonard Corporation

Published in 2013 by Backbeat Books
An Imprint of Hal Leonard Corporation
7777 West Bluemound Road
Milwaukee, WI 53213

Trade Book Division Editorial Offices
33 Plymouth St., Montclair, NJ 07042

All photographs are from the author's collection unless otherwise noted.
Front cover illustration © 2013 Cal Schenkel

Printed in the United States of America

Library of Congress Cataloging-in-Publication Data

Kaylan, Howard.
    Shell shocked : my life with the Turtles, Flo and Eddie, and Frank Zappa, etc. / Howard Kaylan with Jeff Tamarkin.
        pages cm
    Includes index.
    ISBN 978-1-61780-846-3
1. Kaylan, Howard. 2. Rock musicians—United States—Biography. 3. Flo & Eddie (Musical group) 4. Turtles (Musical group) 5. Mothers of Invention. I. Tamarkin, Jeff. II. Title.
    ML420.K226A3 2012
    781.66092—dc23
    [B]
                                    2012044564

www.backbeatbooks.com

Contents

Foreword
Turtlefucking Mothers

BY PENN JILLETTE

Boston was a million miles from western Massachusetts. Boston was a hip city and had hip music, and my little dead factory town of Greenfield, Massachusetts, had jack shit. We had nothing. Getting a driver's license meant music, and music meant Zappa. I drove to Boston to see and hear Frank Zappa and the Mothers of Invention at the Music Hall, October 6, 1971. I was sixteen years old and I'd had my driver's license for one month. It was the first place I drove out of my hometown.

Chuck Berry was Frank's opening act. Chuck did "My Ding-a-Ling" and had the audience singing along with the winking, coy, cheesy, burlesque, little- (or maybe big-) dick joke. The idea wasn't sophisticated, and neither was the music. But Chuck Berry had been part of inventing rock 'n' roll, he played his ass off, and he was opening for Zappa. He had Zappa's imprimatur, so I was reverent regarding Chuck's dick jokes.

Then Zappa's band hit the stage, and there onstage with Frank and the real musicians were two of the Turtles. I couldn't tell, maybe the bass player was also a Turtle, but there was no doubt that the two main Turtles were out there in tie-dye and they were now Mothers. The show was the best show I'd ever seen, but I was a child then. It's still at the top of the list of best shows I've ever seen and I'm old now. Not as old as those guys in the Turtles but still wicked old. I've seen a lot of shows, but that Mothers show was life changing. It didn't just have the potential to change lives in the abstract—it changed my life in ways that can be measured.

❖ ❖ ❖

I learned to juggle when I was twelve years old, and I was funny. I formed a juggling group called the Toss-Ups ("We were originally called the throw-ups but we weren't as popular"—actual joke from the Toss-Ups' show). We were cheesy, vaudeville, and as showbizzy as we could be in a shitty little town. We entered talent shows and won them. We played nursing homes and even did a juggling and unicycle show at the jail where my dad was a guard. We were as close to showbiz as we could get and still live on the wrong side of the tracks from Centerville. It wasn't a real nice place to raise your kids.

Zappa wasn't doing cheesy juggling shows. He was a real musician. Yup, he had funny lyrics, but the music was serious and the funny was subversive and smart. It was Lenny Bruce humor—Zappa's wasn't the humor of the cheesy vaudeville jugglers I watched on *The Ed Sullivan Show*. I was scratching and clawing to get into showbiz and Zappa was in art. So what the fuck were those motherfucking Turtles doing on that stage? The Monkees had come into my family's living room, grabbed my mind, and led me right to Zappa. I had only a quick stop at the Beatles and the Velvets. Zappa was real art.

No one in my family had ever tried alcohol. I had the longest hair in my school and wore eye makeup, but I never even touched recreational drugs. I was an atheist. Zappa was atheist. Zappa made fun of people on drugs, and he was an artist. He was my hero. He was an artist. He was a smart, sober, funny artist. Wow.

What the fucking fuck were those Turtles doing onstage with Zappa? Zappa could do no wrong with me. When the back of his albums told me to listen to Edgard Varèse, I went to the library and listened to Varèse. When he demanded I read "In the Penal Colony" by Franz Kafka before listening to a side of a record, I turned off my mom's record player and rode my bike back to the library and read that story before I listened to the piece. Zappa was teaching me art and now he had fucking Turtles onstage. In my fast trip from the Monkees to the Mothers I didn't stop at the Turtles for a moment. I heard "Happy Together" on the radio, but it didn't mean jack shit to me. Weren't those the same pussies that made my other real artist, Dylan, sound singsongy?

❖ ❖ ❖

Boston 1971: The most important concert of my life and there were the Turtle guys onstage with the man who had taught me to love twentieth-century classical music and real literature. And one of the Turtle guys wasn't rock 'n' roll skinny like I wasn't rock 'n' roll skinny, and he had hair just like mine, long but not hip. Children in my school had said I looked like the fat guy in the Turtles with the long hair and glasses, and there he was, with the other Turtle guy, both singing their asses off with Frank Fucking Zappa. Did this mean I had to like these Turtles?

Years later, brilliant voice actor Billy West would say, "There's one show business." I didn't have those words for it then, but Frank Zappa, Howard Kaylan, and Mark Volman taught me that there was only one showbiz that night in Boston. These lightweights were onstage with the heavyweights and they were doing the best show I would ever see. Their voices were beautiful. The music was hard, and they were still having fun. Some of the jokes were very serious and over my head (what the fuck was going on singing in German about a sofa?). Some of the jokes were just stupid jock cock jokes that I would sneer at in my school. It was all mixed together. It was a show that was smart and stupid, heavy and light, beautiful and more beautiful.

They were doing a show with cheesy jokes, and it was also art. How could that be? It wasn't stuffy—it was funny, entertaining, showbiz, vaudeville, and fun, and it still had content. Those turtlefucking Mothers with those motherfucking Turtles.

They did "Happy Together" in this Mothers show, and it was a really good song. And the music was more sophisticated than I had ever thought. Those perfect AM voices doing art. I loved hearing something I knew from the radio in a smarty-pants show. Were they making fun of it? Yes. Were they also playing it for real? Yes. Were they playing it because it was fun? Yes. My view of showbiz and art came together. It was that moment, during that show in Boston, that the line between showbiz and art was erased for me. If Turtles could be Mothers, maybe a hick juggler could speak his heart in a magic show.

I drove back to Greenfield and now did my best to look as much like the Phlorescent Leech as I could. When people said, "You look like that guy," I said, "Yeah, the guy in the Turtles, he's also in the Mothers now." I was proud of being in showbiz and I was proud of how I looked, and I knew what I wanted to do in life. That's a lot to learn from a couple of Turtles.

I went back and explored the Turtles' music that I had dismissed. They had that California sound, but there was a wink. "Call you up, invest a dime"; "how is the weather?"; "pride and joy, et cetera." And "Happy Together" wasn't as foursquare as the Beach Boys would have played it. It didn't swing like Miles, but at least they dotted the eighth note. There was fucking hip and smart all over this band; once I looked, those fucking Turtles had some depth along with the pop and the funny.

◆ ◆ ◆

I followed Flo and Eddie and they taught me how to live. Each of them had a lifelong artistic showbiz partner, and they showed up anywhere they wanted. They could act, write, sing, do radio, cartoons—there was one showbiz and they were in all of it, and turtlefucker, I was going to be in all of it too. If a couple of goofballs from an AM band could make art with Zappa, a juggler/magician/comedian could do goofy shows with his lifelong artistic partner and feel like it was art. A magic show isn't art? Fuck you, those Turtles are artists! Penn and Teller could try to be artists. Penn and Teller played the Music Hall in Boston, and we've been back there many times. I was in showbiz enough to use the dressing room used by those turtlefucking *Mothers*.

I became friends with Howard and he sat backstage with us and told us stories. I've repeated those stories. I treasure those stories, and they're in this book. Reading this book is like sitting backstage in the Penn and Teller Monkey Room and hearing stories, with all Teller's stupid stories about teaching Latin cut out. This book is way better than hanging out backstage with us. You're about to read Howard's Turtles, Mothers, *and* Flo and Eddie stories without the Penn and Teller stories.

Howard knows I've never done any drugs, but he also knows I love hearing stories about drugs. I'm not sure I would have wanted to hang with him when he was high, but I sure like hearing about it all now that he's sober. This book will teach you that Hendrix was a *Three Stooges* fan, and you wicked need to know that.

And who doesn't love the groupie stories? Howard and I may have disagreed about drugs, but we never disagreed about sex.

This is a great book. By a cheesy vaudeville showbiz entertainer.

And it's art, and don't you fucking forget it!

Acknowledgments

HOWARD KAYLAN

This life was molded by Michelle Dibble Kaylan; Mr. Robert Wood; Mark Volman; Sid and Sally Kaplan; Allan Kaplan; George Carlin; Evan Cohen; Mel Carter; Paula Guran; John Shirley; Joe Stefko and Therese DePrez; Herb, Martin, and Evan Cohen; Penn Jillette; Alexandra Kaylan; Emily and Max Rothenberg; Poochifer Robin Jub-Jub Dibble Kaylan; Ernie Kovacs; Pickle Suzanne Kaylan; Claudette Granahan; the Kingston Trio; Soupy Sales; Frank Zappa; Marc and June Bolan; Jerry Lewis; Harry Nilsson; all the girls; all the dealers I still owe; Dick Clark; Tom Smothers; Scott Walker; Mr. Art Ferguson; Jeff Tamarkin, Janet Rosen, and Sheree Bykofsky; Mike Edison and Bernadette Malavarca; Louis Prima and Keely Smith; Howard Stern; Alan Gordon; Rev. Bleepo Abernathy; LeeLoo Nightmare Kitty; Sid Caesar; Green Buddah Patient Exchange; Stan Freberg; Sam and Dave; Mrs. Koontz; Miss Gretenberg; Mr. Oliveri; Harlan Ellison; Mary Tyler Moore; Ken Barnes; Dubdie the Matriarch; and Harold Bronson.

JEFF TAMARKIN

Jeff Tamarkin is greatly indebted to Howard Kaylan; Michelle Dibble Kaylan; Sheree Bykofsky; Janet Rosen; Mike Edison; Bernadette Malavarca; Gert Tamarkin; Dave Tamarkin; Lydia Sherwood; Larry Rossman; and Caroline Leavitt and Max Tamarkin, my reasons for everything I do.

But First:
A Rock Group Inside
of Enemy Territory

I was snorting coke on Abraham Lincoln's desk in the White House. Yes, *that* Abraham Lincoln and *that* White House. A bunch of hairy peacenik dopers from California though we were, it seems that Tricia Nixon, daughter of Tricky Dick himself, was a fan of the Turtles and had requested our presence. Our first instinct: You've got to be kidding! No way in hell!

Yet here we were, our noses vacuuming lines off the surface of Honest Abe's very own work space.

❖ ❖ ❖

We had gone through several managers during the past five years and been on the charts far more often than anyone would ever have guessed, considering that we were the only ones looking out for us, and that White Whale Records wasn't much of a label.

There had been the folk-rock years, and we had been lucky enough to score a few big hits; we were among the earliest children of Bob Dylan, putting our cover version of his tune "It Ain't Me Babe" into the Top Ten.

Then we had become the good-time-music boys, influenced by the Lovin' Spoonful and determined not to protest anything. We'd made it to number one with a song that's still recognized today as one of the classic rock 'n' roll love songs of all time. "Happy Together," indeed.

And, now, finally, we had engineered our own success with "Elenore," our first self-penned Top Ten record, and "You Showed Me," which we had changed from a Beatlesque rocker into a lush ballad.

We were lucky and we knew it.

Of course, now we had the big-time management to prove it.

Gone were the friends of friends—we'd realized that we really weren't in any position to manage ourselves—and hello to the new Superstar Management Team.

We had been courted, successfully, by Ron DeBlasio and Jeff Wald, who were, at the time, top reps for the Campbell-Silver-Cosby Corporation.

That's right—Bill Cosby.

Mister Pudding Pops.

Fat Freaking Albert.

Bill, his own self, was a full partner in the firm that represented him.

And us.

And others.

And his sweaters.

And he was the number one comic in America.

Across the hall was the office of the appropriately named Artie Mogul, who ran the in-house record company, Tetragrammaton, home to Deep Purple and more.

Of course, he had nothing to do with us. Neither did Mr. Cosby, but his name promised to open a lot of doors in Hollywood, and that was exactly what we needed.

But what, I asked, could these guys bring to the table for a band that had been around the block and, hypothetically, overstayed their welcome?

We didn't have to wait long to find out.

We had heard, through the grapevine, that the Turtles were Tricia's favorite band, and we'd all had a good chuckle over that.

Old Man Nixon was the creepiest Dick of his generation, the least popular president among the under-thirty crowd that had ever been, and a killer of our young men and women, as far as we were concerned.

We were deeply antiwar and deeply self-conscious. We weren't Nix-onites, that's for sure. We were everything he stood against.

So when the hand-engraved invitations to perform at Tricia's coming-out party arrived at the Cosby office, we were none too thrilled. In fact, we flat-out refused to play.

They started to freak out.

"What do you mean, you refuse to play?! Who the hell do you think you are?! This isn't a political thing. It's like a goddamn royal proclamation, you idiots! You play the White House because you're an American!"

Blah, blah, blah . . .

They shamed us into it.

Not only that, but to add insult to injury, management now was requesting that we each go out and buy a classy new suit. Can't play for the president looking like the sewer rats that you really are.

Perfect. There it was, again.

Too bad Johny Barbata wasn't the drummer in the band anymore. He'd have loved the sight of us clumsily trying on the very Brioni suits that he'd been trying to get us to wear for three and a half years.

Now we had each bought one. Talk about fish out of water.

❖ ❖ ❖

Came the big day, May 10, 1969, we flew into Washington, DC, on the taxpayers' dollar. There, we were met by five separate cars, each with a driver, all flying the American flag, and taken directly to the White House. Once there, we discovered that the Secret Service had dossiers on each of us. They kept us in a holding lounge while going through our intimate details individually.

After we had all been cleared, it was time to unload the equipment that we had brought with us all the way from L.A.

But we didn't do the unloading. Instead, the Secret Service guys did. And they didn't know the first thing about large equipment cases. So as they began to unload the trap case (the large case that holds the snare drum, percussion goodies, and miscellaneous items) from the drum set, they tipped it to one side and unknowingly triggered the tiny switch on the electric metronome/tuner that we always carried with us.

". . . tick . . . tick . . . tick."

Out came the guns.

"Up against the wall!"

Oh, we went there. Up against that wall it was as they carted off our little black box. We stood there, a rock group inside enemy territory, the Nixon White House, looking through the crosshairs from the wrong direction. Guys in hazmat suits were brought in to deal with our little plastic tuner, and their freak-out escalated yet another notch when someone hit the tuning switch and the 440-cycle A tone started shrieking from the metronome.

The term *shitting a brick* comes to mind.

My knees were shaking and the sweat was rolling down my face. And it was only May—the fucking cherry blossoms were blooming on America's Lawn and I was about to be shot for treason.

We looked at each other and we looked at them. It was like a Peckinpah movie.

I could almost hear the feds mumbling to each other as they got to work, but I couldn't understand what they were saying. I only perceived a gushing in my ears, as though I were underwater. The only other sound I recall was my way-too-fast heartbeat.

That little fog started to set in, the one where you think you might just pass out.

Now the guns were cocked and ready to fire. They schlepped off our little plastic box for further examination. When they returned it ten minutes later, they had pried the faceplate off and the box was dripping water.

"It's a metronome," they declared. Good work, guys.

That was the longest ten minutes of my life.

Many months later, we received a check from the White House for seventeen dollars.

◆ ◆ ◆

The party itself was pretty crazy. I heard reports from a couple of the band members who actually went up to the roof of the White House with some CIA guys to smoke a joint before sound check, but I wasn't part of that bunch. (In fact, I actually read it in one particular Turtle's autobiography. Someone had to test those mics, and I guess that's what I was doing.)

However, later, when we returned to do the show, we were given President Lincoln's library to use as our dressing room. Unbelievable! In fact, we were told that the entire first floor was okay for us to explore: Just as long as we didn't enter the private quarters, everyone on staff was to let us have the run of the place. And we did. It was amazing. We were loaded—high from smoking pot back at the hotel and a wee bit tipsy from all the French Champagne that was being freely dispensed—and we were roaming around the most important home in America unsupervised.

One member of our crew still had a few tricks up his sleeve, however, and not only did I get to take a few precious tokes of his mystery stash before the show started, but we were able to actually lay out lines of coke on Mr. Lincoln's desk. As the powder flew up my nose, I wondered if this was exactly what the founding fathers had in mind. Land of the Free, indeed. Well, I felt free and on top of the world.

Now I think, Jeez, they *must* have had cameras, but back then, the thought never crossed my mind.

The show was wonderful. Hey, what can I say? We were always a great band. And although our other vocalist, my career-long partner Mark Volman, had a few balance issues—he fell off the stage a few times, much to the amusement of all present—the actual concert was a huge success. Just looking around the room at the dignitaries, the emissaries, and the luminaries was like LSD to a stoner Democrat like me. That made things even more fun. I was smiling from ear to ear. Even the Temptations, who were also on the bill, were drinking and singing and laughing right along with us.

And we were funny. We didn't hold back just because of the venue. Hell, I thought, we've been thrown out of better places than this! But, of course, we hadn't been. Jokes at America's expense . . . literally.

Right after the show, Mark decided to hit on Luci Baines Johnson, former president Lyndon Baines Johnson's daughter, which would have been questionable under any circumstances, but was especially so with her husband, Pat Nugent, growling at Mark from inches away. Spittle was flying. I'm not exactly sure how peace was restored between them, but man, there was an almost incident that was happily avoided. History would have loved that one.

Tricia and her friends seemed to love us. Most of her acquaintances were college kids and, probably unbeknownst to her, were busy spending their evening passing out subversive SDS flyers to the crowd.

Much to our relief, Tricky Dick was off on a foreign mission somewhere, getting our troops killed, and so he never made an appearance. I've always been thankful for that. I am absolutely positive, considering our states of mind that evening, that I—or some other equally messed-up Turtle—would have given him an earful of contempt and probably would have ended up in Gitmo.

snap

They took some photos. One shows five shaggy guys, one psychedelic road manager, Ron DeBlasio, Jeff Wald and his wife, the singer Helen "I Am Woman" Reddy, and there in the center, looking like a Hummel fig-urine in white, Tricia Nixon herself. Another depicts only four shaggy guys—all of the Turtles except me—and Tricia. That one made it to the cover of *Parade* magazine. Read into my missing visage what you will. Was I up to something subversive? I wish I could say I was, but I was probably just exploring the presidential restroom or something. It all kind of makes you proud to be an American, though, doesn't it?

How in the world had I gotten here?

ONE

Howard Kaylan, with a Y

I wasn't born at home. That would have been too easy. Seems like even the moment of birth cosmically had me out on the road. Not far from home, mind you, but in postwar New York City, the distance between boroughs must have seemed enormous. Sid and Sally Kaplan lived in Brooklyn. He was first-generation and born there. Grandpa was Isadore Kaplinsky, who came from the old country and proudly joined the union as a plasterer. My grandmother on my dad's side had been gone for many years and Ike, as we called him, was on his second wife when he entered my memory.

They lived on Tapscott Avenue, right above one of those wonderful old candy stores where you could buy a foot of paper dots for a penny and get a two-cents plain, maybe with a spritz—seltzer water with some chocolate syrup—at the soda fountain if you were lucky.

Mom was born Sarah Berlinsky in Russia and dragged to this country during a very famous revolution. Her mother and father had both died in the war, and her sisters raised little Sarah Berlin—as her name became upon entering the United States, before everyone started calling her Sally—in Providence, Rhode Island. She traveled to Manhattan to attend beauty school but wound up in a police uniform keeping the NYC streets safe in wartime as part of something called the City Patrol. There she met my dad, just back from England and Germany, and set up house in a government-sponsored cardboard community in Brooklyn called the

Linden Houses. Enter Howard Lawrence Kaplan on June 22, 1947—born in the Bronx because my parents were visiting my aunt at the time. Little Allan was to follow in three years' time, but hey, this isn't his book.

My earliest childhood recollections are of those Linden Houses, little boxes in the suburbs filled with knickknacks, each with its own little yard and the illusion of privacy for people who had grown up in the concrete jungle with little hope of a sky view. I remember my dad walking me to the bathroom to do my business like a man—I must have been two or three—and me trying to hurry the process and getting piss all over the bathroom and myself in a mad rush to see the fire engines going by.

My other most prominent childhood memories came courtesy of television. We were the first in the entire development to have a set, and she was a honey: a round-screen, seven-inch black-and-white console that would become my window to the future. I would spend hours on end with my only true friends: Howdy Doody, Uncle Miltie, Arthur Godfrey and Kukla, Fran and Ollie, the denizens of the eponymous puppet show. Another show I loved was *Super Circus*, with a tall blond circus lady in a sparkling one-piece bodysuit. She was hot! I would also watch whatever my parents turned on, without question, even if it was *Meet the Press*, and my television habits have hardly changed over these many years. These days, locked in a smoky hotel room, that very same "take what you can get" philosophy has gotten me through some pretty barren nights—this was my preschool.

There was a little girl my age who lived next door. I think her name was Connie. My mom called her my "little girlfriend," but my only recollections of her are the photos that my dad took of the two of us riding my tricycle. I don't think that I had any other friends. Come to think of it, the two constant themes of my early youth, media viewing and hanging with a chick, are the overriding threads that still hold my life together.

Sid and Sally didn't have a car. Of course, if you live in New York City, even today, you are a moron to own one. We were pedestrians and proud of it. Or they were. I got to be pushed around in my dinky little stroller with the food tray in front of my face. And they all wondered why little Howie seemed to be gaining weight. It's not like the pop-down tray was filled with apples or grapes. No, instead, my father would refrigerate these wonderful confections known as Bonomo Turkish Taffy bars. He'd let the candy harden in the fridge overnight and then smash it into

Howie-size pieces and place it in my tray, ostensibly to keep me placated during our strolls through the five boroughs.

Bridges were my mother's passion and we must have lived very close to either the Manhattan or the Brooklyn Bridge—I never did know which one—because we were always rolling into the city. As we passed the humongous hangar where the Goodyear blimp was tethered, I would stare in disbelief at the spacecraft hovering above my world and chew my taffy religiously. Or we'd go to Coney Island, the legendary amusement park where I was to record my very first song.

I don't recall learning this song, but I still have the scratchy proof that I did. It cost twenty-five cents to step into the tiny recording booth. The red light would go on and you had about two minutes to transcribe your message or tune. Then, just like with the photo booths that still exist in arcades and movie theaters, you would wait outside for your vinyl prize to drop out of the slot. The smell was exciting to me. Hot vinyl. And you could watch your disc being made and see threads of plastic falling into the bin below as your voice was carved into the grooves. My first record was of a song called "Very Good Advice" from Disney's *Alice in Wonderland*. It's still a great song and, not to brag, but my little effort wasn't half-bad. A few weeks later, we returned to Coney Island for my second session. This time it was a kid's song called "I Am a Fine Musician." Several years ago, my seven-year-old grandson, Max, had to learn the same song for school. Talk about a rush.

I would take these little nuggets of plastic home and play them in my room on the tiny record player till the grooves were smooth and there were no sounds but that amazing hiss and my little voice, but in by mind, I was making a record just like the ones my parents owned. The new plastic smelled wonderful. I would write my name across the paper label—*Howard Kaylan*, with a *y*.

My parents thought I was stupid or, at best, a bad speller. But for some reason, even at that very early age, I knew that I was a Kaylan. Whatever that was. I had no reason for it. I was a really little kid and I had never heard that name before, but it was already defining me.

❖ ❖ ❖

It was the early 1950s. My mother had given up her beauty shop dreams and the City Patrol was disbanded after the war ended. She had become a nuclear-age housewife and Sid was repairing televisions for Sylvania when opportunity knocked and rocked my little boat. There was this job, it seemed. And the pay was great. It wasn't repairing, it was creating, and my father was as excited as I'd ever seen him.

One day, my mom got fat and the next day, as I recall, I had a brother. It got very loud around our little house, and eventually even my mom had to admit that we had outgrown our surroundings. The good news was that I finally had someone to beat up. Then one day my dad got the job offer he had been waiting for since returning from Europe. The bad news, and you could see it on my mother's face, was that the offer had come from an unlikely geographic region known as Utica, New York. Upstate. Cold. Away from everything and everyone they knew. And we'd need a car, too.

TWO

Music Juice and the Sounds of Pounds

When I think about Utica I think gray. That's the color of the sky, the buildings, and most of the people. Okay, I was very young, but a kid's first impressions are what he or she takes away to file in the dusty cardboard boxes of adult memory. We moved into the upstairs of a gray house on Genesee Street. Dad drove his new pride and joy, a black 1947 slope-backed Chevy, to his daily job as an electrical technician at General Electric. I have no idea what he actually did there, except that it brought him little joy.

Mom would walk me to school in the mornings and we lived close enough that I could walk back all by myself. Customarily dressed in flannel shirts and corduroy pants with the cuffs rolled up, I made a zippery sort of noise as I shuffled down the block. On one miserable occasion, I just wasn't fast enough, and despite all my bouncing and grabbing, I found myself blocks away from the big gray house with a lapful of wet. Oh, man. I was only five, but that hot-faced moment of embarrassment was fated to become a feeling that I would butt heads with throughout my life.

One day, Miss Daisy's kindergarten class at Utica Elementary took a field trip.

Both parents signed my permission slip allowing me to accompany the seventy-five-year-old teacher and the rest of the class on a walk—not a bus ride, mind you—to the nearby Wonder Bread and Hostess cake factory. To a pudgy six-year-old, not even Coney Island held such promise. The factory was huge, like four or five gigantic blimp hangars all connected. We soaked up the sights and smells hungrily and were all treated to hot slices of bleached white bread and, in another hangar, got samples of Twinkies and Sno Balls. I peeled off the idiot coconut marshmallow crap and flung it across the room. I've always taken my cream-filled doughballs straight—like a man, damn it! And the elderly Miss Daisy, smelling of lavender and mothballs, glowed with a prideful smile at our youthful antics.

With full tummies and pockets bulging with cellophane-wrapped samples, the happy class was led out of the bakery's doors and headed, ostensibly, back to school. Only we weren't walking in the right direction—even I knew that. Miss Daisy walked all thirty of us through a residential district and into one of Utica's prominent and well-kept cemeteries. There were frightened whispers and some of the girls started crying. Miss Daisy grouped us all around one particular headstone and addressed the class brightly.

"Children," she said, "I'd like you to meet my husband. Darling, here are the children I was telling you about. Aren't they special?"

We were freaking.

"Boys and girls, some day, after you have all lived your little lives, you too will be here with my husband and me, under the ground, where it's cool and quiet and no one can bother you anymore. It's a wonderful place, children. Let us all pray that we see each other in heaven."

Miss Daisy didn't return to school the next day. We never saw her again. Evidently, more than a few kids had told their parents about the bakery trip and more than a few calls were made to the school. Farewell, old lady. I felt bad for her, but she was old. Really old. And it was 1953.

❖ ❖ ❖

The following year, Dad finally had the down-payment money together for the purchase of our first home. Of course, the price we paid for our own piece of the pie was a steep one. The washhouse cost $10,000, but it wasn't in Utica, exactly. It was in a suburb of Utica. Who knew that Utica had suburbs? This wide spot on the two-lane highway was called Marcy. Our new house was a two-bedroom ranch with its own garage connected by a breezeway, one of my mother's favorite words. It sat about a hundred yards back off Cavanaugh Road and backed onto a working farm, replete with cows, chickens, and the traditional red barn with the obligatory childhood hayloft. Only a double strand of barbed wire separated my brother and me from myriad adventures.

Dad built us the best tree house in the world. There, we could read comics, tease the cows, drink cocoa, and plan our futures. All we needed to do was shimmy under the electrified fence into our own magic kingdom. We chased and tipped the cows and had Robin Hood fights in the sweet-smelling hayloft. On the roof of the barn were faded letters spelling out Marmendy Mill. I have no idea what or where Marmendy Mill is or was, but the name intrigued me so much that many years later I wrote an auto-biographical song about this golden era.

The community fire station was only a few houses away. It was the center of our lives. Halloween was the best: We'd bob for apples at the firehouse, and I'd get to wear my cowboy clothes without threat of a beating. We really didn't have many friends out there, and although I was far past my corduroy days, I wasn't then, nor am I now, a fountain of confidence. Awww, see little Howie on the big yellow bus for the first time in his life, all bundled up in layers of wool and nylon. And mittens. You can hear the laughter. I don't need to draw you a picture. Life sucked.

Except for television. That was cool, glued to the tube again and eating something, probably wearing cowboy stuff. I had great fringy pants and double six-shooters. The hat was standard-issue Roy Rogers but the vest . . . ah, the vest. That was a fashion touch all my own: Hoppy would never wear a vest like that. Nope, old Hopalong Cassidy always dressed in black. I knew, even back then, that yes, I am fashion.

I might have been eating chocolate pudding. God, I loved that shit. When my mother wasn't around (and strangely, she wasn't around a lot in the afternoons when I would return from school—she would always say that she was "playing mah-jongg with the girls," but I don't remember any girls), I would make my own dessert treat. If pounds made sounds, you could have actually heard me getting fat. I would make Royal choco-late pudding for the entire family on the frequent days of her absence. Of course, everybody would get a little bowl, and I'd get a nice big one. Plus, I'd have the advantage of "licking the pot," which, when I did the cooking, involved a substantial mound o' goop. When I was a baby, I would call pudding "dubdie" for some reason still unknown to me. The cutesy little name stuck. My parents used it forever. I now have a Manx kitty named Dubbie and she too is cutesy.

The snow falls deep out thar in the country. One day, my dad was doing something at the end of our driveway that I had never seen him do before. He was shoveling snow. It was amazing. I stood there all bundled up again and at rapt attention. He was cursing like—well, like he always did as this mongrel-looking pooch came from somewhere up the road and began to bark and snap at him. I heard the sound of the shovel, a yip of surprise from the animal, and yet more recognizable nouns from my father. Not more than two minutes later, this guy came along and asked, "What the hell is going on here?" To which I replied, "I saw my dad hit your dog over the head with a shovel!"

"What?!" my father screamed. "Get in the house!"

Well, he was sort of hidden from my view behind a snowdrift. I honestly thought he hit the dog. I really did. Dad never really denied it to me either. I don't know how he weaseled out of the situation with the dog owner, but I got spanked. Big-time. And I was never allowed to forget it. Ever. Into my forties, I heard about the dog and the shovel. But you know what? I still think he did it. I saw my dad hit the dog over the head with a shovel. And I'm sticking to it.

❧ ❧ ❧

About twice a year, Mom and Dad would shake my brother and me awake in the dead of night, dress us in our warmest sleeping-bag jackets, and cart us off to the train station. We would then board the 6 A.M. New York Central for a trip back to the city to visit Grandpa and his wife, who everyone called Tante. On one particular trip, we somehow managed to get tickets to see the filming of a television show in Manhattan. I'll never forget it as long as I live. It was *The Phil Silvers Show*, or, as it was known at the time, *You'll Never Get Rich*. I remember the episode vividly. It was the one where the troops in Ernie Bilko's barracks convince the eternally bald sergeant that he is somehow regrowing his hair. I've seen that very show in reruns many times in the years that followed, and I swear to God, I can hear my nine-year-old self laughing a little too loud and a little too long. I loved Bilko and I loved showbiz.

One second-grade afternoon, I got pissed off with everything and decided to run away. So I started walking toward school—the only direction I had ever gone—picking up empty bottles along the way. It was a two-mile walk to the town of Whitesboro, where I traded the many bottles in my paper bag for an ice cream sandwich, a Pepsi, and a Superman comic. It took me forever to get home. It was dark and there were no lights on Cavanaugh Road. My dad was pissed off. I got another beating. He was definitely getting better at this.

Each day, I would ride that stupid yellow bus home from Whitesboro High School, where we little kids were tolerated on the town's only campus, and rush inside just in time to watch Kate Smith on TV. I really can't explain this one. Kate Smith was a coloratura soprano of amazing voice and girth. I swear, the woman must have weighed in at three and change. She had a daily variety show where she would warble "God Bless America" and her trademark, "When the Moon Comes Over the Mountain." I hear that stuff now and I can't believe that I was ever, ever into it, even as a fetus. But she was great. Kate was old-school, with a laugh to match her intake, and, for whatever reason, I needed her. You know when your body craves vitamin C and you've got to get your juice on? That's what big old fat Kate was to me, music juice.

The other television ritual that my family routinely enjoyed was Uncle Walt's anthology program originally called *Disneyland* and later *Walt Disney's Wonderful World of Color*. Week after week, my brother and I watched as Walt supervised and thousands of workers built the fabulous resort destination from out of a Southern California orange grove. They dredged canals and turned farmland into Tomorrowland. Steamships and castles and cowboys and Mickey. Man, did I ever love Mickey! I wanted to be there more than anything else in the world. Mom showed me where Anaheim was on the big map of America and then she showed me the location of Marcy, New York. My heart sank. I would never get to Disneyland and that was all that there was to it. Uncle Walt was now handpicking a bunch of talented kids for his new *Mickey Mouse Club* show. There they were, rehearsing for Disneyland's big opening day. They were going to be in the big Main Street Electrical Parade. Man, those little girls were cute. They all had their names on their shirts. I closed my eyes and tried to picture it, but the vision never did come. There was never going to be a Mouseketeer named Howie. I was light-years and

3,000 miles away. I wrote off my chances and got back to the reality of my snow-filled days.

❧ ❧ ❧

When I was in third grade, Mom was absolutely convinced that Dad was having an affair with the lady next door, Jennie. My parents would scream at each other for hours at a time and my brother and I would hide in our double-bedded room and play records. The best thing that my folks ever did for me was to sign me up for something called the Children's Record Guild. Every month I would receive a new record that I could play on my very own record player. Now my dad could listen to his Lou Monte albums and the hits of his generation in absolute peace. And I could crank up the volume on some space travel adventure or Davy Crockett or *A Midsummer Night's Dream*. I think Dad was having that affair with Jennie. They had that look when they were around each other. Jennie's husband put up a chain-link fence and bought an enormous boxer dog.

A few months later, I skipped a grade and we moved away. I was suddenly thrust into fourth grade. I knew no one in my class or the next grade either, and I really didn't care. Those Disney songs and Kate Smith saved me. Those wonderful recordings were my only safe place as a kid. That and my newfound joy of cooking. Of course, those activities were no substitute for actual parental contact. If only my parents had spent a little more quality time with my brother and me. I was already the youngest old bachelor I knew.

THREE

Westward, Toward the Matterhorn!

I was the world's luckiest kid. My father had been offered a job with General Electric in Los Angeles. I was going to Disneyland! It was a miracle. The household was frantically packed and my father traded the '47 slope-backed Chevy for a 1951 slush bucket model with four doors. This was the kind of car in which a family could drive across the country in style. Westward, toward the Matterhorn, ho!

The journey took two weeks. We stopped in DC; at Carlsbad Caverns, in New Mexico; to visit my mother's sister in Phoenix; and, finally, in Sin City, USA. See little Howie in Las Vegas. We had dinner show tickets to see Jack Soo in *Flower Drum Song*. It was amazing and hilarious. This is a great many years before he was in *Barney Miller*. Allan and I had Shirley Temples with little red umbrellas in them. We walked down the then sparsely developed Vegas strip and literally wandered into the best show in town without knowing it. Seeing it changed my life forever.

The show was in the lounge of the Sands Hotel, so my dad didn't mind. He didn't have to come up with any cover or minimum charges for a lounge show. In we walked. We spread ourselves out at a tiny table for four just as the house announcer introduced, "Ladies and gentlemen, the Sands Hotel is proud to welcome to the stage Sam Butera and the Witnesses with Louis Prima and Keely Smith!"

Louis and Keely invented a style of cabaret that my singing partner Mark and I later adapted (all right, we took it, okay?) and still use in every single performance. Louis would clown it up, big-time, while the lovely Indian maiden, Keely, would stand as stiffly as a mannequin and sing in her mesmerizing style, seemingly oblivious to her husband's mad antics. Only eight or nine short years later, those two fat front men in the Turtles were cashing in by doing the very same thing. If you don't know who they were, maybe you remember David Lee Roth's big hit "Just a Gigolo/I Ain't Got Nobody"? That was a note-for-note cover of Louis Prima's arrangement. Seriously, if you're still drawing a blank, get a DVD or go on YouTube and check out their nightclub act from the '50s and '60s. They were amazingly ahead of their time. Hey, Sinatra loved them. The whole business loved them. They molded me.

❖ ❖ ❖

We arrived in L.A. with no place to live, so we spent the first months of my tenth summer staying with my cousin Beebe and her family in Panorama City in the central San Fernando Valley. Right away, we went to Disneyland. I was not disappointed. I had arrived. It was like I had accepted my new, sunnier state quite naturally. Zip-a-dee-do-dah. We found an apartment in Culver City, not far from the airport, and my dad continued to be a G.E. employee. Our place was tiny and upstairs in a ten-family unit. My only solaces were a teenager named Judy who lived downstairs and taught me how to roller-skate, and Johnnie's, the takeout restaurant on the comer of Sepulveda and Washington whose sign proclaimed it the Home of the Original French Dip Sandwich. Johnnie's is still there. It rocks. I lost no weight in Culver City.

We stayed there for a year. My dad hated G.E. and luckily landed a gig with Hughes Aircraft. We moved about five miles south to the suburb of Westchester, where LAX is located. And into a real house, at 5994 West Ninety-Sixth Street. The entire area is now airport parking. I pass my former home site every time I rent a car from Hertz. It's weird.

I was still in fourth grade. Six weeks later, I was bounced up to fifth grade. My teacher was Mrs. Koontz, who nominated me to appear on this television program on the local CBS television station along with three other panelists from my grade. We were to compete with another

12

fifth-grade class from somewhere else in Los Angeles, and the winning school would receive a TV set. The show was broadcast live on a Sunday afternoon, and the host was a very well known local news anchorman. I was nervous. I couldn't speak. I froze. I answered no questions. My school lost. I was the goat. I was Charlie Brown. I was depressed and humiliated in front of my parents and the world. But afterward, Mrs. Koontz took us all out to lunch at the legendary Brown Derby. I wasn't hungry for the first time in my life. Then Mrs. Koontz forced me to order their famous Cobb salad. It was the first time that I'd ever seen an avocado. Since then I've loved avocados. So the day wasn't a total loss.

❖ ❖ ❖

We all had to pick a musical instrument to learn. It was a school thing and a great one at that. My uncle Lou had been a violin player, so my father pushed me toward the rosin and the bow. I couldn't do it. Next, I wanted to be a trumpet player. They were the loudest in the band and always got to play the melody. Plus, the case was small and I was already too lazy to want to drag around anything larger. But I sucked on trumpet. It made my cheeks hurt and I sounded awful. Then I found the clarinet and it came naturally to me. My fingers felt exactly right on the keys and, after I'd practiced my embouchure for a few weeks, my notes actually outnumbered my squeaks.

I took clarinet lessons from Mr. Art Ferguson at the nearby Westchester Music Center for five years. The man was a saint. I joined the Westchester Youth Band under the directorship of one tough lady, Fern Jarris, and learned to march in formation and read much off of tiny lyre-mounted sheets of music. We marched in every parade held in Southern Cali without fail and won tons of awards. We wore purple and gold with giant *W*s on our chests. We would practice behind the music store. My parents came to almost every parade.

There was this trumpet player girl in the band. She was twelve years old too. She was adorable and somehow familiar, but I couldn't place her face. I would just stare at her. She was the one who finally got up the courage to talk to me, wandering over at a break during rehearsal to introduce herself. Her name was Sherry Alberoni, but she was also known as Sherry Allen. When she put on her T-shirt and went to work she became

Mouseketeer Sherry. Yes, oh yes, oh yes! We hit it off. We went on little-kid dates to the movies and for burgers. I would often ride my bike past her house and sit there for hours just waiting for her to look out her window or wave to me. I wrote a song for the two of us and we practiced with a backup band and performed "Sort of In Between" at the band talent show. She was great and really sweet to me. And suddenly I didn't feel like such a nerd. Got a little respect from the kids in school too. Only twelve but mack pimpin' already! I saw Sherry recently at some concert. She looked terrific. We shared a moment of something bigger than the two of us, and then she was gone.

❖ ❖ ❖

During the daytime, I was all study and serious, but after school the animal was changing. I had been given one of those newfangled Japanese transistor radios, and with its help I would while away the summer hours mowing the back lawn or lying on the hammock, gazing at the clouds and listening to the Dodgers.

Sometimes it was difficult to hear the game on the tiny speaker, so I would twist the dials for the best possible reception. But the only station that came in with any volume at all was this bizarre rhythm and blues station called KDAY at 1580 on the AM dial. KDAY was the coolest thing I had ever heard. With the assistance of Art Laboe and other rock radio pioneers, I was introduced to the Spaniels, the Del-Vikings, the Crests, the Marcels, Fats Domino, and Jerry Lee Lewis. I had found my music. Some part of me already knew. Now, school days couldn't end early enough. I would rush home, crank the set to channel 7, and anxiously await Dick Clark and his *American Bandstand*. Now I had a new goal. I had to get on that show, even though it was still broadcast from Philadelphia at the time.

I was still ripping the labels from the records I truly loved and replacing the artist's name with mine—Howard Kaylan.

I would play disc jockey in my room and introduce my songs with lines like, "Here's the new hit from Howard Kaylan—this kid's going places." Stuff like that. My folks left me alone a lot.

However, there were already obstacles in my young path, namely, my impending bar mitzvah. My folks were twice-a-year religious, so this going-to-Hebrew-school stuff was brand-new to me. It was a pretty easy thing: I would just walk to classes after school at the now defunct Airport Junior High. This huge guy named Les would harass me every time I walked there, but since another bully, Dale, used to beat me up when I walked home in the other direction, I never felt strongly about making a choice. Dale would resurface later in my life, and Les was the guy who taught me how to smoke. Once he realized that I wasn't running from him anymore, he gave up and offered me one of his Marlboros. We'd sit on the stairs of some apartment building, shielded from the street, and pretend to be hoods. We weren't. Les was fourteen. It must have been sad. I rocked at my bar mitzvah, but I abhorred all the hoopla and I jumped off the organized-religion train that very day, never to return.

❖ ❖ ❖

Another school friend, Harvey Miller, persuaded me to get into shoplifting with him at the store where he used to buy his own cigarettes. He told me to watch what he did and to copy him exactly. It was all going to be fine. I strolled through Jet Liquors about five steps behind Harvey. He'd put a pack of baseball card bubble gum in his jacket and wait for me to do the same, but I just couldn't. Harvey started to whistle nonchalantly. It only brought attention to us. Who were we kidding? There went a package of corn nuts into Harvey's jacket and still I couldn't do it. Then Harvey picked up a carton of milk from the cooler and waltzed out the door. The automatic bell dinged loudly and the proprietor looked up just in time to see me place a dill pickle wrapped in wax paper in my jacket pocket. I got nabbed. He called my parents and told me to stay out of his store forever. Then Harvey walked in and pretended to be shocked at my predicament. But the owner recognized him. Seems Harvey's dad and the dude were in the same lodge. Harvey's parents got the call and he was admonished too, and I suffered the indignities of a criminal for a damned pickle.

But the pattern that was to follow paved the way for my higher education. Elated by the buzz of the capture, and buoyed by my parents' reaction of unbridled laughter at any subsequent mention of the word *pickle*, I began my mini life of crime. I am not proud of this; I am merely reporting the facts. I graduated to records. The first 45-rpm single that found its way into my pudgy little paws was "Tossin' and Turnin'" by Bobby Lewis. It only cost eighty cents—I started small. The first album was Ray Charles's *Genius + Soul = Jazz.* Thanks to KDAY, I had heard this remarkable man's two latest hits, the novelty "Hit the Road Jack" and the cool instrumental "One Mint Julep." I couldn't wrap my mind around the fact that they were by the same guy. I thought you either played or sang. I didn't know you could do both. In any case, I had to have his album. I loved that album. Still love that album. I walked into Westchester Music like a forty-year-old. I had a folded newspaper in my hand. I put the album inside when Fern's son Dave Jarris wasn't looking. I strolled out. Clean. I can't speak for Internet pirates, but I can tell you this: Nothing sounds as sweet as your first stolen song.

It's not like I stole *every* record that I owned. I did have a paper route. Twice a week Dad would help me fold paper-thin copies of the *Westchester News-Advertiser* in which my mother wrote a community service column. I'd hop on my trusty two-wheeler and schlep the rags through the neighborhood and then collect a quarter each from the residents who took pity on me. It wasn't bad, actually. I was good for about twenty-six big ones a month. And, back then, that bought a lot of Kingston Trio and Bobby Darin. (I won a radio call-in contest once. KRLA gave me two tickets to see Bobby Darin at the Coconut Grove. I took Mom as my date and we sat at the same table as Tony Butala of the Lettermen.)

❖ ❖ ❖

Dad just didn't get the music I was devouring. When it came to comedy, though, sometimes we spoke the same language, but not always. He thrived, as did my mother, on our Sunday afternoons spent listening to Stan Freberg's brilliant radio satire. I'd laugh myself silly, sometimes almost enough to forget about the impending boiled meat or tasteless chicken dinner. My father's laugh was infectious and I really never heard enough of it. He shared my love of Ernie Kovacs and Sid Caesar, but he never understood why I never laughed at Red Skelton, who scared me. Victor Borge I got. Every morning, Dad listened to Bob Crane on the CBS station and he was truly hilarious. Danny Kaye made Dad laugh. Jerry Lewis didn't. I love Jer. He never got Soupy Sales either, and no one, in my opinion, was funnier—or a nicer guy—than Soupy. I was president of the Soupy

Sales Fan Club when I was fourteen. Five years later, I was in Soupy's apartment, higher than I had ever been. Life is full of possibilities.

My brother Al and I also had our first real friends in Westchester, Mark and Arnie Levine. That side of my childhood was pretty idyllic. Mark was my age and Arnie was Al's. It was cool. We'd play catch and talk about the Dodgers. We had another tree house, too, only this one had a secret hiding place for the special magazines that we'd lift from the barbershop while we were making discount deals to sell our used comic books. I came of age, so to speak, while rocking back and forth to the radio and thumbing though my mother's paperback copy of *Peyton Place*. I remember the line "She moaned as if she were hurt." I had no idea what that meant.

FOUR

Destiny Calls

Mr. Ferguson had a battered old silver alto saxophone that sat on a stand in the corner of the practice room upstairs at Westchester Music. During each lesson, as the patient tutor led me through the rigors of "Clarinet Polka" or some such old persons' music, I fixated on that ancient sax. In my mind, I was hearing "Tequila" by the Champs. Yes, I had been playing Dixieland jazz with a group of locals for veterans or at the shopping center, but that wasn't it—there was no passion in Dixieland. I wanted the raunch. I wanted to make the music that I found myself listening to. The sax solo in Bobby Lewis's "Tossin' and Turnin'" was holy to me, and the Coasters' "Yakety Yak"—well, that was the way music was supposed to be. A person certainly couldn't get far in music in those days if he was wearing lederhosen.

So I persuaded Mr. F. to loan me the silver sax on an overnight basis. And he thought that if I continued with my clarinet, learning saxophone, with its similar fingering, wouldn't send me directly to hell. I think I wound up honking on that funky old horn for all of about three weeks when I received the phone call of destiny.

"Who is it, Howard?"

"It's Destiny, Mom."

And I answered.

The call was from some dude I had never met by the name of Chuck Portz. He explained that some friends were putting together a rock 'n' roll band. He'd heard that I played saxophone, and asked if I was interested in joining. Hell, yeah!

❖ ❖ ❖

The band, and I use the term loosely, was called the Nightriders—quite an attitude adjustment from the austere business cards that my mom had printed for our Dixieland band, the Belvederes. I know, I know. The name was not my idea. I still don't know what a Belvedere is.

But I did know that the Nightriders was a name to be reckoned with. And, as anyone alive or dead could tell you, a band's name is half of its success. So the band was me, honking away on alto sax; Chuck Portz, the guy who had drawn the short straw and made that call to me, on bass; Al Nichol, newly transplanted from Ohio and now living in Westchester with his parents, two USC professors, on lead guitar; and a redheaded lanky-bones named Glen Wilson on drums. We played music that Al had glommed from Midwestern rockers like Johnny and the Hurricanes, who had enjoyed national success with an instrumental version of "Red River Valley," and songs by the Ventures, like "Walk Don't Run."

It was a guitar-oriented band, for sure. I honked through the chords and, once a song, got to play an improvised solo of my own too. I learned quickly. I loved rock 'n' roll. We never got too many paying jobs, but we knew that we were headed in the right direction.

One afternoon, we were all watching this local teen dance party. It was live from Pickwick Park in Burbank and was hosted by a DJ of some repute named Bob Eubanks. Hell, we thought, we can do that, and knowing no fear, we called the show's office. Yes, we do court local bands, we were told—but only if they have a record out. Um, so if we had a record out, we could play on TV too? That's right, said the man. We borrowed $125 from Al's dad, went to a little Hollywood studio, and recorded two sides that sounded amazingly identical. One side was called "Radar" and the other was "High Tide." We sent the record to the television office and we played on Bob Eubanks's *Dance Party* the following week. Or, more truly, we lip-synced. It was amazing. I still have that record. It's still terrible. But now the bug had bitten.

I was still a real nobody in high school. I was just that porky guy with the A average who wore sweater vests and hung out with my buddy John

Laughlin instead of the popular kids. Those ample-bosomed babes who ate their school lunches sitting in the stands of the football field and feeding grapes to athletic seniors were just things to gawk at. They were so out of my league. Even Sherry the Mouseketeer, who now was doing movies and television, had moved on, so to speak. I was in scholastic social limbo. The one girl I really liked, Linda Gunderson, indulged me and would actually talk to me in the hall, but when it came time to ask someone special to the prom, Linda had herself a college man and I was broken. Then, bless her heart, at the last minute, she offered up her younger sister, Jane, to be sacrificed. I treated that pretty little kid like a queen. We did the entire limo-and-corsage thing and afterward, I treated her to dinner and a show at the Crescendo on the famous Sunset Strip, where this new young comic, Bill Cosby, was delivering the laughs.

Double foreshadowing here.

I took her home, kissed her good night, and didn't see her again until 2009 at some show. She looked great.

But mostly, I kept my head down, concentrated on school, and found myself daily looking forward to my favorite new class, a cappella choir, taught by the best teacher I ever had, one Robert Wood. So influential was Mr. Wood on my life and my music that many years later, my partner and I would name our ASCAP publishing company Mr. Wood's Music. He was just that good. The music was difficult and Robert Wood demanded perfection. My years with Mr. Ferguson went a long way in this class, as we spent a great deal of time sight-reading new musical charts—wonderful practice and invaluable lessons here. We'd have guest directors. One year, a gentleman by the name of Jester Hairston conducted us in his arrangement of the African-American classic "Hold On." It had soul. At least, it had as much soul as could be wrung from the throats of a hundred or so white-ass beach kids.

This, after all, was Westchester High, a flagship destination for Wonder Bread adolescents from L.A.'s beach communities. Hell, sometimes we'd go back to class after lunch and sometimes we wouldn't. With the beach only half a mile away, most afternoons were spent goofing off or watching some highly touted action between two rival surfing clubs as they battled it out at the Trees, which was literally just that—a group of trees that had sprouted up on Manchester Avenue on the way to the ocean. The battles were little more than excuses for beer parties, and even outsiders were allowed to root for their favorites with no pretense of popularity. Many of the surfers who belonged to the local clubs weren't even that serious about surfing. The club was the thing. Acceptance in high school was the name of the game. So there were many pretenders hanging out—gremmies, they were called by actual wave riders. Some were really good surfers; others were clowns.

❖ ❖ ❖

One day, during a cappella choir practice, I found myself standing and singing next to one of those guys. He was a clown, all right—the *class* clown, in fact: an olive-skinned, frizzy-haired, bespectacled surfer kid who was even portlier than me. And he was a crack-up. Honestly. Mark Volman was the last kid in the row of male first tenors and I was the first kid in the row of male second tenors, singing just a bit lower on the scale. So we stood next to each other. We shared the same music sometimes. And we broke out laughing constantly. In fact, between us, we found a way to get thrown out of almost every class we shared. But I was an A student and Volman was barely a C student, and wise Mr. Wood knew that it was in the choir's best interest if we both took a powder on afternoons when he actually wanted to teach. Mark and I would wander the halls with legit passes almost daily. We both got As in choir anyway. Mr. Wood was pretty strict about testing, and he didn't want to lose his two best tenors.

Mark and I hit it off instantly, and during one of our first conversations he asked me about the Nightriders. The conversation went something like this:

"So I hear you're in a rock 'n' roll band."

"Yep."

"Um, do you think I could join it?"

"Well, what do you do?"

"Nothing."

"Nothing?"

"Nope."

"Sounds good to me. I'll ask Al."

And that was how Mark got to be in our band. He was telling the truth. He couldn't do anything. We weren't a vocal group; we played instrumentals. I, of course, was the esteemed saxophonist. But we really could use a roadie, I told him, someone who could haul our instruments around and get us sodas while we played. And that's exactly what Mark did. Eventually, his father, Joe, got really pissed off at this arrangement. He'd say, "What the hell, fellas? You guys are all making money playing at these little shows and Mark's not getting a penny. How come?"

"Because your son doesn't *do* anything, Mr. Volman. *We* play instruments."

"Okay, well, what if I buy Mark an instrument?"

"Then he can make money too."

The next day, I accompanied Mark and his dad to a music store in downtown Los Angeles, where he purchased an alto sax. By now, I was honking on my own tenor, and together, provided that I could teach Mark to play, we had a nifty little horn section going. It was mind-numbingly coincidental that for many years, Mark had been taking clarinet lessons at Westchester Music with no one else but the sainted Mr. Ferguson himself. This was truly kismet. We learned choreography together and began doing steps onstage as we rocked and rolled. We were sounding pretty damned good, actually.

The band now consisted of me on tenor sax and vocals, Mark on alto, Al Nichol on guitar, Chuck Portz on bass, Jim Tucker from Torrance on rhythm guitar, and Don Murray from Inglewood playing drums; Don designed our logo, too. Volman sang a little in the very beginning on the dirty songs and played tambourine. Al and Chuck liked having Mark in the band because a) he was hilarious and b) he knew all the surf kids. Instantly we had a built-in audience, and besides just loving to dance, these kids ruled the community.

❖ ❖ ❖

This exact band would soon enough become the Turtles but for now we were the Crossfires. We had righteous cool business cards printed in yellow and red with a burning Iron Cross motif, and booked our first shows as I was about to turn sweet sixteen. First, I had to get my driver's license. We only had one car in our family, as my mother didn't drive. It was a 1951 four-door Chevy with a standard column shift, and my dad drove it to work at nearby Hughes Aircraft every day. So I wound up taking my driving test in Al Nichol's push-button automatic Dodge Dart, a car I had never driven before. No problem for the Kid. My father bought another Chevy, gave the '51 slush bucket to me, and the next day I drove to my first real show as a Crossfire at a fraternity house party at nearby UCLA.

The frat guys had tubs filled with this amazing concoction called the Red Death, which, I later learned, was nothing but Hawaiian Punch mixed with everything alcoholic and poured over smoking dry ice. Volman had a few glasses and fell down the stairs with an armload of guitars. We all laughed. I downed one or two potent cups before I was told that my Chevy was blocking the driveway and that I would have to move it. Well, it was rush week at UCLA, meaning that all of the campus houses were packed to capacity with hopeful freshmen and there weren't any parking places for miles. I felt no fear just the same. In fact, I'm not sure that I felt anything. But I had to move the car. Yep. Had to move it. I thought I saw a space up ahead and I thought that I could fit into it. Didn't see that other car backing up. Yikes! You got it. I crashed. Big-time. I gave the other driver my information, though his car looked pretty good. My car, on the other hand, was toast. I coasted downhill to the nearest Mobil station, called my dad, and had him pick me up. In the days before cell phones, I had no way to get in touch with the band guys, so I just went home. My night sucked. I paid to have the car fixed and painted it canary yellow.

I had begun my obsession with the Kingston Trio, and on top of the rock stuff that we had been doing, Mark, Al, and I became the Cross-wind Singers, along with a girl from the choir named Betty McCarty. I wrote folksy tunes, Al played guitar, and the four of us sang. We sounded pretty good for that time and place and were chosen to open the show when national folk heroes Joe and Eddie played in the auditorium. My songs were called "Let the Cold Winds Blow" and "Wanderin' Kind"—both of these would be recorded later as the Turtles became a national act, but for then, we were just happy to be on a real stage.

The Crossfires were gaining in local popularity. We were playing a dance at the Westchester Women's Club when our devoted high school followers showed up to cheer us on. This group of rabid fans called themselves the Chunky Club, named after a song of ours called "Chunky." It was just a standard four-chord rocker with a break where everyone yelled the word *chunky* arbitrarily. It meant nothing. But these kids showed up with huge soupspoons and ladles. They were dirty dancing, making obscene gestures with the kitchen implements toward the genitalia of their female dancing partners. It was perverted, but it was hilarious to watch from the stage. The Women's Club thought otherwise and we were famously banned from working in our own hometown. For a local band, this might have been a devastating blow.

Luckily, we had gotten an offer to play in adjacent Inglewood for teen dances at Darby Park Recreation Center and brought our following, intact, with us. More and more kids started showing up and our reputation grew. When we saw an advertisement in the local paper for a battle of the bands at a teen club in Redondo Beach, about ten miles away, we came, we played, and with the help of our Chunky Club fans, we conquered. Almost overnight, we became the house band at Reb Foster's Revelaire Club at 312 South Catalina Avenue. Reb was a big-time DJ on KRLA, the very same station that employed Bob Eubanks. (In fact, Eubanks was the first DJ to promote a Beatles concert in Los Angeles. He brought the Fab Four to the Hollywood Bowl in 1964.) Reb really didn't know much about us at first.

It was his cousin, Bill Utley, who actually ran the Revelaire, but Reb's name was used both at this club and at the Rendezvous Ballroom in Orange County, where another group, Eddie and the Showmen, held down the house band position. It was a great gig, really. We played on Friday and Saturday nights, three sets a night and—this is the best part—we got to back up all of the national artists who came to perform as guest stars on a weekly basis. We learned all of their songs and were quite prepared to have the big stars simply walk out onstage and do their shows with our accompaniment. And, when necessary, Mark and I would put down the saxes and sing the background parts. We performed with the Coasters and the Drifters, Dick and Dee Dee, Bobby Vee, the Rivingtons, and countless other soul groups and surf bands. We were getting to be instinctive players, learning different musical styles and testing our flexibility. Bert Bertrand, father of Eddie Bertrand—of Eddie and the Showmen—became our de facto manager. He also managed a girl singer by the name of Nita Garfield, who was simply breathtaking to the young me. I vowed to have her, much to the amusement of the band. And I did. We remained an item for several years. Check me out: in a rock band and with a girlfriend—and a rather spectacular one at that. The turning point had been reached and passed. The potato of a guy was on his way to being Spud of the Year.

❖ ❖ ❖

I was feeling much better about my place in the food chain as 1964 washed up on shore. Then the Beatles came along and everything changed. Mark and I put the saxes away and began using our natural vocal gifts to sing rock 'n' roll. Oh sure, we had always done "What'd I Say" and "Money," those classic dance songs that merely require audience participation to work, but now we were singing "From Me to You" and "You Really Got Me" and "Glad All Over." It was bloody wonderful! And, not to throw a sexual light on the procedure, but the ladies that were now waiting backstage and hanging around after the show took our little band to a new level of showmanship. "What the road ladies do to you" are the words that Frank Zappa would have me sing many years later, and this was my first taste of it. They made us better.

The Crossfires learned the hits of the day and spewed them back at a waiting public with great accuracy and passion. We loved it, man. We sang everything. As college loomed ahead and I took the SATs, I knew that I was already past it, at least psychologically. My parents, however, took a slightly different stance on the matter.

UCLA is the single most intimidating place on the planet. It's been forty years since I attended that college, and the statement still remains true. I had graduated from high school early, having won the Bank of America Fine Arts Award for music and literature, and had won a full ride to the University of California, which made my parents extremely happy and proud. Neither of them were graduates, my father having enlisted in the Army Air Corps as World War II began. I was the shining hope of the clan, but I started my days of higher learning already full of doubt. The classes were tremendous: There were often 2,000 students in the lecture halls. Then the classes broke down into smaller work groups, about 150 students. Too big. Too fast. Too much. I was freaking out. The shock of being an A student in high school and receiving a D on my first anthropology exam shook my world.

My only solace was to be found in the student union building. That place was like a mall: great food, a wonderful atmosphere that didn't choke me, and a curious blue index card on the corkboard asking for student DJs for the campus radio station. Now *here* was something that I could get into. I walked into the radio station and right into the general manager's office. He slapped me on the air that very day after hearing me introduce a Beach Boys single. I knew their names, I knew their dad, and I had hung out with them and hit on their girlfriends. I was in and Howie the K. was born.

My show was on Tuesdays and Thursdays at first, but I enjoyed it so much that I volunteered to do daily shifts even though my classes clearly conflicted with my new schedule. Screw the classes; this was way better. I was a virtual encyclopedia of useless knowledge on KBRU, as that was what it was called at the time. Bruin Radio. And what I didn't know, I manufactured. Then things started getting silly. I would ask Mark to come on the show, introduce him as my cousin Gerry Marsden from Gerry and the Pacemakers, and proceed to ask him questions right out of the real band's official biography. Volman's English accent was the absolute worst, but somehow the shows worked. I got better and better, the show got more and more popular, and I stopped going to more and more of my classes.

One lunchtime, I came home from school early, as I had no intention of visiting my afternoon classes: Much to my dismay, I found my father had also come home for a midday meal. I was busted. When he asked what the hell I was doing there, I told him flat out that I was going to quit school because I just wasn't interested. He went red—not just sunburn-y red, but red like a fire engine, like a beet, like a madman.

"We work and we slave for you—we've given up everything and *this* is how you repay us? Just what do you intend to do with your life, idiot?"

A fair question.

So I told them that I intended to make hit records instead. The silence was palpable. My parents were suicidal. So I promised them that if, for some bizarre reason, I didn't get a hit record within the next six months, I would return to school and never bring up the music business again. However, I was underestimating myself. It didn't take that long.

❖ ❖ ❖

The Crossfires were doing their weekly thing at the Revelaire, but we were not very happy. Al Nichol had to get married and there was no way in hell that our meager little rock 'n' roll stipend could support his entire family, so, sadly, I was elected to take a note of resignation upstairs to Bill Utley, the nightclub manager. This was bad and boded poorly for a guy who had sworn to become famous in a matter of months. But here's where it gets weird. These two guys in suits who had been watching the entire show approached me as I headed up the stairs. They said that they were starting up a new record label and that our version of the new Byrds hit "Mr. Tambourine Man" had so impressed them that they wanted to take us into the studio and make a record. At first, I didn't put too much stock in these guys or what they were offering.

We had actually made records in the past. We had released an instrumental called "Dr. Jekyll and Mr. Hyde" on a little label owned by the guy who had a huge international hit with a novelty song called "Alley Oop," but it did nothing. Then we had put out an original Kinks-style knockoff called "One Potato Two Potato" on a label called Lucky Token. That one had actually charted in San Bernardino and Riverside and got us on television locally, on *Sam Riddle's 9th Street West* dance party. Still, exciting though it had been, it wasn't exactly fame.

But hey, now we were getting one more, probably last chance to make a record before we sputtered out. What the hell, why not? That was our attitude and that is how we came to record my original folk songs from the Crosswind Singers days. My folk obsessions had also led me to Bob Dylan, Tom Rush, Fred Neil, and many others, and it was on a Dylan album that I found "It Ain't Me Babe." I had absolutely no idea that it had been recorded by Johnny Cash as a country hit, but my original take on the song wasn't the same as Cash's anyway. I heard the song "angry," not a plaintive cry as Cash and, in fact, Dylan had done. In my brain, I heard it the way Colin Blunstone of the Zombies would have done it, à la "She's Not There." So my version of the song has a soft, innocent, Blunstonesque verse followed by a driving four/four chorus sung in a much harder fashion. This pattern, by the way, remains true to even "Happy Together" and "Elenore." Hey, what can I tell you? It's my thing, man.

❖ ❖ ❖

The label, which didn't have a name yet, now had a record by a group that didn't have a name yet. "The Crossfires" certainly wouldn't work for a folk-rock band. Enter Reb Foster from out of the shadows. Watching from a nice, safe distance, Reb had come up with a plan.

"I've had this name rolling around my head for months," he told us. "Your new name is . . . the Turtles!"

We laughed at him. Right out loud. We rolled on the ground and held our sides.

"You have *got* to be kidding," we chided. "Turtles are fat and ugly and cold and stupid. Why the hell would we want to be called that?"

And Reb explained, "Look, you're on a new label. The Beatles are putting out records on all of these weird little labels." He was correct. "And the name has an *l-e-s* ending, just like the Beatles, and it's an animal name too. The public is going to think that you guys come from England, and England is really hot!"

Well, we couldn't argue with that logic. And I'll be damned if Reb Foster wasn't absolutely correct. "It Ain't Me Babe" came out exactly four months after my fateful bargain with my parents. It all happened so fast we didn't know what hit us. One weekend, we were playing our standard shows at the Revelaire with the little girls crying over the onstage banner, which read FAREWELL TO THE CROSSFIRES, and the following week we returned to do the exact same set with the addition of "It Ain't Me Babe" and wearing the lime-green velour shirts and matching caps that Reb had picked out for us.

We sat in the parking lot of the club before our first show, munching potato chips and listening to the radio as the disc jockey on KRLA announced that the new Bob Dylan record had debuted at number seven, and we remained hopeful that, maybe next week, our record might have a shot too. "Like a Rolling Stone" was magnificent, and we prepped for our little show with resignation.

And then the announcer said, "But wait, we have one record that debuted even *higher*!" "It Ain't Me Babe" came on the radio and we screamed and hugged and lost our minds. It took a minute to get our shit together. We still had a show to do. Inside the familiar Revelaire, the new banner read WELCOME THE TURTLES. We played that show and then we were gone.

"It Ain't Me Babe" became a national Top Ten record. I bought my parents a huge color TV and a trip to Hawaii and never heard about bad career choices again.

❖ ❖ ❖

During one of our last days in the studio, Lee Lasseff and Ted Feigin, the two suits who ran White Whale Records, came into the booth, a rare occurrence already, to finalize the credits for the album and the single.

Everybody gave them the correct spellings of their names as well as the names of those who had written the songs on the record. When they came to me, I had to spell my last name for the two executives. And I spelled it *K-a-y-l-a-n*.

What?

The band looked at me like I was insane. "What are you doing, man?"

"I don't know why." It wasn't to mask my being Jewish. It wasn't anything. I had just known since childhood that I was supposed to be Howard Kaylan.

The label didn't care, and the band didn't think that we had a shot in hell with this album anyway, so they let it slide with only a few giggles and some hurtful asides.

But there it was now, in stone, or print, as the case may be. The B-side of "It Ain't Me Babe" was "Almost There," written by Howard Kaylan.

I was now officially Howard Kaylan.

Two years later I went to court to legally change it. But right now, this was good enough for me.

❖ ❖ ❖

To be reflective for a minute, looking back, the years fifteen through twenty were—as they probably are for most people—the most formative years of my life. Mainly, during this time, I learned to make my own decisions. Had I truly realized how important this time in my life was, I probably would have taken greater pains to be more serious about choices that obviously affected every facet of my future. But these are the days of impending adulthood where no kid wants to hear that he is acting impulsively. I personally don't think that I had any choice in the matter. I was destined to do this entertainment thing from a very early age, and I knew it. And when anyone is that certain about anything, and is prepared to stay the course for his or her convictions, that path is a righteous one and that dream is destined to come true. Honestly. I truly believe, and I'll go down fighting on this one, that this is true.

So, if you're a parent, listen to your kids. By the time they are old enough to know what they are doing, they are already doing it. It's too late for your input. I am of the opinion that the worst thing a parent can do is to offer the advice to "have something to fall back on." I have heard this all of my days. It is my experience that, if a child has something to fall back on, they will fall back. Absolutely. When any passion takes over your child's life, that is the strongest voice that he or she will ever hear. For God's sake, encourage them to listen to it. It is passion that is missing from so many of our humdrum existences. We go to work, come home, eat dinner, watch TV, and go to bed. Maybe your son or daughter deserves more. Maybe they are aiming just a little bit higher. Please don't attack their dreams. Talent is like a flower and it needs encouragement as much as sunlight or water. At this age, listen to your children—they know more than you do.

Of course, as I turned eighteen years old, I wasn't thinking like a parent; I was becoming a rock star and figuring out what exactly that meant. It was the mid-'60s and I had a massive hit record.

In 1965 and 1966, the Turtles spent most of our waking hours on the road when we weren't recording back in Los Angeles. We traveled in two station wagons, usually pulling a U-Haul trailer behind us filled with our equipment. We were folk-rock darlings when we first went to New York City to perform for a week at the Phone Booth, where the Young Rascals had been the house band before their recent success. It was here that we met Bob Dylan. After a particularly energetic show that climaxed with "It Ain't Me Babe," we were led past him in processional fashion. When I got my chance to shake his hand, Dylan said, "Hey, that was a great song you just played, man. That should be your single." Then he passed out into his food. I didn't see him again until 1984.

FIVE

The West Coast Ambassadors of Good-Time Music

Well, life is certainly different when you have a hit record. And I had it all in 1965, before my eighteenth birthday.

Gone was the '51 slush bucket Chevy I had inherited from my dad, though I'd give a lot to have that baby now. I had moved on up to a used Cadillac convertible, thanks to my cousin Ruby Bird at Budget rental cars. He told my dad it was a nice, safe ride.

And, lest we forget, I had Nita Garfield as my girlfriend and she was, by anybody's standards, one hot chick.

The very next week after my birthday, Reb had us booked at the very same Crescendo on Sunset where I had seen Bill Cosby onstage less than one year before. The DJ who introduced us was named Dave Diamond from the AM rock station KHJ. He had us all jumping around behind him chanting, "We are hot 'cause we smoke pot!"

Which we didn't.

Nor did he.

But the riots on Sunset Strip had begun just down the street at Pandora's Box and anything less than revolutionary wouldn't have attracted any attention at all.

So now we were a Hollywood band, commuting from Westchester, but not for long.

I moved away from home. This was traumatic for my folks and a blessing for my brother, who got his own room at the age of fifteen. As far as I was concerned, mentally I had left a long time ago.

Mark and I moved into a house together in fabled Laurel Canyon on Lookout Mountain Avenue, across from Wonderland Avenue School. Everybody who worked in a Hollywood band seemed to already be there. Our pals Danny Hutton (later of Three Dog Night) and the great photographer Henry Diltz were neighbors. The famous Zappa log cabin was there as well as the burned-out ruins of Houdini's mansion, where vigils were held each year on Halloween to invoke the magician's ghost. We were moving up quickly.

❖ ❖ ❖

As our little record climbed the national charts, much to our surprise, Lee and Ted had us in the studio recording our debut album. Both had been record promoters in the L.A. area for years, much as Sonny Bono had, and they had gotten together in Aldo's, the Hollywood Boulevard bar that sat downstairs from KFWB, the big AM rocker in town. Lee told Ted that he'd leave his job at Liberty Records if Ted would give up his at London Records and together they'd scour L.A. for the right band and begin their own label. After all, they knew everybody and, apparently, were due a few favors.

Thank God for those favors. And here's where the luck comes in. These clowns could have thrown us into any studio with any old engineer and probably without a producer either and we wouldn't have known the difference. But, like I said, they knew people.

So we wound up recording at the world-famous Western Studios on Sunset Boulevard, in Studio 3, which, although we didn't realize it, was already legendary for being the sonic home to the Beach Boys, Jan and Dean and, soon, a host of others. Lee and Ted had positioned themselves to be "the producers," although they just sat near the console nodding their heads.

But it was the engineers who were the true stars of those early sessions.

The brilliant veteran Chuck Britz, who had recorded our ridiculous "Dr. Jekyll" record the year before, was once again at the console. But the head engineer was a tall drink of water named Bones Howe, who knew exactly how to get the sound that we and, more important, Lee and Ted were looking for.

Bones had been used to working with L.A.'s famous Wrecking Crew, though they weren't called that yet. This was the crème de la crème of Hollywood's session players and they played on everybody's hits. No shit, everybody: all the Beach Boys' stuff, Phil Spector's records, the Mamas and the Papas, the Fifth Dimension, the Monkees, all of it. The list is stupid long.

These guys were one-take pros. Record companies couldn't waste their money on valuable studio time nurturing their new crop of long-haired long shots. Slap a singer on it, put some shaggy guys on the album cover, and invent a name. Shit, it worked for the Grass Roots—the band wasn't even put together until after their first record had become a hit.

Ah, but that's not how White Whale did it.

These guys were cheap. And—at this point, at least—presumably poor. So we played everything ourselves, just like on our little demo records. We were ignorant. We thought everybody played on their own records. Thankfully, we had Bones. And the fact that there was still an opportunity for actual teenagers to play on their own records must have appealed to him.

The songs we had recorded in the past had all been rather primitive, as were the recording techniques employed. The Nightriders' demo had been done using one microphone set up in the middle of the room, in one-track mono. The Crossfires had done our records with Larry Johnson on two tracks and with Chuck Britz at Western on three, still mixed down to mono. By the time Bones recorded us, the industry standard was the Ampex four-track.

The band was in the studio together to do the basic instrumental tracks. Al and Jim's guitars were usually put on the same track, Chuck's bass and Don's drums were combined together on a single track, and my work vocals were saved on third. Later, I would go in to do the actual vocals, the entire band would be mixed down to stereo, and we'd have a track left over to which we'd bounce guitar overdubs and background vocals from a second, or slave, two-track machine. Of course, all of this bouncing and combining made for some hissy-sounding recordings as two separate performances had to be moved over to an open track, freeing up the spots where they had been for even more recording. But we learned how to be economical about our choices and how to cut and edit actual magnetic tape, an art that is dying in our present digital age.

Also, in the era before we had vices, our little band was remarkably focused. And that was a lucky thing. We were a folk-rock group by default. So where was the material for the album coming from? We were hardly prolific, and our sudden success had taken everybody by surprise. Luckily, I had a few trusty gems left over from the Crosswind Singers days and, along with some Dylan and a few public domain folk relics that we rocked up and took credit for, we had the bulk of an album that White Whale could release as our first national tour kicked off.

But, everyone agreed, there wasn't a second single.

❖ ❖ ❖

White Whale's office was in a beautiful building on Sunset near Beverly Hills that they shared with ABC-Dunhill Records and Trousdale Music, both operated by Lou Adler, a brilliant entrepreneur and one smart cookie. He was responsible for the Grass Roots.

Lou had signed a new writer named Phil Sloan and Bones brought him backstage to meet us after a show at the Crescendo.

He introduced himself as P. F., produced an acoustic guitar from thin air, and proceeded to sing his new song, adding how great this would be as our Dylan follow-up. And we gasped.

Phil, or P. F., or Flip—or whatever he was calling himself that day—sang us "Eve of Destruction" for the very first time. We didn't know how to react. We weren't stupid—we all realized that this song was earthshaking and absolutely a monster hit record, but it scared the shit out of us. What did we know? We were all white, middle-class kids of the *Leave It to Beaver* mentality. Whoever released this record would have a lot of explaining to do, and we knew that we weren't those guys. What the hell did we have to protest anyway?

Bones was crushed. He was going to be a hero and we had shot him down. But fortunately, Phil was no one-trick pony. He had another song for us to hear and this one, "Let Me Be," was definitely a gentler, while still confrontational, option. It was written from the point of view of a kid imploring his parents and the over-thirty bastards that were ruining the world to leave him alone to grow his hair long and think for himself.

Plus, Phil had patterned the song to echo the formula of "It Ain't Me Babe," with soft minor verses followed by angrier hard fours in the chorus sections. This we could do. And it fit our new so-called image to a T. Now we had a follow-up.

Our first real concert as the Turtles was opening up for Herman's Hermits at the Rose Bowl in Pasadena. Sonny and Cher were there too. Nearly half a century later, we still frequently open shows for Peter Noone of the Hermits. Some things never change.

And now, with a single entering the Top Ten in America and our first album in the can, we flew off to Chicago for our first tour, Dick Clark's Caravan of Stars. It ran from August 1 through September 6, 1965, and was our first experience away from Los Angeles. Hell, we had never even stayed in a hotel before as a band. We were meeting the entire entourage, in progress, as the cross-country bus tour hit the Windy City at the Hilton, a snazzy place. The lineup included Tom Jones, fresh off "It's Not Unusual" and "What's New Pussycat?"; Peter and Gordon, also from the UK with a slew of Beatles-related hits; the immortal Shirelles; singers Brian Hyland, Ronnie Dove, and Billy Joe Royal; and crooner Mel Carter, who did "Hold Me, Thrill Me, Kiss Me." When Dick Clark wasn't on board to intro the show, there was an MC named George McCannon III to vamp.

The tour was doing great business and we were giddy to be a part of it. In a happy trance and thrilled to be on the road at last, Al Nichol went across the street to an inviting park bench to take pictures of the hotel after check-in and was promptly mugged. Wallet gone, cash gone, camera gone. He returned to the hotel to report the incident, only to be met by hundreds of conventioneers from the Shriners, who had the rest of us intimidated in the restaurants, lobby, stairwells, and elevators, shouting obscenities and calling us long-haired fairy boys and worse. There was much shoving and a few very tense moments as we got our first taste of life outside Hollywood as a rock group. Still, the following day, we were welcomed onto the tour bus for the short drive to the Convention Center and went on, as scheduled, before the first-half closers, Peter and Gordon, to perform our big hit and our new follow-up. And they sounded exactly the same.

The following day, we were all assigned our permanent bus seats and couldn't believe our incredible good luck. I was actually sharing a bench seat with the great Gordon Waller in the back of the bus, and even I knew that was the place to be! And Mark had done even better, getting to sit next to Tom Jones for the next several weeks. We were happy, but we were ignorant. As night fell, and we left Chicago heading for the great unknown, Gordon looked at me and announced, "Right then, here we go!" I stared at him blankly, not knowing what was expected of me. Tom Jones stared at Volman and nodded toward the floor.

Ah, I see. Now we understood. When it got dark outside, the "stars" got to spread out on the seats to nap the traveling hours away in relative comfort, while the lackeys were forced to sleep at their feet in the tiny spaces between the seats. From my position on the bumpy floor, I could see Mark looking back at me in the darkness. We shared a "What the fuck?" moment and tried to get some sleep.

The concerts were great and our first taste of actual stardom, although it was baby stardom in our case. However, the perks were undeniable. Namely, girls. That's right, I said girls. Did I mention girls? Hey, I'll admit, sometimes it felt like I was merely inheriting Tom Jones's rejects, but this whole groupie thing was totally new to me, and that actually wasn't such a bad thing at all. I found that even a potato of a guy such as I could do pretty well with the ladies as long as he had a hit record. This knowledge would serve me well over the next few decades.

By the time I got to Columbus, Ohio, the following week, I had learned how to shuffle my schedule around to accommodate multiple liaisons on a daily basis. Hey, it wasn't like I was cheating on Nita—we never had exclusivity that I was aware of. I was emerging from the hive I was never allowed into, not even in high school. I was spreading my wings at last. I was a newborn baby bee, ready to pollinate any flower that landed on my radar. Regrets? Not a one.

◆ ◆ ◆

As life-changing as the random ladies were, it was a guy who actually had a more profound effect on my future. And no, not in *that* way! I guess that the Turtles had been rather obvious about our innocence aboard the bus, but we couldn't understand what a lot of the onboard giggling had been about. Still, we were pretty sure that it had been directed at us. Paranoid? Not yet.

One night in Memphis, Mel Carter called my room and invited all of the Turtles up. This was unprecedented, to say the least. The tour had experienced an inordinate amount of resistance from hotel managers and restaurant owners as we worked our way across America's heartland, all due to the integrated nature of rock 'n' roll. We were thrilled to be on the same bill as the Shirelles and Mr. Carter, but this was still 1965 and the country was not yet ready for the races mingling so happily. Often, the entire busload was turned away at diners and motels that wouldn't accept black entertainers. These were usually the same assholes that made fun of our long hair. We hated them all, but there was nothing we could do about it. Small people with small minds have always run this country. Still, everyone on the tour was united, and we were pissed off. So maybe this meeting in Mel's room had something to do with that.

When we got there, we could hear voices inside and smelled the subtle aroma of incense that signaled a party. We knocked and Mel opened. Things got quiet. There were two very large black men in dark suits and sunglasses sitting on Mel's sofa. And between them, on the floor, was an ominous brown paper bag. No one made a move to camouflage the obvious, and we could see the long, green buds protruding from the container.

Anything worth doing is worth doing right, so it took us a while to figure out how to inhale this stuff correctly. All of us were coughing and spewing and trying not to embarrass ourselves as the large, scary guys fought to contain their laughter.

"Naw, that ain't it!" Mel was trying his best to be patient with us as the precious smoke was lost in the ozone. Finally, in desperation, Mel motioned to me to come nearer. He took a mind-blowing hit of the weed, grabbed me by the shoulders, and breathed the entire hit into my mouth, which he covered with his own. In this uncomfortable and nonerotic frightening moment, thoughts were leapfrogging through my brain. Am I high? Am I gay? Am I going to be sick? The noise had been sucked out of the room; I was, literally, in a breathless vacuum of weirdness, not knowing what was going to happen next.

And then I felt it. With the cleansing exhale that followed, the world came back into view with a new and better focus. Mel pulled back to see the expression on my face and his smile made me feel even better. Whatever this was, sign me up! It wasn't only me, either. We were like kids in a candy store: "Me next! Me! Me!" The band lined up like we were receiving the blessed sacrament. Which we were.

We hung out with Mel for an hour or so until he announced that he had some business to take care of with his "associates," and we somehow found the way back to our rooms to talk about our newly awakened perceptions. The next day, we each purchased small amounts of weed from Mel, who seemed more than ready to accommodate us. Needless to say, the rest of the tour was significantly more fun. There were no more giggles. I guess we had been accepted into adulthood in bus terms and were allowed to join everybody's hipper-than-hip little club.

The Caravan of Stars was a learning experience. Tom Jones was an education all by himself. Every day, when the tour bus arrived at our venue, there were hundreds of waiting, screaming teenage girls, and Tom taunted them mercilessly from behind the safety of his window. He actually pulled out his legendary-for-good-reason schlong, which he had nicknamed Wendell, and waved it at the befuddled girls, who hooted, hollered, and pushed their friends aside to get a look at the one-eyed monster.

"Ooh, you'd like to meet Wendell, wouldn't you, ladies? Arrrgh, here he comes, girls." Tom was very advanced.

❖ ❖ ❖

It's hard to calculate exactly how much we learned on that first six-week outing, but we could now play to any crowd in America with confidence. And we knew how to amuse ourselves between shows, too, a talent we'd soon need, as yet another bus tour was about to loom large.

And keep in mind, we're not talking about your contemporary, upscale rock 'n' roll tour bus here. Picture my nose mere inches from Gordon Waller's postconcert stocking feet. And Mark had Tom Jones to contend with. Tom, you snore! These were your Greyhounds, your Trailways: bench seats and a stinky pisser two rows behind me.

While we were still out on the road with the Caravan of Stars, our next booking came in, a little three-weeker called Wrap-Up '65. This one was a doozy. And already the six of us were beginning to appreciate how fortunate we had been mere weeks before.

The lineup was Jewel Akens, who had a monster hit called "The Birds and the Bees"; the Larks, a vocal quintet with a dance record called "The

Jerk"; and Shirley Ellis, who famously had the world playing "The Name Game." Now, add to that urban mix Bobby Goldsboro, who'd had a hit with "See the Funny Little Clown," and then insert us. Not making much sense, is it? Audiences and promoters had the same reaction: confusion.

It was as weird on the bus as it was off. Shirley had her arranger and accompanist, Lincoln Chase, with her, day and night. And it was plain to us, now seasoned druggies, that these guys were bombed 24/7 and, whatever they were on, it sure wasn't weed. Coincidentally, the Larks also seemed afflicted by this glassy-eyed medication. Those guys stayed pretty much to themselves, leaving us and Mr. Goldsboro to amuse ourselves—he just played country acoustic and made cricket noises. The pot waited until we got to our shared motel rooms.

After that one, we made a group decision *not* to do any more bus tours if we could help it. And we pretty much stuck to our guns. Once in a while, we'd wind up joining an existing tour in progress, replacing another act for a week or two if there were prior commitments involved.

We jumped on one Dick Clark Caravan to fill in for the Standells. But, jolly sorts that these gentlemen were, the lads had gone on their way letting the entire tour believe that the Turtles were infamous junkies and to keep their eyes open for suspicious behavior. Well, we didn't know that. And on one auspicious evening, as the rain pelted our Holiday Inn balcony, Al and I found ourselves pinned to the floor of our shared room by some wicked weed that had come from a local fan. We couldn't move. Which at first was hilarious. And then it wasn't. And then the tour manager started pounding on our door and yelling something about being late and leaving without us. Hell, the shower was still running in the bathroom and neither of us had unpacked yet, let alone dressed for the concert.

So we didn't. We just crawled to the door and somehow made it onto the bus, where the brilliant Ian Whitcomb ("You Turn Me On") was playing his ukulele and regaling the tour with bawdy English drinking songs. I lost it. Al lost it. We all lost it. Uncontrollable laughter, convulsing tears, gasps for air. Later, at the show, my senses went into overdrive. Somehow, I had convinced myself, in the middle of "Let Me Be," that I hadn't been singing at all; I had merely been lip-syncing, miming to the record, just as we had done on countless television shows. And then I forgot the words. So, naturally, I waited to hear what the singer was going to do before I could pretend to sing along. Only the singer was me. It was bad. I don't think anyone noticed, and that was even more disheartening. But I somehow caught up and the rest of the set was, evidently, fine. We stuck to a rented station wagon and pulling a U-Haul trailer after that.

And we were, for the most part, on our own. Traveling for the first time ever with Bill Utley behind the wheel was at once both totally freeing and really frightening. He was an awful driver with a horrible temper, which would manifest itself more violently to us later. Bill tried to be our buddy for his percentage's sake, but he really had little patience for our juvenile behavior and eschewed our pot-smoking ways. He didn't last very long as a touring manager and quickly foisted us off on his brother-in-law, who would act on his behalf, if not ours. We played ballrooms in the Midwest, school dances, mall openings. Sometimes we had dressing rooms. Sometimes, we'd change in the car.

❖ ❖ ❖

Our show was pretty silly. We did our folk-rock album stuff plus some Crossfires dance standards, when called for, and always remained self-deprecating and accessible. They loved us in the heartland. And we loved them back. Lots of them. Some nights, two at a time.

We would do a tour, come back to L.A. just long enough to do our laundry and record for the second album, and take off again. Now, when we played at the Whisky a Go Go, we were the obvious headliners and house band. We would do a couple of weeks at a time. Crazy Vito Paulekas and even crazier Carl Franzoni, Sunset Strip fixtures with white beards and gypsy clothing, would bring their commune down to our show to dance and play tambourines and frighten off the general population. Among their tribe was one very young and hot little blonde, always in a see-through top. This was a fifteen-year-old Pamela Miller, soon to be Miss Pamela of the GTOs. Our opening act was an upstart band of miscreants who called themselves the Doors. The *L.A. Times* hated them, but they sure loved us. And we sure loved the Doors.

But we were starting to doubt ourselves a little bit. We had a Top Ten record our first time out of the box, but "Let Me Be," while respectably making it into the Top 30, was a follow-up: no less and no more. It did nothing to solidify our career. And now, with yet another folk-rock album in the works, we began to question, yet again, what the hell we were protesting.

Barry McGuire's recording of "Eve of Destruction" had become an international number one record—we all knew that it would—but, as predicted, there would be no follow-up to that one.

Folk rock was already showing signs of either wearing thin or becoming fodder for parody and we were clueless about our next move. You had to have a next move if you really wanted to be America's Beatles and that we certainly did.

❖ ❖ ❖

We pulled into New York City, my ancestral homeland, for the first time to play at Steve Paul's Scene, the biggest happening club in the city. It was star-studded and we killed. Almost immediately, we were asked to fill in for a week of shows at the Phone Booth, just as the Young Rascals were about to embark on their first trip to L.A. to play the Whisky.

On our nights off, or even after our shows, the whole group would head off to Greenwich Village to hang with the hippies and smoke pot in Washington Square. Our pals from L.A., the Mothers of Invention, were playing ridiculous shows at the Garrick Theatre, and we'd hang there night after night. One lucky evening we happened into a dark, smoky nightclub called the Night Owl Cafe and got our first glimpse of the Lovin' Spoonful. They were amazing. And more than that, they were really having fun. Onstage! They were actually smiling at each other and at the adoring audience. And they weren't protesting anything—they were singing happy songs: "Good Time Music," they called it. Shit, that's what we wanted to do too! Spoiled little bastards that we were: We want *that* now.

So we returned to L.A. and, right then and there, told Lee, Ted, and Bones that we were finished with folk rock and were now the West Coast Ambassadors of Good-Time Music.

They could have panicked. They should have panicked. But instead, Bones in particular nodded knowingly and plucked a 7-inch demo record from his briefcase.

"This is the new one from P. F. Sloan," he announced.

Oh, no. Another protest song?

But then the drum pattern started and Don Murray smiled for the first time in three years.

The song was "You Baby." It became a Top 20 hit, broke the sophomore curse, and changed us, literally overnight, into the West Coast Ambassadors of Good-Time Music, just like we wanted. That song marked another sea change in the band's destiny as we suddenly became more adult-friendly and television-accessible. Now Merv Griffin's office was on the phone and Mike Douglas came out to talk to us between songs. The bigger television shows were lining up to air bands with a little longevity and here we were. There were a ton of teen dance shows on the air in the mid-'60s, and the Turtles were regulars on all of them.

I can't tell you offhand how many episodes of *Where the Action Is* we did for Dick Clark, but we did a lot. And *American Bandstand* too, the very show that I had rushed home from school to see all those years ago. Man, what a feeling that was! Local KHJ DJ Sam Riddle had three shows; Lloyd Thaxton over at channel 13 became a close friend; Clay Cole in the East and Jerry Blavat—"the Geator with the Heater"—in Philly. There was *Upbeat* in Cleveland, and on Saturday night Dick Clark had a prime-time rock show back in Hollywood as well. The biggest of the L.A. shows by far was *Shindig!* and it was a great and prestigious national network mainstay. After that one, we almost felt big-time.

If you did *Shindig!* on the West Coast, then it was a given that you'd do *Hullaballoo* in New York. That was NBC's national prime-time equivalent. They set up the cameras to shoot our segment through a fully stocked aquarium, and posed between us were the famous *Hullaballoo* models standing mannequin-still in full scuba attire. They were magnificent. One in particular caught my eye, a stunning pixie-haired blonde, and with my new self-confidence and a sense of nothing to lose, I approached.

Her name was Heidi and I somehow scored her number. In fact, she invited me on a tour of the city and I took a taxi to her apartment the following day. The bad news—Heidi had a boyfriend. The good news—Heidi also had a roommate. And this was a statuesque honey-haired ballerina with the unlikely moniker of Melita Pepper. She was aloof and artsy and couldn't have cared less about rock 'n' roll, so of course I was immediately attracted to her. She was everything that Nita was not.

Nita had been a petite little porcelain girlfriend with an amazing body and aspirations of stardom. Melita drank Lancers wine from a ceramic bottle, planted country daisies in her Upper East Side flower box, and spent hours listening to the rain on the roof while Tim Hardin played on the stereo. It was so damned New York. And it was spring: cherry blossoms in Central Park, the hansom cabs and the omnipresence of the Spoonful at the Night Owl.

I'm not sure exactly what I fell in love with, but it hit me hard. I spent a couple of extra weeks in the city before I returned to Laurel Canyon, where I spent many more weeks on the telephone.

❖ ❖ ❖

Back at home, the big buzz was that the Beatles were coming to Los Angeles to play at Dodger Stadium and, of course, we were stoked! Having purchased a new Pontiac LeMans convertible a few days before the show, I agreed to drive. It was just me and Jim Tucker at the show itself, lost in the crowd of other insane fans and not able to hear anything over the teenage din. Still, we had seen the Beatles and braved the traffic and that had been enough. Afterward, we stopped off at the Whisky to check the local hot action. And David Crosby came strolling up.

"Hey, you guys *are* coming to the party, right? 'Cause I know that Derek had you on the list."

"What party? What list?"

The party was at the Beatles' rented house on Blue Jay Way in the hills just below Laurel. Derek was Derek Taylor, who was the Beatles' as well as the Byrds' PR guy at the time, and Crosby was one of the guys who was helping Derek put this party together. Oh, man. This was going to be unbelievable. Tucker and I headed for the door only to be stopped by former Beach Boy David Marks, who we had both known from our old surf days, looking for a ride. Apparently, he was on the list too. Why not? The more the merrier.

Down Sunset and left turn up to the foothills, where there were police checkpoints at every corner. My heart was pounding as I apprehensively approached checkpoint number one.

"Kaylan? Uh . . . let me see." The uniformed cop was actually being quite cordial, considering the state of affairs between Hollywood's Finest and the local hippie contingent.

"Ah, here we are. You're good to go!"

Amazing. I was on the list. We were minutes away from actually meeting the lads. Up to the second checkpoint. And the third. Now we were right outside the house itself—I could see George Harrison drinking something in the living room. He was wearing an Indian scarf.

There was a knock on my window and I rolled it down.

"You can't park here, son. Gotta turn around and go back a block."

Okay. No biggie. I nodded and inched up to the very next driveway to turn around when all the lights in the world came on.

"Trespassing, officer. I told you!" Some lady in a fuzzy blue bathrobe had another cop's ear. "All night long, cars in my driveway. I can't stand it!"

"Sorry, fellas. You're gonna have to—"

When from the backseat comes the sound of David Marks:

"Fuck you, pig! Oink, oink!"

"Out of the car, punks!"

Right there in the bathrobe lady's driveway: hands against the vehicle. Pop the trunk, please.

"But officer, it's a brand-new car."

". . . And what do we have here? A marijuana seed?"

What? In the trunk of a car that had never been opened? They schlepped us down to the Cole Street Station in Hollywood and started in.

"The Turtles, huh? Boy, your fans are going to love this! You guys are going away for a while."

They held us all night. They called my folks since I was underage. Even my parents laughed. A seed? They let us go for illegal search and seizure. They just wanted to hassle us. The bastards kept me from meeting the Beatles.

Back at Lookout Mountain, news of my little adventure had triggered a small but evident case of paranoia. I was probably more nervous than Mark was, but I was certain that, because of the celebrity taunting I had received at the police station, we were being watched.

Richie Furay was living with us now, sleeping in the living room as he assembled his new band, the Buffalo Springfield. They were rehearsing here too. So cars were in our driveway at all hours and Stephen Stills, Neil Young, and Dewey Martin would come and go at all hours. They smoked too. It was risky business as far as I was concerned. If the noise was too much, I knew the cops would come to check it out. My name was on the lease and I now had a "record," so any consequences would be indirectly my fault.

I felt shitty. I bit my lip and kissed my canyon goodbye. Richie moved into my bedroom and I slunk into a bottom-of-the-barrel "luxury studio apartment" on Hollywood Boulevard to lick my wounds and feel sorry for myself. Nita hated it and so did I. But I remained there for a long, long time. Self-punishment is my specialty.

❖ ❖ ❖

"You Baby" legitimized the Turtles. Now we were three-hit wonders, and that meant credibility. Suddenly we were co-headlining concerts with the Yardbirds and, yes, the Lovin' Spoonful. The three acts worked really well together and did a bunch of shows throughout the Midwest that summer. And a big thank-you to Eric Burdon for showing us groupie games in a Hammond, Indiana, motel room that I still find unspeakable forty-five years later.

We had momentum on our side and then . . . White Whale couldn't find a follow-up. Again.

Al and Chuck, cashing in on the Beatles' new interest in Indian music, had written an Eastern-sounding jazz raga in 5/4 time called "Grim Reaper of Love." It wasn't commercial. It wasn't melodic. Shit, it was barely a song. But Lee and Ted owned the publishing, were getting greedy, and had nothing else. So they released it and almost ended our brief career.

What was radio supposed to do with that? Not much, it turns out. And for the first time, our newfound success seemed to be slipping away.

Frantically, Lee and Ted started putting out limited runs of singles, hoping against hope that one of them would stick. They didn't. "We'll Meet Again," the Vera Lynn World War II classic from *Dr. Strangelove*, was a hit in Canada. They tried a poppy number called "Makin' My Mind Up," which failed. Things were getting tense.

During a taping of the Jerry Blavat show one Saturday, Don Murray became convinced that the entire band was conspiring to replace him, talking behind his back, and trying to mess with him onstage. None of these allegations were true, but Don walked off in the middle of the show, screaming accusations. It was quite theatrical. He was quite nuts.

Now we had no drummer. Our Hollywood pal Joel Larson sat in on a few gigs while we began the arduous process of auditioning drummers. We were having trouble finding someone as good as Don had been, and word was all over town that we were searching. To the rescue, one Gene Clark, now formerly of the Byrds. He had a guy. . . .

Johny Barbata auditioned for the band at Western Studios, where we were ready to cut yet another single attempt. He played a Buddy Rich solo, flawlessly. The best I'd ever heard. We hired him on the spot and, since he was already set up, we recorded him on "Can I Get to Know You Better," another P. F. Sloan "You Baby" clone that charted, but not well enough.

Sensing the impending end of the band, Chuck Portz also jumped ship to become an abalone fisherman, of all things, which he still is today.

I couldn't remember being this scared before. I felt the band slipping away. What was it "they" said? Oh, yeah. The average life span of a successful rock band is eighteen months. If that were so, we were already living on borrowed time. And just when it seemed that things couldn't possibly get any worse, on the very same day, both Mark and I got our draft notices.

Shit!

SIX

How Is the Weather?

Maybe it was because we lived in the same house or were born in the same year, but for whatever reason, the local induction center requested our presence on the very same morning. Misery might love company, but neither Mark nor I was prepared for this sort of dilemma. I was panicking big-time. Three hit records in a row, an actual career making rock music, and it was all about to go away forever. I knew that if, or when, I returned from whatever fresh hell Uncle Sam had in store for me, there would be no Turtles and I'd be back in school studying for some half-assed life that I didn't really want.

It was 1966 when we got the letters. I wasn't in college anymore, so I couldn't use that deferment. I wasn't married. I wasn't supporting a family. I was in big trouble. I was going to go to Vietnam. I was going to die there, just like my high school friend Kenny Hanson would the following year. We went off to tour and Kenny went off to war. He never came home but we found his name on the Vietnam Veterans Memorial wall in Washington, DC, and it still makes me cry.

I was blind with panic. Utley said there was nothing he could do and sort of smirked about it in a very irritating way. You'd think he would have had a bit more compassion for his meal ticket. Lee and Ted were a lot more concerned, but totally clueless.

These were tough times for America, and we could feel the friction in the air. Although he didn't get his invitation to don a uniform until well after Mark and I did, Gary Lewis is a perfect example of how a side trip to the military could screw things up for a rock star. Gary had had a giant number one hit with "This Diamond Ring" and scored big with several other Top Ten singles, and yet his father, the amazing Jerry Lewis, a lifelong idol of mine, had refused to help him escape the dreaded draft. President Johnson even offered a deferment to Jerry on Gary's behalf and Jerry turned it down. Jerry was a patriot, although he was strictly showbiz and had never been in the military himself. Gary got the call in early '67 and was sent off to Nam the following year. He watched his best friend get blown away in a foxhole next to him, and returned to Hollywood. Gary's career had petered out long before he went away, but when he came home there was nothing here waiting for him. He never forgave his dad, and vice versa.

My parents were as afraid for me as I was and, in the end, it was my mother who turned everything around. "Why don't you go see your cousin Herb?" she said. I barely knew my cousin Herb Cohen. I knew that he had come to my bar mitzvah. I knew that he managed Frank Zappa and had worked with Lenny Bruce. I had heard in whispers, throughout the years, about his involvement in smuggling deals throughout the Middle East, rugs and guns and maybe more. And I knew that he had operated one of the first hip coffee houses in L.A., the Unicorn, starting in 1957. I had absolutely nothing to lose. Mom got me the phone number and Herb agreed to meet me in Laurel Canyon, in fact at Frank's house while the Mothers were out of town.

Herb was a human lawn gnome who never wore anything except those Cuban guayabera shirts, cargo pants, and an Indiana Jones fedora. If the cliché had existed back then, he would have been the model. He answered the door, directed me to a chair, and made certain that I understood he had no time for any crap.

I explained and he tried to settle me down.

"Stop worrying! I got Zappa out, I got Tim Buckley out, and I'll get you out." He handed me a notepad and a pen and told me to take notes.

"First," Herb began, "you can't bathe. I mean, for days. You should be ripe. Are you getting this?"

I nodded.

"Next, do you have drugs?"

I actually started going through my pockets.

"Not here! Jesus! You might not even need my help!" He looked at me as if I were an idiot. "I mean, do you have any drugs at home?"

Of course I did.

"Well, take them. Take all of them! Why the hell not? They got doctors there in case you OD. And remember this next bit: They are military and you're not. That means you're a civilian and they can't tell you what to do. It doesn't matter if they're a private or a general—it doesn't mean shit to you. Just keep disobeying. If they say, "Go right!" you go left. They say be quiet, you make a lot of noise, get it? There's nothing they can do. Also, fail the test."

"Huh?"

"They give you these little tests, you know? Like, basic logic. Identify the shapes, primary colors . . . don't do it."

"Don't take the test?"

"What? Wait. No. You have to take the test. Just don't pass the test. Man!"

I was scribbling down every word as if my life depended on it. Which it did. I'm certain that Herb thought I was a mental case.

"Is that it?"

"That's it. Oh, and act a little queer. They really hate that."

Mark and his girlfriend Pat Hickey had been fighting and he had taken an interim live-in lover named Pam Hermanson. On the eve of our draft board confrontation, it was the three of us at the house on Lookout Mountain and none of us had slept, washed, or changed clothes in over a week.

The weed wasn't skunky—we were. We smoked everything in the house. We took every pill we could find. We played checkers with them. We made elaborate smoothie concoctions with booze and yogurt and cough medicine and chocolate syrup. Hash and uppers and more weed and downers; by the time Pam drove us to the draft board in downtown Los Angeles, we didn't know who we were.

They divided us arbitrarily into alphabetical groups: A–L and M–Z. I whispered a hushed "See ya" to Mark as we parted ways for the day. I was told to line up with my group against a puke-green wall to await the exams. That was my cue to test the waters for the first time as I left the orderly line to stroll down the hallway, opening each and every door to stick my head in and taunt the inductees. My fellow victims were all motioning me back into formation, but it took a rather large corporal or two to corral me back.

We were led to our first test room, which resembled an eighth-grade math class with those uncomfortable one-piece desk/chair combos. This test was all about common sense: Which one of the following shapes does not belong: a circle, a square, a triangle, a rectangle, or a horse? Well, obviously, the triangle. I continued with my winning answers, adding numbers incorrectly and making apples into peace signs, all the while remembering Herb's sage words of wisdom. When I handed in my paper, the sergeant at the desk took a perfunctory look, shook his head, and made a "tsk-tsk" sound with his tongue. Then he placed a red plastic tag around my neck with a piece of string.

"What's this?"

"It's a moron tag, moron. Just follow the red line on the floor."

Which took me to the medical testing area. Here, my fellow paranoids were stripping down to their skivvies and holding their clothing in front of their naked little bodies for dear life as they approached the clerk in charge for the old turn-your-head-and-cough. But not me. I went up to the desk fully clothed in my stinkiest *schmattas*.

"What the hell do you think you're doing?"

"I'm not going to get undressed out here with all of these strange men. Are you kidding? But if *you* want to undress me, that's different. We can go into one of those little rooms and you can do anything you want to me—anything at all!"

The clerk threw up in his mouth a little bit, I'm sure.

"Jesus Christ, Dorothy! Another one! All right, sweetie, here you go!"

And with that, he stamped my paper SECTION 8 and pointed down the hall to another set of offices, where I was given more paperwork to fill out. Next, I was introduced to the admitting psychiatrist, who had a few additional questions.

"So, under drug use, you checked yes; then you unchecked it, and then you checked it again. I can see that your eyes are the size of saucers. Are you high right now?"

"What? Wait. No. I don't do drugs anymore. Oh, sure, I used to do drugs, lots of them. But now I find that I don't have to. I can close my eyes and wish myself as high as I want to be. You should try it. It saves me a fortune."

"Uh-huh. What's this here? Under suicide, there seems to be some confusion."

"Oh, no. That was a mistake. No suicides. I mean, once in a while I'd find myself just walking into the ocean, but that was just the old acid, I think. I'm totally in control right now. And I want to do my bit for my country."

"Your bit?"

"Shit, yeah. I want to jump out of that chopper with my guns blazing, man. I want to kill everything that I see: women, children, dogs, you name it. They all gotta die, man. This is for America, you bastards! Blam! Blam!"

"Yeah, well, I don't think so, Mister Ka—"

"What? You mean I don't get to go over there and kill them gooks, them motherfuckers?

"Not today, son. You get to go home."

They stamped my draft notice 4-F, NOT QUALIFIED FOR SERVICE and motioned me toward the exit door.

I did it! I beat the system. I wouldn't die in Nam.

I had never before, and have never since, been so happy.

And check this out: For some reason there was a huge parade in the streets of downtown Los Angeles on that very afternoon! I believe it was the Puerto Rican Festival. Whatever it was, I joined right in, marching and cheering at the back of the procession. I was absorbed by the revelers for a few blocks and peeled off when I spotted a phone booth, where I called my dad to come and pick me up. I couldn't wipe that smile from my face for days. Later, back at the house, I learned that Mark had undergone a similar experience, had also scored with his acting skills and, just like me, was free at last, free at last. Great God Almighty, we were free at last!

Free to be Turtles again.

❖ ❖ ❖

We had won our freedom to persevere and continue the quest for another elusive hit record. Unlike a lot of the other new bands of the late '60s, we didn't write our own A-sides. We *wanted* badly to be the Beatles, but the problem, according to White Whale, at least, was that John and Paul were great songwriters and we were not. We wrote our B-sides and album cuts, but only because White Whale owned our publishing. These guys were really old-school show-business creeps who believed that kids were good enough to sell records, but the writing belonged to the professionals. To this end, they recruited every Brill Building writer that they could, cuz after all, who in our band could deliver a tune as well as Carole King or Barry Mann and Cynthia Weil?

We were actually quite content going through the stacks of submitted demo recordings. We might not have known how to write a hit song, but as a group, we had an uncanny knack of choosing the songs that we could perform best, and we knew our limitations, or at least what the label wanted us to believe. Hell, Peter Noone didn't write his hits. The Hollies and even Gary Lewis sang Brill Building songs, and Lee and Ted were always playing on our insecurities. To them, we would always be The Boys. We were never taken seriously as songwriters until years later and even then, the label considered it a fluke. They would often just hand us a demo and tell us to learn it because it was going to be our next single. We resented them. But what could we do? I can't help but feel like deals were being made under the table without our knowledge or participation. Shady deals. In the end, we were very lucky guys despite them.

But now we found ourselves backed into a corner. After a few failed attempts at a new single, and shaken up quite a bit by the personnel changes, we realized that if we didn't find a killer hit—and soon—we would be just another three-hit wonder. I, for one, wasn't ready for a day job. Thus began the now familiar task of hunting for a single. This entailed listening to literally hundreds of acetates: demos sent by publishing companies to record labels and artists in the hopes that these songs would be made into hit records.

The process took days. After a while, your ears sort of burn out and you're not sure whether you can even make a good judgment call anymore. We were about at that phase of the listening process when we placed the phonograph needle on a rather worn-out looking hunk of vinyl sent from New York. On the demo, you can hear the composers trying their best to convey the emotion of their little song: one guy strumming an acoustic guitar while the other sings in a bizarre falsetto while pounding on his legs to get a semblance of rhythm going. The voices were abysmal; the record itself was scratchy and sticky and, we later learned, had been passed over by everyone on both coasts, from the Grass Roots to the Vogues.

And we loved it.

Despite the sound of the record, we knew we had to have it. We got White Whale to contact the publishers who, coincidentally, were the producers of the Lovin' Spoonful, and they flew the Manhattan-based writers out to L.A. for a meeting with us at the Beverly Hills Hotel, where they were ensconced in a $2,500-per-night bungalow. Oh, man, I couldn't wait for this!

Garry Bonner retrieved his guitar from the bedroom and Alan Gordon began to slap his knees in time to the strumming. They sounded even worse than the demo. But it didn't matter. We wanted this song, and they and their publishers certainly wanted us to have it.

The publishers were Charles Koppelman and Don Rubin and, indeed, they had been responsible for recording some of the greatest music of the past few years, in our band's humble opinion. Good-Time Music. We were finally closing in on the source. We just *knew* that Erik Jacobsen, who had produced the 'Spoons for Koppelman-Rubin, would be assigned to us too and that we were about to laugh our way back to the top of the charts. But instead, after forcing Lee and Ted into what must have been an uncomfortable meeting with Bones Howe, we were handed over to a relative newcomer, one Joe Wissert.

Who?

Joe, it seems, had been the child genius engineer responsible, at the unbelievable age of fifteen, for engineering some of the biggest hits to come out of Cameo-Parkway Records in Philadelphia. These included hits by the Orlons, Bobby Rydell, and Dee Dee Sharp. We remained nervous, but Charlie and Don assured us that we were golden.

Still, we weren't quite ready yet to make another record. We weren't even really a band anymore. Not yet. We enlisted the help of Chip Douglas, a bass player and vocalist we had known for years as part of the L.A. club scene.

We spent the next eight months on the road perfecting our new song, "Happy Together." Chip arranged the background vocals and even wrote out the horn parts, and he played bass too. It's difficult to assess whose contribution to the production was more important, although that very heated conversation continues to this day between Joe and Chip. I believe that the record is a total synchronicity of its parts and players and wouldn't have happened if the wrong butterfly hadn't have flapped its wings somewhere.

Everything about recording "Happy Together" was just a little bit different for us. For the first time, we weren't at our familiar and beloved Western Studios. We were now at Sunset Sound, with a lot more wood and glass than our old stomping grounds. And not only was Bones gone, so was Chuck Britz. The legendary Bruce Botnick was the engineer at the helm, helping out the new kid on the block, Joe.

The actual recording went very quickly. In fact, my lead vocal was done in one take with Lee and Ted grinning at me through the glass partition. I tossed in the line "How is the weather?" from Alan Gordon's original throwaway demo and everyone laughed. I knew that I'd have a few more chances to sing the song without a joke ending. But no, they all loved it and it became part of rock history. I was just being a jerk.

Still, by the time we had put on the background voices and Botnick cranked the track, powered by Johny's fantastic and tasty drumming, we all heard the magic. Add Chip's orchestra and Wissert's airy mix and, voilà! A sound that has never been duplicated.

The record is justly included in the Rock and Roll Hall of Fame, although for political reasons, the Turtles, as a band, will probably never be. But that's a different book for another time.

"Happy Together" remains the only time I've left a recording session *knowing* that I had just made a number one record. It was not only the Turtles' biggest hit record, it changed just about everything for us!

It still defines me.

SEVEN

Beat the Beatles

Here's a tip for those times when you're a little down and out: Have a number one record! It really does wonders for one's self-esteem. Talk about your sea change. Had it not been for the women who were already beginning to complicate my thoughts, these would have been the smoothest seas I had ever sailed. But first, I had to tell Nita about my love in the city.

It had been your cliché slow-motion, soft-focus Elvira Madigan kind of daydream. Sitting down with Nita and her mother in their Culver City apartment, I was only peripherally aware of their double heartbreak. Look at me: I had never had anyone outside of my immediate family who gave a shit about me one way or the other, and here I was, kissing off the most beautiful chick I had ever seen because I had fallen in love with the idea of being in love. I was a rat. Truly. It was a selfish and pompous act on my part and the beginning of a very long list of life errors. It also wasn't the last time that I would be such an asshole to the girls in my world. I guess I had a lot of living to do.

So, as "Happy Together" began its meteoric rise to the top of the charts, Melita and I pursued our long-distance love affair. And, of course, I was also getting laid every time I turned around. We all were. Karmically screwed forever.

Our song was everywhere in a big hurry. I heard it every half-hour on every radio station in L.A. By the time it hit the Top 20, Bill Utley's phone was ringing off the hook.

And the inquiries were growing classier. We got the first clue about our emerging status with a booking on the very prestigious *Smothers Brothers Comedy Hour*. Having grown up a folkie, I knew the brothers' comedy shtick by heart. Mark and I had sung "Marching to Pretoria" and performed the rest of their act in his father's den on our drunken overnights. And these guys had the ear of the underground. Tommy Smothers was John Lennon's friend. Getting this show was a huge deal. All these years later, it still is. Tommy loves to smoke weed. He did then too. And he's a brilliant guy who, like the rest of us, desires a little credit for thinking outside the box. So we thought that it was fantastic that Tommy took us under his wing and introduced us to the national television audience as his good friends and recent discovery.

We had the best time ever doing a TV show at CBS's Television City in Fairfax, next to the farmers' market and across the street from the Farmer's Daughter Hotel—hourly rates available. I sang live over the actual backing track from the studio sessions.

Everyone else could relax and lip-sync their parts, but I was realizing now that I would have to stay alert and be in great voice if I was going to be singing live from now on. Just a few weeks later, the brothers brought us back again, this time to proudly announce that their discoveries had the biggest record in America. We had a lot more confidence this time around.

❖ ❖ ❖

I moved into a tiny little jewel box of a house on Kirkland Avenue, back in Laurel Canyon. I didn't need that low-self-esteem Hollywood Boulevard flophouse anymore. I was done punishing myself. For now. Everything was better. The Midwest ballroom gigs were being replaced by actual concerts in beautiful theaters. We were invited to perform at the Expo 67 world's fair in Montreal. It was amazing. We played at the Alaska centennial ceremonies in Anchorage. We did *The Tonight Show*, got the nod and the wink from Johnny, and got asked to play Jerry Lewis's telethon by Ed McMahon himself. Not to be outdone, *The Joey Bishop Show*, with a young Regis Philbin, phoned. We were often flown to remote locations in tiny private planes and met at the airport by waiting limousines. This was the life I had always imagined that rock stars lived. Now it was my turn. When *The Ed Sullivan Show* called, we were only one degree of separation from our heroes, the Beatles.

The following week, "Happy Together" knocked "Penny Lane" out of the number one slot in America. It stayed there for three weeks in late March and early April of '67.

The Ed Sullivan Show was the pinnacle of success in show business, not just for rock acts, but for all acts, from Judy Garland to the Harmonicats to those plate spinners and ventriloquists. Everyone watched, every Sunday night at 8 P.M. on CBS. And I mean everyone. I always had. My parents had watched Ed as far back as I could remember. I was still living at home when we had all watched the Beatles together. Now my parents would get to see their own son, in living color, on the giant TV he had bought for them.

CBS put us up at the Plaza Hotel, which would have been spectacular had it not been for the construction going on below our room on Central Park South. I met Melita there and my nerves were already frazzled going into the week of rehearsals for Sunday night. The jackhammers were an unnecessary addition to the mix. I couldn't sleep and I was losing my voice. CBS called a doctor for me, who prescribed a sleeping aid to ensure that I would relax enough to regain some vocal strength before the live performance. It was a lethal-looking maroon-colored gelcap containing 500 milligrams of a substance called Placidyl. Welcome, my friend—you and I are about to spend quite a few fun-filled years together.

Mr. Sullivan, famous for his confusion on-air as well as for his malapropian introductions, brought us out on live television with the words, "Ladies and gentlemen, and they're all from California!"

The program went very well indeed. You can still view it online or on DVD. The Smothers stuff too. It's all still out there. You can't outrun your past. My voice kicked in, the band looked great, and when the song was ending and the cameras cut to Ed, Mark and I boldly walked up to the man himself to present him with an oversize prop flower. He accepted it, but he sure wasn't expecting it. Flower Power, man! The Turtles were the new poster boys for the movement of peace and love as the most important summer in musical history began. Ed must have liked us, because we returned a couple of times to play our new releases. It got much easier and a lot less stressful.

❖ ❖ ❖

I had made it! Life was good. I drove a Mercedes 280SL and wore velvet and lace onstage. I had a fuzzy top hat I had appropriated from Western Costume and a sweet walking stick I carried as an even more outrageous affectation. "Happy Together" was now a number one record around the world. My parents loved me and Melita was talking marriage.

Meanwhile, Chip Douglas had been talking to his pals Micky Dolenz and Davy Jones. He quit the Turtles, despite having a number one record, to produce the Monkees. Their first record together was "Daydream Believer," so the partnership obviously worked. It was now up to us to find his replacement. And we knew just the guy: our L.A. friend and former lead singer and bassist for the Leaves, Jim Pons. He slipped seamlessly into our band and our hearts and would remain there though many subsequent incarnations. It's Jim you see in the aforementioned video clips; Chip had no desire to be a part of any democracy.

All the while, a strange fever was sweeping through our little bubble. It was called marriage. First, Al had gotten hitched to his post–high school sweetheart, Diane, and they had a child instantly. He was already quite the family man by 1967. Then Mark married his high school girlfriend, Pat. Jim Pons invited us all to Oregon to witness his vows to one Nan Gary. Don Murray married Kathy and although Tucker was unaffected, I was also swept up in the madness.

Melita and I were planning a June wedding, even though I had not yet turned twenty. She picked out this pretty little Rudi Gernreich number and, with her long honey-colored hair flowing in the wind, she was all the inspiration that I needed to return home from what was to be our first European tour.

We returned to Sunset Sound with Joe Wissert at the helm and Bruce Botnick at the controls. There was never any question about what our next recording would be. Even though we had discovered quite a few wonderful songs in our demo listening, we were now a Koppelman-Rubin act. They had chosen wisely for the Lovin' Spoonful and we could only assume that they knew more than we did. They picked another song by Garry Bonner and Alan Gordon: a zippy little number with vaudeville razzmatazz called "She'd Rather Be with Me," and, cute as it was, none of us were under the delusion that there was magic here.

But White Whale wanted it, we had a big tour ahead, and we were in no position to start arguing abstracts like magic. So, in late May, with "She'd Rather" climbing the charts both here and abroad, and having dethroned the Beatles on our home turf, we finished playing a late concert in upstate New York and met Bill Utley at JFK Airport for a cheesy non-stop Air India flight to London.

EIGHT

We Rule This World! No One Can Touch Us!

The flight was amazing. The smells were exotic and foreign and so were the passengers. We sat in the rear of the old 707 in what was, back in the day, the smoking section. They served us little green curried snacks that were indescribable and inedible. And, I swear, although I might have imagined this part, there were people traveling with live chickens in cages jammed into those tiny overhead luggage bins. Everyone had turbans and no one spoke the Queen's English at all.

Why, we couldn't help but wonder, did our record company stick us on this weird and depressing airline when we were, obviously, the next big thing? Seems that it was impossible to get paid for Indian sales, but if you took your payment in trade—like airplane tickets—that was no problem. They all did it; it wasn't just White Whale. Besides, we weren't on White Whale Records in the UK.

Our first records, "It Ain't Me Babe" and "Let Me Be," had been released by Pye Records, a British indie label that had the Kinks, among other luminaries. We were just thrilled to have our songs released globally; we'd never expected hits. When "You Baby" was released, it was on Andrew Loog Oldham's Immediate Records, with much more prestige attached. Oldham loved us—still does—but it didn't help propel our good-time song into the Brit charts. When "Happy Together" came out and began its meteoric rise up the American charts, Decca Records in the UK called Lee and Ted and promised them an international hit if they'd sign an independent distribution contract. Decca was massive, as was their subsidiary London Records, which released American artists. We were finally on a major label.

"Happy Together" was already a huge record in England as we crossed the Atlantic on our stinky chariot. Tucker got plastered on the flight over, alternately yelling about how we were bigger than the Beatles and passing out in his coach seat. Utley, of course, flew first class. We read all the British music magazines on that flight: *Sounds, Disc & Music Echo, NME* (*New Musical Express*), and *Melody Maker*. This Yank called Jimi Hendrix was on the cover of a recent *Melody Maker* with a big article about how he was single-handedly changing the rock scene forever, but we didn't know who he was or what the big deal was about him.

What really caught our attention, however, was a column called Blind Date, in which a celebrity was played a bunch of random new releases and reviewed them without knowing who the artists were. This week's guest artist was the singer Lulu, of "To Sir with Love" fame. And one of her reviews was of our follow-up single, "She'd Rather Be with Me." She recognized our voices instantly, which I guess was a good thing. And then she proceeded to attack. "Oh, these are the Americans who did 'Happy Together,' right? Um . . . too bad. I had expected so much more from them. Oh, well." And that was that. Dismissed. We were momentarily depressed but then realized that it was only Lulu talking here and that probably no one cared. Fortunately we were correct. "She'd Rather" became a much bigger hit in Europe than "Happy Together" had been—go figure. And maybe her review, in some small way, had helped.

We landed at Heathrow sometime after 8 P.M. and took taxis to our assigned hotel, the Stratford Court, a stuffy businessman's rest on Oxford Street. Definitely not a rock hotel. We were still wearing the clothes we had worn on the flight over. The message light on my telephone was blinking when I first entered my tiny room. Calling the front desk to retrieve my message, I learned that I had received a call from Graham Nash of the Hollies. I called Graham instantly and he happily invited the entire band over to his flat to hang out and have a smoke. No one even changed his shirt—we quickly hopped into a cab and embarked upon our first international adventure.

❖ ❖ ❖

Nash had a beautiful apartment with Oriental rugs and hanging art. Sitar music was softly playing and, to complete the surreal picture, there was Donovan, the "Mellow Yellow" man himself, dressed in Indian garb and sitting cross-legged on one of the aforementioned carpets, smoking hash from a hookah. Just hanging out, the way we had imagined things would be if we ever made it to England. It was all "Hello, lads" and "Welcome!" and we settled down to enjoy some London hospitality. After an hour or so, when we were all sufficiently baked, Graham asked us if we wanted to hear something brand-new. We were all psyched, thinking that we would be among the first to hear the new Hollies album, and voiced our approval and anticipation.

"Sorry, lads. No Hollies tonight. This is the new album from the Fabs!"

What? The new Beatles record? We had heard about this for months. How the hell did Graham have the new Beatles record? It wasn't even out yet! Graham grabbed a 7½-inch tape reel from his shelf and threaded it into his machine.

"George gave this to me last week. It's bloody amazing!"

And, Donovan said, "It'll blow your mind."

Which it did. *Sgt. Pepper's Lonely Hearts Club Band* was, and is, the greatest rock album ever made. We knew it that night and it's still true almost half a century later. Our collective jaws were on the floor. Song after song, trip after trip, we were whisked away on a cloud of hash and music and celebrity. And when "A Day in the Life" finally ended with the world's longest chord, we were smiling and exhausted. Tucker said, "Man, those guys are gods! If I could meet them, I swear, I could die a happy man."

"Hope you've got insurance, Tucko, 'cause your dreams are about to come true!" This says Graham as he reaches for his keys and his jacket. "Fancy popping 'round for a pint, lads?" We were on our feet in a heartbeat, ready to follow Nash anywhere. And on the way out, Donovan wisely cautioned, "Beware of Lennon!" I didn't know what he meant at the time, but I should have listened.

We wound though the wet London streets with Nash at the wheel till we reached an inconspicuous-looking building in the middle of a business district—not quite what we were expecting. The tiny sign read THE SPEAKEASY, and an arrow pointed to the entrance. We went up the narrow stairs and the sounds of music pulsing from the club grew more intense with every step. Graham yelled over the music, "Stick around late enough and you'll get to hear Eric jam tonight."

Al asked, "Burdon?"

Graham laughed. "No, son, Clapton!"

The club itself was divided into two sections. The band onstage performed to a full house of trendy mods at tables and on the dance floor while a separate glassed-in area was kept relatively soundproof and designated as the restaurant. We were greeted at the door by a bearded gent in a bowler hat who met Graham with a hearty handshake and directed us past the bar to the showroom beyond. At the bar, Nash paused to make a quick introduction.

"Justin Hayward, John Lodge of the Moody Blues, I'd like you to meet the Turtles from America."

We all shook hands and exchanged pleasantries. I think it was Mark who approached the two and congratulated them on their success. "You guys are really cool. Nice to meet you. Which one of you sang 'Go Now'? 'Cause that's one of the greatest songs of all time!"

"Uh, yeah, thanks, I guess," replied John. "But that was Denny Laine and he's no longer with the group."

Volman tried to backpedal. "Oh, sorry. I didn't know. So, what are you guys doing these days? Still in the music business?"

"We are currently working on a major symphonic piece of vast proportions with the London Festival Orchestra. It's a multidimensional journey into the psyche called *Days of Future Passed*."

"Called what?"

"*Days of Future Passed*."

"Ha! That's great. Really catchy. Uh, yeah. Well, good luck with that."

And with that, Mark set off on his way, following the pack into the club, shaking his head and mumbling. "Oh, yeah, that's catchy all right. What pompous jerks."

"Bloody tourists!" from Justin and John.

❖ ❖ ❖

Inside the Speakeasy, all the girls looked like Twiggy, the iconic pixie-haired waif model whose London fashion had taken the world by storm.

We must have walked past fifteen look-alikes on our way to our next destination and we actually heard the Beatles before we saw them. It was just like being in *A Hard Day's Night*.

"Aw, come on, John. Leave the candles alone. You're gonna start a bloody fire in here."

"I can't see anything down here, Paul. It's as dark as a hooker's heart." And then, a female voice.

"Please, Paul. Don't humor him anymore. This is getting ridiculous. I'm going to leave."

Graham led us around the corner, where the Fab Four were hanging with their dates at a private table in the back of the room. Well, actually it was the Fab Three—George Harrison was not in attendance. (For those of you familiar with the 2003 movie that I wrote chronicling this evening, *My Dinner with Jimi*, Harrison was added to this scene for dramatic effect. I regret fictionalizing some of those moments to this day.) The deal was, Lennon was actually under the table taking Polaroid pictures up the skirts of his female companions while Paul lent a hand. Ringo laughed at everything, and Paul's then girlfriend, Jane Asher, was doing her best to drag him out of there. Dressed in Carnaby Street's finest, the Beatles were dimly lit, and a halo of light illuminating their mop-top hairdos added just the right ambiance to make this already bizarre scene even more surreal.

Paul was ducking under the table himself now, helping his business partner illuminate the proceedings with his disposable lighter, and Jane was searching the booth for her coat as we approached them, with Graham in the lead.

"I'll be leaving now, Paul," Jane said through clenched teeth as she pushed her way out of the booth and stood there, staring him down.

"Hi, Jane." Graham was friendly but she didn't even acknowledge his presence.

"I'm going home, Paul. And I don't mean your home." She made her way toward the exit as we all walked up in a pack. Jim Tucker actually grabbed her arm to stop her en route.

"Hey, Miss Asher. Hi. My name is Jim Tucker and I worked with your brother." Jim was referring to the Dick Clark tour we had done with Peter (her brother) and Gordon. He extended his hand, only to have her push him away.

"Piss off, wanker!" Jane just blew him off and brushed past us on her way out of the club. Jim stood there examining his hand for a long moment.

"Hey, guys," Graham greeted as Paul frantically scrambled to his feet.

"Jane! Jane! Aw, come on, baby. We're just having a little fun." Jane kept walking.

"Boys, I'd like you to meet the Turtles, all the way from America."

"Pleased to meet you." Ringo was the first to shake our sweaty hands. Then both John and Paul settled back in their seats and greeted us in similar fashion.

Paul said, "I really enjoyed your record." And then, to me, "Great voice, man. Nice set of pipes." I was bursting.

Then Lennon. "Yeah, that's a lovely bit of Flower Power in the middle there with those ba-ba-bas." And then all three of them sang the ba-ba-bas. And we were all beside ourselves with swollen pride.

"So, where did you learn to sing?" Paul asked me.

"High school choir, I guess. Then we formed the band and started playing local clubs, you know, a little bit of R&B stuff—"

"What kind of R&B stuff."

"Oh, you know, 'Money,' 'What'd I Say,' 'Justine' . . ."

"'Justine' by Don and Dewey? I love that song."

And then Paul began to sing the Crossfires' trademark soul song. I joined in on the answers and the chorus. Ringo played spoons on the tabletop while the customers watched and Lennon looked on as if bored to death. When we were done, there was a smattering of applause and Paul said, "That was great. I'd love to do that with *my* band some day. You sing great."

"Oh my God, thank you," I gushed.

"Still, it *is* a bit sappy on your record there when you sing 'invest a dime' with that cry in your voice. A bit light in the loafers, if you ask me."

"What?" Yeah, I became defensive all right. "We're just trying to be the American version of *you!*"

"Touché" said McCartney.

"Well, that's not bloody likely, is it?" Lennon piped in. His eyes skipped from Turtle to Turtle, checking us out for the first time. "And what do you call that guy over there?" John pointed at Tucko, who was cowering in his wrinkled brown suit, thrilled just to be noticed.

"That's Jim Tucker, our rhythm guitar player"

"Bad suit, son. And an even worse haircut. Did you tell your barber to give you a Beatle cut? It's awful, man. You give rhythm players a bad name."

Tucko, oblivious, stumbled for words. "You're like a god to me, man. You guys changed my life."

Much to his credit, Pons tried, in vain, to turn the conversation around. "We just heard *Sergeant Pepper* and I've got to thank you on behalf of the entire world for the greatest album of all time!"

Paul graciously nodded thanks and toasted us with his beverage. But John was not to be denied.

"Tucko, is it? I could have a lot of fun with that name. Let's see . . . Tucko Tucko, bo bucko, banana fanna fo fucko . . ."

Tucker winced and Lennon saw the weakness and went in for the kill.

"There was a boy named Tucko, a very stupid fellow—"

Finally, Jim realized that he was the butt of Lennon's abuse and could hold back no longer.

"What is your problem, man? You're supposed to be the Beatles! I fuckin' *loved* you guys and you turn out to be assholes."

Lennon feigned shock and recoiled at the words.

"Tsk, tsk . . . such language. What would your mum say?"

"She'd say you were a dick, that's what! Man, was I wrong. You're a total shit! I'm sorry I ever met you!"

Lennon shook his head slowly, savoring every syllable. "You never did, son. You never did."

And with that, Jim Tucker walked away from the table, up the stairs, and into a cab. And, following the few British shows we had lined up, Jim flew home and never played music again. The Turtles would continue on as a five-piece band from that time forward. The other guys followed Jim upstairs, and our goodbyes were a lot sadder than our hellos had been.

"See you, fellas," said McCartney. "Sorry!"

Lennon narrated the egress. "And there they go, ladies and gentlemen, the Truffles from Salad California!"

❖ ❖ ❖

I was devastated. This had been the most important night of my life and it had gone to hell. I refused to cab it back to the hotel. I just watched, heartbroken, from the Speakeasy's front door and felt like I wanted to cry. That is, until a voice broke my reverie.

"Excuse me. Can I please have your autograph?"

That voice just couldn't be talking to me. I looked up to see a silhouette framed by the outside lights. It was an immaculately dressed hippie type with long blond hair and a blue velvet suit. He had a sheet of paper for me to sign and, without thinking, I took it from him and scrawled my name.

"Who should I make this out to?" I asked.

"Brian would be great, thanks."

"Is that why you're dressed like Brian Jones?" I asked, intelligently.

"No, I'm dressed this way because I *am* Brian Jones."

At last, I left my torpor long enough to look up and, what do you know? It was, indeed, Brian Jones of the Rolling Stones. I couldn't believe it.

"What? What do you want with my autograph? *I'm* nobody."

"Are you serious? You're Howard Kaylan from the Turtles. I love your stuff. I've got all of your records going back to the folkie stuff. It's great, man. I love California music: you guys, the Beach Boys, the Mamas and the Papas. The Turtles have the best harmonies in the business. Isn't that right, Jimi?"

"You can say that again," said a voice from the stairway. With the lights in my eyes, it took a minute for me to make out the features of the dude on the stairs. I recognized him from the cover of *Melody Maker*. It was Jimi Hendrix.

"We're going to grab some food," Brian announced. "Would you care to join us?"

"I sure would!" I answered, a bit too anxiously. And the three of us all tried to cram ourselves into the doorway of the club at the same time—very Three Stooges.

Jimi said, "Why, you, I oughta!" à la Moe.

We all laughed and extricated ourselves as Brian went, "Nyuk, nyuk, nyuk," and we walked back into the Speakeasy. Once inside, we approached the glassed-in restaurant and Jimi started making out with one of the waitresses as Brian found a lady friend and disappeared into the crowd.

"Is he coming back?" I asked naively.

Hendrix laughed and said, "I don't think we'll see him again this night. It's cool. Wanna eat?"

I did. We were seated at a semiprivate table with a view of the stage, although all we could hear though the glass was the booming of the bass and an occasional screech of feedback. I think Adam Faith was onstage, but I wouldn't swear to it. Jimi ordered for both of us, since he knew the club's offerings without the assistance of a menu. Spinach omelets. I had never had one before. Not a big spinach fan.

Then the drinks started coming. Scotch and Cokes. Everybody was drinking them. I can still taste that acidic, sickeningly sweet flavor at the back of my throat. We spoke of many things, mostly music. I tried to document the conversation in the movie decades later, but it really wasn't very enlightening. Jimi asked me what success felt like and explained how he had come to play his guitar upside down. We talked about girls and marriage and cars and his upcoming gig at the Monterey Pop Festival in June. He was really nervous that the American critics weren't going to understand what he was trying to do, although he was already revered throughout Europe. He told me about being a paratrooper and about his father and Seattle. But mostly, we talked shop, all about the audience and how to work a crowd. He was smart and soft-spoken and a real mensch. I was impressed, not only with Jimi's conversation, but with his tolerance for alcohol, which was amazing.

The drinks kept coming and then the omelet arrived. It wasn't bad. A bit too creamy, I remember thinking. The restaurant manager came by and offered many glasses of complimentary cognac, which numbed the situation down a bit, and then Jimi broke out a joint. It was a huge bomber of hashish and tobacco: That's what they were smoking in England, not marijuana, and I became instantly paranoid.

"Hey, what are you worried about?" Hendrix asked. This is London and it's gonna be the Summer of Love—that's what the writers are calling it already! We're young and we have hit records and all the pussy we can handle. Shit, man! We rule this world! No one can touch us! Now smoke up and don't waste it."

And smoke we did. And drink. And eat. And talk until the room started spinning and I began to feel like an American amateur, in way over my head.

"Ooo, Jimi. I'm not doing so well, man. Where's the loo?"

"The loo? The can? The potty? The powder room?" Jimi was not funny. And sadly, and much to my regret, my only response was, "I'm not gonna make it, man." I proceeded to throw up violently, all over Jimi's classic and beautiful red velvet suit.

He jumped to his feet, screaming.

"What the fuck, man! My suit! Shit! What the fuck?"

I passed out cold, right there at the table, in a pile of my own sick. I don't know how I got back to the hotel that night. Not at all. But I do know that Hendrix jammed at the Speakeasy later in the evening. With Eric!

Clapton, not Burdon.

Sergeant Pepper came out the next day and I had one of the roadies buy me a portable phonograph so I could play it over and over as I nursed the world's worst hangover. We had to cancel a few shows; Tucker stayed a few days before he flew home alone.

❖ ❖ ❖

Once we were able, on the following Sunday, the Turtles played at the Speakeasy and Jimi was there to root us on. He never mentioned the suit, but I do know that he had to retire it. I think he had others made, but that particular red velvet number was never smelt or dealt with again. Brian Jones was at the show too, taking 8-mm movies of us onstage, probably without sound—the complete collector. The Beatles were there too, as were the Moody Blues. Go figure! Luckily, we were great.

Decca assigned us this wonderful lady called Miranda who took us around town, went shopping for clothes and souvenirs with us, and showed us how to blend in a bit with the locals, although we were far too fat to be mistaken for Brits. The trip did pay off, though. "She'd Rather Be with Me" got to number four on the UK charts and we did tons of TV and radio shows, most of which are still online.

Melita met me at the airport when our Air India flight brought us home. But she had cut off all of her long, beautiful hair. Seems like Twiggy's pixie haircut had caught on big-time in the States and, even years later, she never grew it back. We got married that month, June of '67, and the haircut went well with the Rudi Gernreich dress, so I guess it all worked out.

In years to come, we would get to know the Beatle lads quite a bit better and would return to England often, but there was only one Summer of Love and, having ushered it in with quite a bang, we were ready for the absolute best summer of our lives.

NINE

Eht Seltrut

What a wedding it was. Jim Pons, our new bass player and a recent husband himself, was my best man. He drove my Mercedes 280SL and I rode shotgun all the way to the Little Brown Church, a chapel well-used by the stars and their friends on Coldwater Canyon Avenue. My parents and brother, Al, were in attendance, as were Melita's mother, Helen Benson, and whoever she was with at the time—I think it was this cabana boy she brought home with her from a trip to her native Greece. Oh, and a stepfather or two. The woman was a free thinker.

Afterward, Jim rode back with somebody else, and my new bride and I were off to our tiny bachelor pad on Kirkwood. Which, by the way, didn't remain our residence for long. We found a big white box of a modern-looking edifice at the top of Laurel Canyon at the corner of Wonderland Park and Hollywood Hills Road and bought it. Soon there was to be the expected patter of little feet, if Melita had her say about it, and before I knew it, the little Mercedes was replaced by a hulking blue Volvo station wagon. I should have had a clue right then, but I was blinded by the zeitgeist and besides, marriage is all about compromise, right?

In the meantime, I had no intention of remaining a true-blue husband out on the road—I'd seen how it was done—so home was a place I went to between shows and affairs for two weeks at a time while, just like the rest of the band and every other band out there, I was cultivating relationships, or at least one-nighters, with any cute girl who would give the old boy a tumble. I could look ahead at my itinerary and see where I was going to be on any given day before picking up the phone and scheduling my nighttimes around the shows. The shows became secondary, in fact. A good night wasn't judged by the quality of our onstage performance, but by the performances of our nighttime girls. And on a lot of nights, particularly after the success of "Happy Together," I had to schedule my lady visitors so as not to conflict with one another. In retrospect, I wonder when I ever slept. My, what amazing things the young male body is capable of, especially when there are female bodies around that are far more capable.

So, not to brag or compare myself to an NBA player, but it was astounding to me, as a not-so-attractive teenager, how many women I was able to "be with"—and this continued into the '80s: lined up in the hallways, crossing paths in the lobby preceding the shift change . . . Of course, with each lady came baggage. I heard more stories about parents and brothers and unfaithful boyfriends and school than I care to recall. In fact, fortunately, I recall none of them. A switch in my brain could accept a certain amount of palaver without even taking it in. Click. Ah! That's better. Now I don't hear a word you're saying. Oh, is that your bra?

Got pretty damned good at it. I know, a horrible, chauvinistic way to act. If it helps at all, I've learned my lessons, albeit late in life and following at least three decades of Caligula-like decadence. I'm older and wiser now, and besides, I don't have the energy anymore these days, or the inclination. And I don't give a flaming shit about anybody's brother or their schoolwork. I'd kill myself if I had to listen to that crap again. But at the time, it got me into many, many pairs of panties, and that was the game.

❖ ❖ ❖

Man, did we have fun when we got back to touring America during the Summer of Love in 1967. There were chicks in Seattle, Columbus, Atlanta, Chicago, Miami, and everywhere in between. I was the lead singer, so I got noticed and usually laid. But Barbata was amazing. With his Italian suits, perfect coif, and Playboy Club maneuvers, he was a pleasure to witness on a nightly basis. The rest of us were all rank amateurs compared to Johny. He had the girls in and out in like twenty minutes. Next! And these were generally the cream of the crop, so to speak. It's true, some of the ladies complained about Johny's brusque treatment, but remember, they had to complain to someone! And that was usually one of us. So— and please don't be offended—some lucky bandmate would usually wind up with the legendary "sloppy seconds." I apologize, ladies, but I'm here to educate as well as entertain.

The theaters were bigger now and the crowds were a lot more animated, though every once in a while we'd find ourselves doing things like opening up for the jumping horse on the pier at Atlantic City. True, not a lot of prestige there, but that damned horse was amazing. He'd hurl himself and his rider off of the boardwalk and into the Atlantic Ocean. For a lousy carrot, for God's sake. And ten times a day. Like us, he had showbiz in his blood. Or, to paraphrase Woody Allen, he just needed the carrots. We all did.

Melita and I installed a pricey black-bottomed pool in our tiny hillside yard. I still have no idea why. But I had actual tour money for the first time in my short career, and it felt great.

And, because the Turtles had been deemed family-friendly following our first Sullivan show, we were the new "go to" band for the myriad television shows being produced for syndication. Everybody had a show, and we did them all. Let's see: Della Reese had a show, as did Mike Douglas, Merv Griffin, Diahann Carroll, even Woody Woodbury. Then there was *Shebang, Upbeat, The Hollywood Palace, Hollywood A Go-Go, 9th Street West*. It wasn't uncommon for us to do two or three big-time TV shows in any given week. We were getting cockier with each performance, and the wackiness sometimes translated to a lack of caring on our part, but hey, that's what the Beatles did. We did care; we just thought it was cooler and more English to act that way, especially for the lip-synced broadcasts.

By the time we did our second *Ed Sullivan Show*, my nerves had left me: I got high instead of uptight, and I really had a good time. "She'd Rather Be with Me," for all our trepidation, zoomed up to either number two or three, depending on which trade paper you believed. Not bad for a follow-up, especially one that was supposedly lacking that magic.

We were part of the Koppelman-Rubin hit machine now, exactly what we wished for. But as we all know, you gotta be careful about those wishes. The records we released weren't our choice anymore. I guess the Lovin' Spoonful went through the same thing, but they had John Sebastian and we had Bonner and Gordon. And, as brilliant as they were as a song-writing team, when we listened to our next proposed single, it was tanta-mount to beholding the emperor's new clothes. We just didn't get it.

"You Know What I Mean" was basically a tone poem. There was no disputing that it was beautiful and that Joe Wissert's production was flawless, but there was no verse, to speak of, and no sing-along chorus at all. I sang the lead vocal in a single take and there were to be no overdubs—just me, out there in a blue spotlight in front of an amazing full orchestra and, of course, the band playing everything else. It was different. It was, I suppose, a change of pace for us, but as Stan Freberg once famously spoofed, "If they can't bop to it, bombsville!"

You surely couldn't dance to this. But we said nothing. We were scared and we had begged for this. We didn't even think to talk back to either our production company or our label. Management didn't care; they were too busy counting their cash and putting together many more road months for their golden boys. As a band, we feared the worst: There goes our winning streak and soon it'll be back to Dairy Queen, metaphori-cally speaking. But here's the weird part: The record was a hit, climbing to number twelve in the all-important *Billboard* singles chart. Radio played the hell out of it. We were and continue to be grateful, but we never performed "You Know What I Mean" onstage live. Ever. Not even when it was a hit. I still turn it up when it comes on oldies radio, but I doubt that I could remember the words. That record's success was a miracle as far as I'm concerned.

❖ ❖ ❖

And I needed all the miracles I could get, because in 1968, when I was the ripe old age of twenty-one, Melita informed me that we were preggers. All of the wives were. In 1968, if you were a Turtle, your wife was with child. That's cool. It was the thing to do.

It was our turn to live large. We saw all the other hit bands enjoy their success, and we were bound and determined to do the same. Unfortu-nately, we didn't have the benefit of wisdom or direction to guide us. No one helped us set up retirement accounts or invest our earnings in growth accounts. Hell, no. We received our checks and didn't see "management" until they needed something from us. So when we got money, we spent

Brother Al, Howard as Roy Rogers, and grandfather Ike Kaplinsky on the stoop of the Kaplans' home at the Linden Projects in Brooklyn, New York, 1953. This grainy shot is the only surviving photograph of Howard as a child.

Mom and Dad—Sally and Sid Kaplan: first to arrive at Howard's first wedding reception. Westchester, California, 1967.

Promotional photo from 1964 for the release of the Crossfires' "One Potato, Two Potato" single. Note the aprons and potato peelers. The group had to place gaffer tape over the Iron Cross on their drum kit—the label thought it sent the wrong message. Left to right: Howard, Al Nichol, Don Murray, Chuck Portz, Mark Volman, and Jim Tucker.

The Turtles just before taping their first *Shindig!* appearance in 1965, backstage at ABC Studios in Hollywood. Left to right: Mark, Don, Howard, Al, Jim Tucker, and Chuck.

The Turtles on *The Ed Sullivan Show*, 1967, New York City. Left to right: Mark, Johny Barbata, Howard, Al, and Jim Pons.

Howard and his first wife Melita Kaylan at their wedding in Studio City, California, 1967.

The lonely guy in one of his heavier Turtle incarnations, 1968.

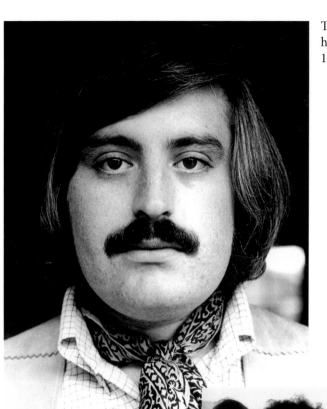

Alternate cover photo for the *Turtle Soup* album. The Turtles: Al, Mark, Jim Pons, Howard, and John Seiter in Malibu, California, 1970. (Photo by Henry Diltz, used by permission.)

Alternate photo for the Turtles' *Battle of the Bands* album interior. Left to right: Johny, Mark, Al, Howard, and Jim Pons in Laurel Canyon, California, 1969. (Photo by Henry Diltz, used by permission.)

Meeting the Kinks' Ray Davies at L.A. International Airport for the recording of *Turtle Soup*, which he produced in 1970. Left to right: Ray, John Seiter, and Howard.

The Mothers of Invention perform the Sanzini Brothers' world-famous Pyramid Trick, Los Angeles, 1970. Left to right: Frank Zappa, Jeff Simmons, Ian Underwood, Mark Volman, George Duke, Howard, and Aynsley Dunbar.

The Mothers of Invention pose at London's Royal Albert Hall, where they thought they'd be performing. Neither the band nor the sold-out audience was in on manager Herb Cohen's elaborate publicity stunt. Left to right: George Duke, Martin Lickert (Ringo Starr's chauffeur, who appeared in the film *200 Motels*), Howard, Frank Zappa, Mark Volman, Ian Underwood, and, far right, Howard's cousin Cohen, in snazzy chapeau. MIA: Aynsley. 1971.

Onstage at the Fillmore East in New York City, 1971. In the shadows, Jim Pons, Mark Volman, Don Preston, Ian Underwood, Aynsley Dunbar, and Bob Harris. Front line: Howard, Yoko Ono, John Lennon, and Frank Zappa.

On the set of *200 Motels*, Pinewood Studios, England, 1971. Howard and Ringo Starr.

Frank on the bus in Europe with unknown friend, 1970.

Frank on the bus in Europe with yet another special mystery friend, with Ian and Mark in the background.

it. We were really stupid, but we were young and no one our age was thinking about their financial future at that time.

Even though we all lived in Los Angeles, most of our concerts were in Middle America, so we all agreed that somehow it made perfect sense to rent out an entire floor of the exclusive Astor Tower Hotel in downtown Chicago—we drew straws or something to see who would get the bedroom closest to the white grand piano in the living room. Very Beatles.

Speaking of whom, we all had seen the Fabs waving to their fans from the BEA plane that they cleverly turned into the BEATLES with a can of paint. It was our turn now. Hell, we had earned this. We had paid our dues. We were twenty-one. So we leased our own airplane. True, it wasn't as snazzy as the Beatles'—it was a wartime DC-3—but it flew. It came with a crew of two, who were now on salary. One was a Nazi. Really. And man, did he hate our guts. Every flight, we held our breaths waiting for our Germanic copilot to grab the wheel, yell "Heil Hitler," and fly us into a mountain. Here's the best part: On one side of the plane we had painted THE TURTLES. But on the other, we had it say EHT SELTRUT. We thought that was hilarious. I don't think anyone else got it.

We weren't done throwing our money away yet. Waiting downstairs from our high-rise Windy City digs were Doc and George, our twenty-four-hour limo drivers. They just sat there, in case Al wanted to go to the nearby Playboy Club or Jim needed toothpaste. And, tick-tick-tick, these guys were on the clock. Could we really justify this excess considering our paychecks for these state fairs and even arena shows? No, we couldn't. But we also couldn't be bothered with those details. It was our turn. Besides, touring kept us away from home for literally months at a time. And this was in a primitive epoch before FaceTime or Skype.

Still, it was amazingly cool. We would wake up late on any given morning—and we needed to, trust me—and roll downstairs into one of the two waiting stretch Cadillacs for the short ride to Midway Airport, where Captain America and Heinrich Himmler would have the engines revving up for the very quick flight to, let's say, Appleton, Wisconsin, or Minot, North Dakota.

Generally, the local radio stations were involved in that evening's show, so they would announce our impending arrival on the air, resulting in a few dozen teenage female fans, at least. Easy pickins. And we hadn't even gotten to the hotel yet. A few hours there, with or without company, was a smokeathon followed by what Al called the Shower, Shit, and Shave, and then we'd get picked up or escorted to the venue.

The shows were great and the crowds were consistently enthusiastic, though once we found ourselves playing an afternoon show on a community college's stage, hastily constructed from a dozen or so cafeteria tables. Picture it: The drums behind me, all of the amps in a tight little line, the mic stands in place, and the kids grooving. Volman's tambourine flies up and, in slow-mo, he jumps to grab it in midair. A split-second shared look of dread and anticipation. Then Mark hits the "stage" and it all collapses around us. It was like a whirlpool, or maybe a vortex. Whichever, Volman was the center of the black hole, and we all caved in around him, with the drums and amps and hardware raining down on our heads. Good thing we were toasted. I remember just hearing laughter among the rubble and it was contagious. We laughed all the way back to our dressing room. I'm not sure what the audience thought, but I seem to remember that the students set the makeshift stage back up again, rescued the equipment with the help of our roadie guy, and that we finished the set, received our cash and accolades, in that order, and flew back to Chicago. It wasn't all glamorous.

Then there was Arnolds Park, Iowa.

There was an amusement park there and our accommodations were little trailers, the sort that carny folks would inhabit. Insert cliché here: The park owner had this daughter, see? I can hear the groans. And you'd be right. So it was a one-night stand with the promoter's daughter in a carny dressing room, within earshot of the calliope and the crowds. I loved the surreal parts, don't get me wrong. And what did I care anyway? I'd be out of there in the morning, and this one would get the same space in my new daily diary as everyone else did.

Cut to Arnolds Park, Iowa again, one year later. I'm in the same trailer, just unpacking my suitcase, when I hear a squealing commotion outside of my door, followed by the dreaded knocking. It was good ol' What's Her Name, as expected, but with a three-month-old—I'm just guessing— infant of some kind or other. What the hell? "And I've named him little Howie 'cause he looks just like you!" Oh, hell no! Bye-bye, baby. It's been real! You've gotta go now. Honest. Down the three creaky steps and back to your own trailer somewhere on the midway.

"But my dad! . . . And you loved me! , . . And you won't get paid! . . . And . . . "

Blah blah blah. I had already flicked the mute switch.

I soon learned from her father that I had nothing to worry about. He told me about his idiot daughter's lunatic boyfriend and their love child and how she had tried the same crap on Mark Lindsay and Davy Jones and how they hadn't bought her story either and he was so sorry and really liked our band. Just another town. Blah blah blah.

❖ ❖ ❖

We had the best times on our little plane. I mean, it was a DC-3: the workhorse of World War II, with rows and rows of upholstered seats. There was a galley we never used and a bathroom that we certainly did, although, much like on a tour bus, the man or woman who dookied would be chastised for the remainder of the flight.

The main advantage of having our own airplane, besides the obvious ease of travel, was that we could get as high as we liked whenever and wherever. Of course, Hermann Goering was not amused and eventually fled for less green pastures, but we didn't care. He was simply replaced.

Our airplane was officially christened when Stephen Stills, even higher than usual, hitched a ride to a mutual show and spray-painted some unintelligible hieroglyphs across the bulkhead.

Class, Stephen. Real class.

Eht Seltrut would land in Des Moines and the girls who greeted us would, in turn, be greeted by a cloud of smoke as we descended from the two-engine prop behemoth with pretty big smiles for that hour of the day. The hotel, the show, the girls, the flight back to the Astor Tower, Doc and George, room service food from Maxim's de Paris or fantastic pizza and barbecue from Mister Chicken. Then, there was the obligatory call home followed by hours of smoking and singing around the piano. It was here that most of our creative juices were allowed to flow crazily. There were never any groupies allowed at these intimate sessions that, I have to say, were some of the happiest times in my life. The dumb song covers that we invented, just to occupy our off-hours, we'd record onto a cassette and pretend that we were our alter egos, the Rhythm Butchers, performing at some empty roadhouse cafe. Stupid fun times. Many years later, Rhino

Records released seven Rhythm Butchers extended-play records, so our childlike exuberance lives on for future generations to ignore.

It was all pretty psychedelic. Finally, our music and our real lives were intersecting. The fourth release from the new Koppelman-Rubin-ized Turtles was a beautiful example of a two-and-a-half-minute acid trip. With its gorgeous melody, "Lucy in the Sky" words, and a lush orchestral arrangement to boot, "She's My Girl" became one of my favorite Turtles singles. And White Whale must have agreed, because they ponied up the dough for an incredible music video shot by Rod Dyer. We had done a rather famous film for "Happy Together" that the BBC had commissioned a full fourteen years before MTV existed, but it wasn't widely seen in America. Now we had a short film that we could send to the smaller cities that weren't on our tour schedule in an effort to saturate America. One small problem:

The opening line of "She's My Girl" is: "Morning, morning glory / If you'd like to know where was I last night . . ."

Sorry. This was still the '60s and morning glories were known to have hallucinogenic properties. It was said that if you chewed on enough morning glory seeds, you'd go on a mind trip you'd not soon forget. And it was true. Unlike the "Mellow Yellow" craze that triggered a nation of banana-peel smokers who dried and scraped and puffed to no avail a few years before, morning glories worked. Evidently, our glorious opening line about this beautiful flower was a threat to America and thus a great many radio stations across the country refused to play our record. Luckily, a great many more did. And the Turtles had scored yet another Top 20 hit despite the controversy.

Which, to White Whale, meant just one thing: It was time to release a greatest hits album!

We were really afraid that these guys were going to drop the ball here. After all, we were a band that sold singles, not albums. No one had cared about the LPs, not really. We were just another one of those groups that racked up a ton of hit 45-rpm singles but was perceived as padding out our 33^1/$_3$-rpm albums with fillers and B-sides. An assumption that was largely true.

But now we had something to actually sell to an album-buying audience. Including the folk-rock stuff and the newer NYC productions, we had a solid commercial product at last.

As a band, we still didn't want this record to look typical: the band guys all wearing bad suits and standing in half-profile with shit-eating grins on their faces. So we went over to the house of our pal and fellow L.A. road dog, Dean Torrence of Jan and Dean fame, who was just beginning to segue from rock into graphics. He designed a surreal cover with our heads floating in space and surrounded by the headless bodies of stylized naked women. What's not to like about that idea? Packed with monster singles as it was, *The Turtles! Golden Hits*, released in the fall of '67, went gold instantly, hit the Top Ten, and became our biggest-selling album.

Bill Utley wasn't traveling with the band anymore. There were a few interim tour managers hired, including Bill's brother Bob, but either we hated them or Bill did. Ah, but then came a guy I'll just call Dave K. A tall, blond, Midwestern drink of water, Dave was a smooth-talking son of a gun who had just the correct amount of gravitas to collect the money for each show with heavy-handed authority, while hanging out with the band like a sixth member. Everybody loved Dave. Hell, we trusted him with our lives, not to mention our money. We laughed together; we loved together. He was one of us: a chosen traveler who we happily invited inside of our exclusive little circle.

In fact, Dave became such a comrade-in-arms that we all decided that the band would be a lot better off if *he* were our manager instead of cranky old Bill, who didn't seem to really have time for us anymore. At least, that's what Dave told us. It didn't take long and, as I mentioned, Dave was charming. By the end of our fourth tour together, he had us thoroughly believing that Utley was an ogre and up to no good.

But, not to worry—Dave had a plan. He would buy our management contract from Bill in installment payments and we would soon be free to become the supergroup he knew we could be.

In reality, here's how the shit went down: Dave needed cash, so he went to White Whale and convinced them that Utley had been the only thing standing between the label and the complete control they wanted to have. Now, however, with *him* as manager, the label got to do whatever they so desired, release whatever they felt like, and even have a financial stake in our touring. All he needed from them was cash—cash that Lee and Ted refused to part with. However, the Turtles had money in their account and they really wanted this deal to happen, so . . .

We borrowed $50,000 from White Whale as an advance against future royalties, and paid it to Bill Utley as the first installment of a $200,000 buyout.

We bought ourselves, and gave ourselves to Dave K., who still owed Utley a stately hundred and fifty large.

So, imagine our surprise when, upon returning from a particularly grueling month of schlepping on the road, we found out that Dave had absconded to Mexico with all of the tour money. Neither Dave nor the money was ever seen again.

Still, we were living the good life, so we sucked it up and attempted to move on. One afternoon, in the midst of a routine landing in Altoona, Pennsylvania, the front wheel of the airplane locked up and we found ourselves hurtling wildly across the runway and off the tarmac onto the grass. Still spinning out of control, we all had the most amazing reaction—we laughed. All of us. Nearing death, it was all we could do. My life didn't flash before my eyes or anything. I could only laugh at how stupid it was to wind up checking out like this. What a way to go!

Needless to say, we dumped *Eht Seltrut* right then and there and went back to rented station wagons and U-Haul trucks. I figure what we lost in glamour, we made up in years of life.

There was a new road manager now, and a new attitude in the group. We were big-time successful. The new guy was named Rick Soderlind and, while we were all looking to calm ourselves in the wake of Dave K., Rick was getting ready to bring another storm of his own.

TEN

Punks Leaving a Trail of Destruction

We turned down the next few Bonner and Gordon songs that were sent to us. One of them, "Cat in the Window," proved us correct. We recorded it, just to make sure it wasn't right for us, but we didn't release it (we later stuck it on our second greatest-hits collection, even though it wasn't a hit). Petula Clark did cut it as a single, and it tanked, so we were feeling all cocky regarding our ability to detect a loser.

But the next one proved us to be not only wrong but world-class morons. It was originally called "Celebrity Ball" and the only cool thing about it, as far as we were concerned, was the fade-out at the end of the song. That song is now referred to as "Celebrate" and it became a Top 20 single for Three Dog Night. You win some, you lose some. We sucked it up, again.

We begged the songwriting duo to come up with something else, anything else. But for some reason, the well had run dry. Bonner and Gordon had a falling-out, broke up as partners, and never wrote another song together. There were a few more submissions, but we were getting Spoonful castoffs now, so again we felt abandoned. Even with our album on the charts and our pictures in the trade publications, the face of music was shifting and we weren't really a part of that change, no matter how cool we represented ourselves to be.

One or two hit records may not take a band very far, but when you string together a collection of seven or more, as we did, you've got something you can actually take to the bank. Or sell as an album. But we were a singles outfit, and we weren't getting airplay at all on the newfangled FM radio the kids were all listening to. During the previous year or so, there had been a marked sea change in music. Bands like the Grass Roots and Herman's Hermits were being eclipsed by newer-style, heavier bands like Cream and the Jimi Hendrix Experience. Hit records weren't important to a new culture that didn't value success. These kids just wanted to groove, man. And if you could play the same chord for twenty minutes and do it loudly enough, you were the flavor of the month and would probably soon grace the cover of that new, hip rock mag called *Rolling Stone*.

So the Turtles were a bit of an anomaly. Hip, just because we were, and square because of the way we were perceived in some places. In New York, we headlined the Fillmore East in October 1968 with Creedence Clearwater Revival opening for us. It was a different experience than in '66 when we played the original Fillmore Auditorium in San Francisco. There Bill Graham, who booked us into both venues, shook our hands and congratulated us, but it had been intimidating—we felt like we were out of our element in that nascent jam-band culture. Funny thing, though: You play your songs, talk to the audience like real people and maybe drop the tambourine a few times and the next thing you know, the kids genuinely like you, and you realize that music is music, good is good and, at least back in the '60s, we were all in this together.

But it was totally frustrating not to be getting the all-important FM airplay where the new "underground" stations were springing up. So, of course, we all started looking around for someone to blame. We decided, as a band like we had always done, to replace Koppelman and Rubin, even though they had given us nothing but hits. We were going to produce ourselves. Heck, yes, that's the ticket!

Only, it wasn't that easy to say goodbye. It seems that White Whale had signed some sort of long-term production deal with Koppelman-Rubin in New York and, regardless of our feelings, we weren't at liberty to decide anything. Which, of course, pissed us off. Results didn't matter—only decisions mattered. And we had made up our collective mind. I don't know what machinations Lee and Ted went through to dissolve their agreement, but I know it cost them, big-time. We were punks leaving a trail of destruction in our path. And it's not like we had an alternative plan. We had bupkes, but we wanted our freedom more than we wanted success.

The label fought us as they never had before, and they were right. We were a band of brats running amok with power. We had never produced anything in our lives and now we were about to take a chart career and throw it away, without a producer or even a song—just because we could. What a bunch of jerks. But we were all they had and, horrified at the prospect of stirring up trouble now, they played the acquiesce card.

Jim had been working on this little ditty called "Sound Asleep," and with a bit of communal assistance—I added this and Al added that, etc.—we came up with a cute little concept piece that featured a bit of everything but, in reality, contained not enough of anything. So to polish this turd we added a handsaw and a falling tree, sitars, a horn section, a marching army, and a chorus of quacking ducks. "Sound Asleep" was a mess, but it's still fun to listen to and it still made the charts, sort of, in early '68. No career damage sustained—yet.

Cut back to the Astor Tower in Chicago. Trying to find that next record. We kinda got psychedelicized by some pot punch brewed up by Elaine McFarlane (of Spanky and Our Gang fame) and wound up writing a group of spaced-out songs that we were convinced would put us into *Revolver* territory. Still trying to be the Beatles. We penned this opus called "The Owl," about a wise old bird who sees all (Jesus, really?), and, together with two other spacey gems, notably "The Last Thing I Remember" and "To See the Sun," were ready to go into any studio with a tape machine and change the world, as long as White Whale was picking up the tab.

Of course, we went big. We booked the famous Chess Studios for a run of days so that we'd have sufficient time for the sitar and tamboura overdubs. (I was the tamboura player—never mind, you don't need to know.) We also managed to book about a dozen local kids from the Head Start program to portray the plaintive children of the world. "To See the Sun" was an opera. They all were amazing little ecology plays in their own way and we happily sent off both the recordings and the invoice to the label, awaiting their response to the next big thing. Which was, "What are you, high or something?" We could see their point.

Meanwhile, the Turtles had decided that we, as a band, were fully capable not only of producing and writing but also of managing ourselves.

All we needed was a spokesman to voice our thoughts and keep us at arm's length from the record company, and that might as well be Rick Soderlind, who was road managing us anyway. He seemed to be a nice guy. So as we struggled in the Chicago studio, where he wasn't needed, Rick was back in Los Angeles, where he had found an attorney by the name of Rosalie Morton. Outraged by our financial state despite our career success, the two of them hatched a plan to secretly shop around and find out what the Turtles "might" be worth to a major label. Well, that's just plain illegal. When you're under contract, shopping around, even casually, is considered an enormous breach of contract. Any lawyer knows that, especially one who was soon to be named a prosecutor. But RCA said we *were* worth something to them and we found ourselves on the horns of a dilemma.

❖ ❖ ❖

Emily Anne Kaylan was born on May 7, 1969, at Cedars-Sinai Medical Center in L.A., and Melita instantly realized that our Laurel Canyon home would be far too small. Besides, what the hell, we could afford it. We found a classic red-barn charmer, as the realtor said, in nearby Woodland Hills. There was an Olympic-size pool (why?), a hayloft, and a frickin' corral. I thought it was a bit much, but Melita and her mother, Helen, both agreed that a child needed room to grow, so we moved to the Valley. Now, every day was spent with Melita and Helen out by the pool with little Emily in the water and Daddy locked in the den, trying to be creative.

There were a bunch of meetings at Rosalie's office and actual signed RCA contracts were dangled in front of our faces. We were so close to actually being on a major label. Not that it would have mattered one little bit at that point in our careers, but we didn't grok that. It was a strange period that felt a lot like limbo, even though we were still out there touring and the bread continued to roll in from our past recordings.

I was a landlord now. We had rented out our Hollywood Hills digs to a couple of starving actresses and on one occasion—and I know this sounds like a scene from an old Jack Lemmon movie—I was given the task of driving to the house, in person, to collect the delinquent rent. It was raining when I arrived at the all-too-familiar edifice. Up the stairs, ding-dong, and here comes little What's-Her-Name, wrapped only in a towel. "Sorry, but I don't have the money yet. Would you like some wine?" Boy, am I a sucker for that obvious shit. Of course I would! And the little pipe. Even the baggage: the boyfriend in a band and his photo on the bedside table, the sputtering candles dripping wax on the carpet I'd just had cleaned, the Stones playing in the living room where Emily had taken her first steps. Fuck it—I wanted this chick! The whole bedroom thing was a bit surreal, but the sex was actually pretty good and, sorry, Melita, I think the rent's gonna be a bit late this month. I wrote a song called "Lady Blue." I put it on *The Phlorescent Leech and Eddie*, the album Mark and I released in 1972 that launched the Flo and Eddie phase of my career. Inspiration has to come from somewhere.

Our track record at White Whale was still pretty good, yet no matter what we released or how successful it became, these clowns who now had a financial interest in us weren't happy. Realizing that we weren't any good at producing ourselves in the studio and wishing to appease the label a little, just to get some breathing room, we placed a call to our former bassist and now Monkees producer Chip Douglas, who was all too pleased to rejoin our happy throng in a new and improved capacity. Chip called his pal, the genius Harry Nilsson, to join us for a session at the fabled Gold Star recording studio in Hollywood.

Nilsson played us a song called "The Story of Rock and Roll" and we were floored. Harry played piano and Chip produced. Mark and I recorded ourselves on track after track, combining our falsettos into a divine gospel glory that Chip named the Incredivoices. The record was really great, got released as a single, and should have worked. Yet, it stalled midway up the *Billboard* Hot 100 chart, thereby fueling the label's anxiety even further. Now they weren't sure that Chip had been the correct choice either.

But we loved working with Chip—he got us, and singing with Harry was like working with Gershwin. It was time to hit the Astor Tower and do some writing.

❖ ❖ ❖

Our idea was to portray twelve completely different groups on a single album. We'd be the heavy metal band, the folkies, the surf band, the mods; we'd write songs in all of these divergent styles and let Henry Diltz, our trusted photographer and good friend, take pictures of us dressed appropriately in rented costumes and makeup. It would be like a variety show where, unlike the Beatles on *Sergeant Pepper,* we could *be* all the bands on the compilation. All we needed was an opener, something to welcome the audience to the show. Let's call Harry.

Harry wrote the title track for *The Turtles Present the Battle of the Bands*. It was all razzamatazz and step-right-up: exactly what we were looking for. There, in Chicago, everyone was working on what would become their contribution to the project. Jim had a tasty country number called "Too Much Heartsick Feeling," Al had this fuzzy instrumental called "Buzzsaw" that sounded like velour wallpaper; even Johny had a drum solo spoof called "I'm Chief Kamanawanalea" that was going to be awesome. Chip contributed the amazing ecology mantra "Earth Anthem," written by his pal Bill Martin, and I had a funny song or two in the mix, but nothing jumped out. And the label, like the hungry, slobbering beast that it was, called out for more, more, more.

"Give us another 'Happy Together,'" the assholes intoned. A litany of garbage chanted by drooling idiots. Give us another "Happy Together"! I couldn't stand it anymore. I bolted to my room, locked the door and, thirty minutes later, emerged with "Elenore."

I had gotten so pissed off that I had decided to show White Whale, once and for all, what dicks they were. So I took the song "Happy Together" and mutated it, just for Lee and Ted. Every time the "Happy" chords went up, mine went down. Every time the melody took a cheesy turn, mine took a cheesier one. Then, to sweeten the deal, I threw in handfuls of pimply teenage hyperboles: "pride and joy, etcetera" was originally "fab and gear, etcetera." "Your folks hate me" and "I really think you're groovy" were meant to inflame the wrath of these L.A. lames and I couldn't wait to sing this new ditty for the band, hear their cynical laughter, and forward it on to our slave-driving masters in the West. But instead, something else happened.

Everybody liked it. Humor? What humor? This is just what we've been looking for! Chip was nearly orgasmic. We worked out the harmonies right then and there. Chip called the label to tell them that we had the hit they had been looking for. We came back to L.A., cut "Elenore" at Gold Star and it was a monster hit, not only in America but in Canada, the UK, even Australia and New Zealand. Couldn't have come at a better time. We had a minute now to finish the album, we had a Top Ten record three years after "It Ain't Me Babe," and back we were on the Hollywood soundstages, doing network TV and still performing, long after the Fab Four had hung up their touring shoes. Yeah, man.

Although "Elenore" was all my doing, we had agreed before this project to write everything as a group, just like the Doors did. True democracy in action. Which is why I only receive one-fifth writers' royalty for "Elenore," the same as Mark, Jim, Al, and Johny. Unfair? Yes. Democratic? Most certainly. Regrettable? Shit, yes. Would I do it again? Not bloody likely.

There was still one slot to fill on *The Battle of the Bands* and Chip was convinced that he had just the tune for the job. The song he had in mind was a Beatles-style Merseybeat tune written by Gene Clark and Roger McGuinn of the Byrds (who was still Jim at the time), way back before they had gotten a record deal or recorded "Mr. Tambourine Man." It was a lot like "I Want to Hold Your Hand." Chip was excited about playing the song for our approval, so Mark and I drove up to his house at the top of Kirkwood to hear him perform it. There was no piano at Chip's and he couldn't play it on guitar. So we wound up listening to the performance as Chip sang accompanied by an old pump organ with only one of its two bellows working—it was broken and playing things only half as fast as they should have been. Remember, Chip kept reminding us, this song is fast: I just can't play it that way. But what we heard was a beautiful ballad with a soaring melody and plaintive lyrics. And that beautiful, broken pump organ. "No, Chip. You're wrong. This is a slow song. This is the ballad that we've waited for. This is a giant hit record."

We included "You Showed Me" on *The Battle of the Bands* and released it as a follow-up to "Elenore." It was, indeed, a gigantic hit record, our final Top Ten single. The album itself sold respectably, but we were still a singles band. *Rolling Stone* reviewed it twice. The writer of the first article absolutely loved it and hailed us as a musical force to be reckoned with. The second called us a schlock Mothers of Invention pretend band, inferring that only Mister Zappa could fuse comedy and music. I've never forgotten that review. Sometimes it only takes one little thing, one negative critic, to color your entire world black. If I ever meet that guy . . .

ELEVEN

Lucifer Laughs

Rick Soderlind was a friend of ours first, unlike Dave K., who had been thrust upon us and ripped us open from the inside. Johny had really been hurt. He had given Dave a shitload of money to open up an exclusive Italian auto dealership in the Bay Area. Johny was going to be the exclusive West Coast distributor of the Italian Marcos automobile, a really fast, fiberglass racing machine. Johny bought one and fell in love with it. He'd rocket through the Canyon at ridiculous speeds, tempting the inevitable daily. Dave also set Johny up with a magnificent geodesic dome house in Marin County. With the down payment supposedly in escrow, Johny drove up there one afternoon to check out his new digs, and was shocked and angry to find it happily occupied by an owner who didn't know what Johny was talking about. Dave was a lovable dude.

Rick, however, had been Johny's friend. So when the band decided that we'd be better off managing ourselves, why not just pay Rick a salary to be our spokesman? It would be the best of both worlds and we would maintain total control of our lives.

Rick Soderlind, meet Rosalie Morton. Oh, man. Somewhere, at that very second, Lucifer laughed.

Rick meant well. I really think he did. But he soon realized his own limitations. Soon, as our de facto "manager," it was Rick who was staying home in Hollywood—at Johny's house, by the way—while Rick's friend Steve took us out on the road. But here's what happened next. Rosalie, as our attorney, received court papers from an outfit in New York called the Martin Phillips Company claiming that they owned us. And we didn't know who they were or what they were talking about.

Flashback to Dave K. and one of his slightly effeminate "friends" from back in the day. I'll call the guy John P. He wore cologne and bad suits and ol' Dave always got defensive, come to think of it, when John's name came up. But he was just this creepy guy. There were always creepy guys. None of us ever thought much of it.

So imagine our surprise, sitting in Rosalie's plush Beverly Hills office, to hear that just before he had headed off to parts unknown, Dave had sold our fraudulent management contract to his buddy and his buddy's invisible partner. It was legal. He owned us. He had purchased us, fair and square, with our own money, and he legally had the right to do whatever he wanted with us. So he did. The threatening papers kept rolling in from New York, but—

We didn't care. We had a lawyer in our corner and a major label courting us, and our Chicago trips were about to change the face of the band. For many of our late-night, post-performance excursions into the psychedelic, we were joined by our dear Windy City friends and fellow road dogs, Spanky and Our Gang. These guys were wonderful, not only as singers and musicians, but as raconteurs and fellow experimenters. Elaine's pot punch fueled many an evening of story and song. Most nights, Johny, who elected to live in his own apartment across the hall, dressed to the nines and took one of the limos into town, either with a date or trolling for one. He thought that our wasted evenings were just that, so as a result, we revelers spent an inordinate amount of time with Spanky's drummer, John Seiter—the Chief, as he was called.

After a time, the inevitable occurred: Barbata felt ostracized and Seiter felt guilty. Johny left the band without too much ceremony. He went on to play with Crosby, Stills, Nash and Young and was on their live *4 Way Street* album in 1970, then moved on to join the final lineup of Jefferson Airplane and stuck around when they morphed into Jefferson Starship. We knew he'd be fine without us, probably able to wear his good suits now for a more discerning audience.

And we had a great new drummer who felt that he was finally in a band where his two cents actually meant something. We had a pot buddy in our tight little circle—not that Johny hadn't been; it just wasn't a sing-along kind of high—and we were proceeding with the notion that it was more important to surround yourself with friends than with talent. Not to take away from John Seiter's drumming—the guy was solid as a rock—but Barbata had been amazing. On more than one occasion at the Astor Tower, we would all be invited upstairs to the apartment of the great Buddy Rich, where, after getting comfortably toasted and electrified, we'd be treated to Johny and Buddy "trading eights," alternating solo drum breaks. Barbata kept up and Buddy was suitably impressed. And we'd laugh our asses off at Buddy's snarky comments and classic showbiz stories. To further complicate life's mysterious plan, by literally stealing John Seiter, the Chief, from Spanky and Our Gang, we effectively broke up the band made up of the closest friends we had. We didn't mean to, honest. There were other drummers out there. They could have gone on. But it wasn't like that. Our Gang had been like a family, all of them coming together from separate folk and blues bands in Chicago's legendary Piper's Alley. Now they had folded. Thanks to us. Great.

❧ ❧ ❧

Emily was getting to be an actual kid. I had never minded the diaper phase, not once I had gotten over the initial shock of that actual infant chore, but I was looking forward to being more of a dad than I had been, what with the road and the weed, the so-called creative process, and the ever-present mother-in-law and that self-satisfied smirk I wanted to knock off of her Grecian face.

We were still riding high in 1969 with "You Showed Me," and Rosalie Morton took advantage of our chart position and longevity—not to mention her under-the-table talks with RCA—to demand a contract renegotiation with White Whale. She probably shouldn't have brought up the blatantly illegal conversations with another label, a detail strictly prohibited under the provisions of *any* recording contract. Things got sticky and very confusing. Her legal standing was questioned. Old court documents were opened. We were now in court with both our label and the supposed new managers out of state. And because Bill Utley hadn't received a payment of Dave K.'s buyout money since his disappearance, he was actively suing us too. The band was often in depositions, courtroom questioning under oath, three days a week. Later on, we would extend these litigious happenings for years. By the way, these are not the greatest circumstances for creativity.

Nonetheless, it was touring as usual for us, no matter what was going on in L.A., and with Seiter in on the hotel and rental car improvisations, it didn't seem to matter much to anyone that we had lost a lot of our onstage snap. As far as the label was concerned, a drummer was a drummer, and besides, on account of Rosalie's ranting and the transparent RCA dealings, we had a new deal with White Whale. We were now not only producers who delivered product to the label, as we had become prior to "Sound Asleep," but a label ourselves. Still mimicking the Beatles, we became Blimp to their Apple. That meant that we had our logo on every record. It meant that we could sign new artists to our label. And, most importantly, it meant that we were making a buck a record instead of the twenty cents or so that we had been earning. On paper.

It would have been a fantastic deal for Seiter as a member of our new corporation, as well as for the rest of us, had we sold records. We were having fun being the Rhythm Butchers full-time, but despite the infusion of John's blues influences, as well as his humor and wisdom, there was nothing at all that was commercial about our group's decision. And deep down, I think that John knew it.

Rick Soderlind was still keeping our shit together, but we all knew that any growth now would be coming from the outside. Which it soon did when Rick brought us a new management situation to consider. Seems that Bill Cosby was forming a super-company. Cosby, the same guy that I had taken my prom date to see at the very Crescendo nightclub where we had danced the pot dance with Dave Diamond. That Bill Cosby. I remember reading about this new company in the trades. He had just launched his own sitcom, and it was a huge hit from the get-go, but he had become fed up with his own representation. Now he was going to make sure that the same treatment wouldn't befall any of the artists that he signed. He hired the great Artie Mogul to head up his label, Tetragrammaton, which immediately had a hit with Deep Purple's "Hush." (In a few years, we would cross their paths again.) He also hired two extremely "Hollywood" agents, Ron DeBlasio and Jeff Wald, to head up the management division, which included us. And Tiny Tim. And Biff

Rose, I think, and a few others. In a couple of weeks, they had us saying things like "outside the box" and "just go with it."

We were back on television, even though we were lip-syncing to old hits. It felt sad and a bit directionless, and then the invitation arrived.

TWELVE

Fuckin' Corporate Sellouts!

Since we'd played our big gig at the White House in May of '69—Tricia Nixon's birthday bash where we got loaded and almost had our heads blown off by the FBI—the Turtles' bookings had been elevated to a new strata of elitism. The agency's phone was ringing off the hook now with offers to play at posh events and upper-crust parties. One of these events was happening right up the coast at an elaborate mansion owned by the president of U.S. Steel on the occasion of his daughter's birthday—she was in her teens; I don't know the exact age. Anyway, I didn't much care. I had gotten pretty political in the days following Nixon's election and I had also gotten unbelievably high. The entire week preceding the U.S. Steel party, I was wasted on the most fantastic orange-barrel LSD I had taken in months. Of course, I didn't get high for the show—that would have been unprofessional, and I certainly was never that. Nonetheless . . .

On the afternoon of the show, two stretch limos picked us up at our hotel and delivered us to the swimming pool entrance to the mansion. Our dressing room was the cabana. Still, I was cool. Business as usual. The audience was all out of a beach party movie: well-scrubbed collegiate types with sweaters draped around their necks, metaphorically. Our "dressing room" was well catered and all of us took advantage of the free-flowing champagne. At least, I did. And I learned a lot about combining alcohol with drugs that afternoon.

The band was set up just like in those great Annette Funicello and Frankie Avalon movies, inches from the action. And the set was to be a low-pressure and low-profile show for big corporate bucks. But somehow, once the show started, none of those facts made sense to me. Here I was, performing for these stuck-up, entitled Stanford brats, and they'd dance or chat or toss each other into the water and we'd play yet another one of our big hits for them. And they just didn't care.

I think it was during "She'd Rather Be with Me" when I lost it. My inner asshole began speaking to me: acid and champagne—recipe for disaster. Here we were, one of America's biggest bands, playing live in these little dipshits' backyard, like slaves, while they dithered about like extras in a *Dobie Gillis* episode. I couldn't stop myself as I felt my blood pressure build along with the song I was singing. What a waste of breath. They didn't deserve us. Then the endless song ground to a halt and I placed the mic back in its stand and waited for the obligatory applause before kicking off the next bit. But there was none. Just silence, except for the sound of a bunch of asshole kids wasting Daddy's money. And I lost it.

"Well, how did you like that song, you entitled bunch of assholes?" I asked into the microphone. "You're all a bunch of spoiled pricks, you know that, don't you? These are hit records, you bastards! You guys are fucked and your girlfriends are fucked and your parents are fucked-up too!"

The band started trying to pull me back as the rich-bitch parents started filtering outside to see what the commotion was all about.

"Fuck you, sir, and fuck you, lady!" I was screaming now at the top of my lungs and tears were streaming down my face, out of nowhere. I threw the microphone, stand and all, into the swimming pool. And then the lawn chairs. And then the food. And I never stopped ranting.

They finally led me, still cursing, toward the dressing room. "And fuck you guys too!" I cursed at my bandmates. "Fuckin' corporate sellouts! I quit, man. I fucking quit!"

I got into one of the two waiting limousines and went directly to the airport. I flew home to Los Angeles, drove to Woodland Hills, and locked myself in my den for two months.

I spoke to no one. No one called me. Not White Whale and certainly not a Turtle. I just sat there on my braided carpet with my acoustic guitar hanging around my neck, trying to write, but the songs were all dark and hopeless. Plus, it wasn't easy to create with the weight of my actions hanging over my head, not to mention the sounds of Emily, Melita, and Helen, endlessly playing in the gigantic pool I could no longer pay for.

The marijuana couldn't help the reality. I was unemployed and damned near friendless, with no future plans and a bank account that had about three months of living in it. I put out a few professional feelers and planned a lonely solo career of playing the nightclubs and passing the hat. I knew a lot of old rockers who were doing that stuff to stay alive at the end of the '60s—I'd just never expected to be one of them.

I finally got my wish for more "daddy time," but I was in a consistently shitty mood, so I'm not sure that my daughter benefited much from my company. My world was gray. I turned off every Turtles song that came on the radio. Maybe I could start a supergroup. I'd call John Sebastian and Harry Nilsson and put together a band that FM radio could get behind, one that *Rolling Stone* would finally appreciate.

Still, there were loose ends to tie up before I could really strike out on my own: checks to sign and contracts to void. One afternoon, I was forced to make the very short drive to Al's house to complete some arbitrary paperwork and was surprised to see the entire band there, rehearsing.

"Whatcha doin'?" I asked.

"Rehearsing," came the answer.

"Rehearsing what?" I asked.

"Stuff!" was the reply.

Really juvenile.

The Turtles had decided to go on without me and were all busy at work on their own material. Each guy was writing his own songs and together, somehow, they hoped to put it all into some sort of cohesive package. I asked to hear a few songs and the guys happily obliged. It was good stuff. "Do you hear a hit?" I was asked. But of course, I didn't. And probably wouldn't have admitted it if I had.

"So, what you doin'?" I was asked.

"Nothin'," I answered.

"Cool." was the reply.

Really juvenile.

"Want to come back into the band?"

"Sure. Why not?"

I was back.

❖ ❖ ❖

The group had six or seven songs they had been working on and I had a few of my own. The plan was for everyone to sing their own compositions on the new album. It would be a different kind of Turtles for a new generation who hadn't grown up with the wide-eyed innocence of "Happy Together" or "Elenore." Jim sang his Western song; Seiter had a tune about this hippie house that had taken him in; Mark and Al were actually writing together. It was a new era, all right.

We were a band with renewed enthusiasm—real or fake, it didn't matter. Now we needed a producer who would share our excitement and take this band, five years on, to the next level.

We tasked each other with putting together a wish list of the greatest record producers in the world and, like the superstars that we imagined ourselves to be, the list was suitably awesome. Included were George Martin, Phil Spector, and, on everybody's list, the amazing Ray Davies of the Kinks. The Kinks had just released their epic *Village Green Preservation Society* album, and we had worn out several copies wallowing in our appreciation for all things Ray. The man was a genius—we had known that since 1964—but he was, it seemed, unreachable. Besides, he only produced records for his own band. We weren't the Kinks. We were dreaming.

Still on the road, we found ourselves in the unlikely town of St. John's, Newfoundland, at the eastern edge of Canada. Trapped by a snowstorm for days, we listened to *Village Green* and drank the local poison, bottom-of-the-barrel dregs known as Screech. Fueled by that and our ignorance, we spent a Sunday afternoon phoning everyone we knew in London, trying to find Ray Davies. We figured that we were as close to England as we were going to get on this continent. Still, it wasn't easy. Many expensive overseas calls later, we realized that only one guy in England knew everybody else, so we phoned up our friend, the brilliant Derek Taylor from Apple, who scanned his Rolodex and came up with Ray's number in a matter of seconds.

"Hiya, Ray. You don't know us. We're the Turtles from America—"

"The 'Happy Together' Turtles?"

"Yep. Listen, we know this is sort of out of the blue, but would you be interested in producing an album for us?"

Crazy, right? I know. It shouldn't have worked. But it did. Lucky for us. And so it was that three weeks later, the entire Turtles band went down to Los Angeles International Airport to pick Ray Davies up from his London flight and chauffeur him to the Sunset Tower Hotel, where he would stay while we recorded our final, complete studio album, *Turtle Soup*.

White Whale loved Ray once we explained to them who he was. We actually had to sing "You Really Got Me" for them before they'd agree to pick up the considerable check. And Ray wanted to do things right. He had done his Turtles homework. We went into Western, Studio 3, just like the old days. Ray loved that room. Our engineer was, once again, the legendary Chuck Britz. It felt like home in there. Still, there was the strange, new material that threw Ray for a loop. He hadn't been told about any of the band's internal strife. All he knew was, these were the Americans who had had a dozen hits. He really wasn't prepared for the drummer to be singing lead. Or the bass player. Or the tambourine guy.

We trusted Ray to do the mixing on his own, since he knew the material by heart and had Chuck by his side. Ray Pohlman did the or- chestral arrangements and we knew his work to be extraordinary, so we let the team go to work and we returned to the studio three days later to hear the final product. And we hated it. Ray had cranked the orchestra so high that the record didn't sound like a band anymore. It sounded like the frickin' Moody Blues. We were awash in strings. Ray was shocked and hurt that we disapproved of his work and was even more insulted when we insisted on standing behind him and literally hovering over a second, hastily done and simpler mix. But we weren't an orchestra, damn it. And we were doing everything we possibly could to still be a group.

White Whale spent a ton (of our money) on *Turtle Soup*. The album was released with a foldout, matte-finished double cover. Henry Diltz took the photographs and Gary Burden designed an Eagles-style package complete with a custom sleeve and the lyrics done in painstaking callig- raphy. Too bad it wasn't a better album. Seiter's "House on the Hill" was released as a single but didn't chart. Al's "Love in the City," a great song, fared better, and my "You Don't Have to Walk in the Rain" was a minor hit. Critics liked us again, but we were all disappointed.

Still, the touring continued and we were already contemplating our next step.

Not that it would make any difference.

THIRTEEN

Put a Fork in Us

The ever-present roadwork continued. The girls were still there in quality and quantity, and being a good dad at home somehow didn't seem to affect my logic when my lower brain won over logic night after night. We had some bizarre things happen, but then again I've read everybody else's road stories, so I know that everybody did. If you've spent any time at all on the road, drug-free or otherwise, I'm sure you've had some interesting times too.

Mine include waking up in the backseat of our speeding station wagon to the screams of everybody there including George, our roadie, who closed his eyes and prayed. We were careening toward two semi trucks, one passing the other. We were dead. No laughing this time. And then it was over. Somehow, they separated and we drove between them—like in a Burt Reynolds movie. We pulled the car over to the shoulder of the highway and wept or prayed or kissed the ground. Everybody got out and needed to walk for a minute. It was a good fifteen minutes before we could resume the ride. I think somebody else drove the next leg.

Another time, the entire group decided to do just a taste of sweet blotter acid that we had taken with us across the border into Canada before a rather prestigious show. We were hired to perform at the Miss Teen Canada pageant. It was supposed to be a classy affair with an audience of suits, press, and proud parents. That was fine with us: We were a classy band, certainly ready for anything. We had suits too. We didn't, however, expect to begin the show in the theater's basement. We didn't see any classy audience. We didn't see anybody. We were in a pit, looking at a cement wall.

The idea was that John was to begin playing the drum lick opening of "You Baby" as we rose, like magic, on the hydraulic stage. When we got up to normal audience level, that's when the song was to start. Well, the show began. We could kind of hear our introduction, all muffled and distant from a floor above us. We got the cue. John started the drumming and as the stage got higher, so did we, or so it seemed. We got our second cue. Now the guitars played the familiar riff. Higher went the stage; now we saw the audience—huge and in multitiered balconies, and the cameras and the Pepsi banners. And everybody stopped.

We just stopped.

And stood there. Like we had no idea who we were or what we were doing there. Then, after what seemed an eternity but was probably a nanosecond, all of us got on the same mental page and picked up the song exactly where we had left off. No one knew. They loved us. The contestants, in their formal gowns, told us so after the concert. Man, how we did enjoy pushing the envelope.

◆ ◆ ◆

We didn't have the Astor Tower anymore. Those glory days were over and we were, once again, a band on a budget. Still, when it came to taking time off, we spared no expense and would usually hang in Manhattan, frequently at the Gramercy Park Hotel in ragged but wonderful suites. We had keys to the gated little neighborhood park across the street. Nice place to smoke.

We often walked in the Village and bought hip clothes. We smelled the incense emanating from one shop from a block away, even over the normal hot dog and urine odors. It may have been the New York branch of Granny Takes a Trip, the famed London boutique. The place was small and hot, but cramped with hangers and the strangest prints and styles we had ever seen: Carnaby Street collars and brocade jackets, paisleys and Nehru coats, and oh so many scarves. Loud bongo music plus that Indian aroma drew us in on a cloud of smoke like Pepé Le Pew. A wonderful British hippie couple welcomed us with hugs. We might have had our sitars with us. No, really. We purchased. We schmoozed. And we heard the strangest music playing. The singer was wailing away in some bizarre foreign tongue. But it was hypnotizing. Who were these strangers from another world, we asked our new salespeople friends? What was this lyrical language?

It was English. The dude was singing in English. Huh? They showed us the album cover, the husband and wife who owned the store. The album was called *My People Were Fair and Had Sky in Their Hair . . . but Now They're Content to Wear Stars on Their Brows*. Well, that was different. It had been recorded by a British duo called Tyrannosaurus Rex. We loved it. We bought it. And there had been others—English imports. We bought them too. And learned them. And sang them. We were fans, probably among their few American acoloytes.

Cut to: the Turtles, on the road again, a one-nighter at the Grande Ballroom in Detroit. And the opening act: Tyrannosaurus Rex. Boy, were we jazzed! Onstage, an Oriental rug, incense burners, candles, and cushions. Out walks a tiny elfin sprite, who we correctly assume is Marc Bolan, and a lanky hand drummer, who we know is Steve Peregrin Took. This was not unlike the night that I stood next to David Crosby at the Palladium in Hollywood and watched, dumbfounded, as the Who performed *Tommy* in L.A. for the first time. It was that heavy for me.

We didn't hang in our backstage dressing room, as usual. We went out into the ballroom and nudged our way into the front row. It wasn't difficult to do. No one had ever heard of these guys, and once they started up, they failed to impress the audience, owing to their lack of both rock and roll.

The boys couldn't help but notice us there, like groupies, and performed with a renewed vigor when they spotted us. After the show, we hung out backstage and had a legendary smokeout at our hotel. Marc's wife, June, was along for the ride and she was a captivating beauty and a lovely spirit. We sang and rolled into the morning and Bolan couldn't believe that he had met us at all, being a huge fan. He knew Turtles B-sides and album cuts. He was far more impressed that we could join him on such album selections as "Mustang Ford" and the early single "Debora."

We were shocked to realize that he had sung on the very cool song "Desdemona" by John's Children that White Whale had released. We traded info and promised to look him up the minute we got to England.

We really never expected to be in England again, but we would soon be proven wrong.

❖ ❖ ❖

It was a weird time. Again. The Campbell-Silver-Cosby Corporation, our management company, was splitting up. What? They can do that?

Now we found ourselves represented by the newly formed DeBlasio-Wald Management. But Jeff was now spending most of his time launching the career of his wife, Helen Reddy. It felt lonely again. These were "big picture" guys who really had no inclination to deal with day-to-day tour minutiae. Plus, we were still in depositions scheduled around these very tours. We would come home, have a day or two off, and then zip right into some courtroom or attorney's office to answer an endless stream of moronic questions from Martin Phillips's or Bill Utley's lawyer. It was pretty exhausting, not to mention exorbitant.

Meanwhile, White Whale, disappointed by the weak showing of *Turtle Soup*, despite the billboard they had paid for on Sunset Boulevard, was freaking out and growing more evil with every day. Now they had another genius idea. They would have hit producer Chips Moman record some great tracks for us and fly Mark and me into Memphis to do the vocals and, presto, a hit record. You should have heard the yelling in that office. Al was not happy. Label or not, we were the Turtles, damn it, and they couldn't tell us what to do. We'd tell *them* what to do!

Indeed, it was time to make another album, but this time, we—not Lee and Ted—were going to run the show. Deciding to stay closer to home, we asked our friend Jerry Yester to produce. Jerry had been in the Modern Folk Quartet with Chip Douglas and had arranged the orchestra for us on much of the *Happy Together* album. He'd also been in the Spoonful for a while, replacing Zal Yanovsky. His brother, Jim, was in the Association. We had known Jerry forever. And John Seiter had been working with Jerry and his wife, folksinger Judy Henske, on an interesting side project that would soon wind up on Frank Zappa's new label. So we began to gather material for a much more commercial album than *Turtle Soup* had ever been.

The album was to be called *Shell Shock* and it was going to be a great one. I was singing a lot more, thankfully, and writing better than I had in a long time. With one piece, "We Ain't Gonna Party No More," I continued my quest to do one autobiographical song on every record. It was an anti-war opus when we needed it the most, and I was anxious for it to be heard. It was a mini rock opera because I had a lot of Vietnam to get off my chest. Some other standouts: Mark's beautiful "There You Sit Lonely" and a Bonner and Gordon leftover, "Goodbye Surprise," a heavy guitar rocker. There were also some "inside joke" cuts, like our a cappella take on "Teardrops" by Lee Andrews and the Hearts and the bizarre "Gas Money," which had been the flip side of Jan and Arnie's "Bonnie Lou" in 1963. White Whale didn't hear a hit.

Instead, they gave us this demo, this awful, horrible demo. The song was called "Who Would Ever Think That I Would Marry Margaret?" by an unknown songwriting team and it sucked. Honestly. Maybe it could have been a B-side for Billy Joe Royal or something, but it certainly wasn't for us. It was country, for God's sake. The kind of thing Chips Moman would have had us record. Hmmmm. We refused to record it. White Whale said record this song or you don't get to finish the album. We buckled. We recorded their stupid song with Jerry producing. It sucked. The label loved it. They released it as a single. It bombed bigger than even I expected. We yada-yada'd and went back to Sunset Sound only to find that the studio doors had been padlocked and we were locked out. Our equipment was still set up inside, but we weren't getting in, that was certain.

Livid, we arranged for an independent audit of White Whale's books by the Harry Fox Agency in January of 1970 and discovered a discrepancy of more than $650,000 for one six-month period of time in 1969, a good but not banner year for sales. Extrapolating their results, in March we initiated a lawsuit against the label for two and a half million dollars, and of course they immediately countersued. Because we had signed our new production deal with them as individuals as well as collectively, we were forbidden to use the name Turtles or any of our individual names, either, to go elsewhere. We were trapped. We had screwed ourselves over.

We sure didn't want to go out that way. What a terrible way to leave our fans. The Turtles were never again to make another record. It was sad. We decided to do a rather unorthodox thing. We begged.

❖ ❖ ❖

Our own label, Blimp, had signed a brilliant singer-songwriter to a contract. Her name was Judee Sill, and she was an extraordinary artist: sensitive, brilliant, and talented beyond my comprehension. Jim Pons and his fellow ex-Leaves member John Beck had discovered Judee, who had a heroin problem, upon her release from a reform school in L.A. for one crime or another. Her husband was, in fact, Bob Harris, who would later be installed as the keyboardist in the Mothers of Invention: The world of professional music is a very small one. Judee was currently in the studio with Graham Nash producing what would be the first album released on Asylum Records, *Judee Sill*.

One of Judee's songs screamed to be sung by yours truly. I humbled myself by appealing to White Whale to do the unthinkable on their dime. I went into Western with Judee playing guitar and sang her beautiful "Lady-O" as sweetly as I could. We added a string quartet and Al and Mark's la-las at the end. It was gorgeous. We begged the label to release it as our swan song. Despite the impending court battles, to them a buck was a buck and they weren't about to throw a new single away. It came out quietly as the final Turtles record even as the new lawsuit began.

Now we found ourselves in court almost every day, fighting at least two managers and our former record company. We couldn't sign with anyone else, couldn't join another band or put our names on another contract. Put a fork in us, folks. The Turtles were done.

FOURTEEN

Around Here, We Have Rules

Darkness. That's what I remember. I don't think I got out of bed for a week. There were only a few calls, some from incredulous friends who had heard, but not believed, the grapevine, and others from showbiz types, quick to admonish me for being a moron. It had been hard enough to quit the Turtles, but somehow this felt a lot more final. There would be nothing to return to now.

None of the band guys called either. It was creepy. Nobody had planned on this. I tried to put myself in my wife, Melita's, shoes. There goes the meal ticket. I'm sure that I was part of it—I couldn't have been easy to be around. I tried to do normal daddy things, but even going to Gelson's, our local market, seemed like a waking dream. We hadn't spoken about it, but it was sort of understood that whatever happened, Mark and I would remain partners. After all, it had been the two of us who had rallied against Al and Jim's sudden swing toward country music, à la the Flying Burrito Brothers. We were brought up on Broadway and the Kingston Trio, not Hank Williams or George Jones—although I had driven to Las Vegas with Pons to see George and Tammy Wynette. Hell, I had also driven there to see Elvis, but I wasn't interested in doing his music.

So I just curled up in a fetal position and pondered my fate. I had plenty of weed. I'd shuffle downstairs in our enormous Woodland Hills house, grab something from the fridge, and sit in the dark corner of my brass-railed mahogany bar with stained glass fixtures and cabinets, where no one had ever come to be entertained. And there I'd feel sorry for myself. But unlike the last time, I wasn't writing songs and imagining my solo career with nervous anticipation. I was turning inward and entering my own Brian Wilson/Harry Nilsson bathrobe phase.

I just didn't care. I wanted to wallow in the bitter taste of my failure. Not even twenty-three and it was over. I knew that I was lucky to have been in a band that had been successful and I counted up all of our hits in my head over and over. I wasn't going to kid myself. I didn't look forward to getting a real-world job, but the unlikely possibility of a Volman-Kaylan duo finding favor in this new FM radio world weighed heavily on me. So I would curl into a tighter ball and await my fate. Change had always come from the outside, and I knew, deep down, that it would again. Something, or someone, would save me.

The phone rang about 2 P.M. on one memorable afternoon. Of course, I was still in bed and everyone else had left the house. I reluctantly rolled over to silence the noisy intrusion. It was Donald Fagen, an aspiring writer from Trousdale Music, upstairs from the White Whale office. Mark and I had sung on the demo recording that had gotten him and his partner, Walter Becker, their publishing deal: a song called "Everyone's Gone to the Movies." Now they wanted to make records themselves, only Donald hated his voice and was petrified about the inevitability of having to perform on a stage. Hence the call. Yeah, hence.

Did I want to be the lead singer in Donald and Walter's new band? There were no guarantees—we'd be playing a lot of small clubs perfecting this new jazz-style rock fusion. It wouldn't be easy. But here was the kicker—they didn't need two of us. They only wanted me. Still, it was a gig; somebody actually wanted me. And that knowledge was all I needed to feel cocky again. Hell, I was still Howard Kaylan and I could still afford to pick and choose the direction of my life. It may not have been true, but that brief infusion of confidence was all that I needed. In my fog, I explained that Mark and I had always been a team and that, unless they were interested in hiring both of us, I would respectfully have to pass. What a jerk! Why was I saying this? Did I have some sort of death wish? Was I not in a panic mere minutes before the call? I don't know. To this very day, I don't know. It just felt wrong. Not for me. Sorry, boys. Yeah, and by the way, good luck with that new group of yours, Steely something or other. And then I rolled over and went back to sleep. Back to feeling sorry for myself.

❖ ❖ ❖

The Turtles had now been officially kaput for one week. The next day, Mark finally made contact, but not for the reason I expected him to.

Back in our New York City hang days, Mark had spent a great deal of time in the company of one Shelley Plimpton, a diminutive sprite of a Broadway actress who had been appearing in a featured role in *Hair*, the tribal love-rock musical that was a huge success in Manhattan. We went to see the show quite a few times in between those Zappa performances at the Garrick. Shelley was a great girl who brought us backstage in the show's early days when it was still part of Joseph Papp's Shakespeare Festival at the Public Theater in the East Village to meet the show's creators, James Rado and Gerome Ragni. We laughed, we smoked, and we forgot about it. Until they too heard of the Turtles' demise and offered Mark and me the two lead parts of Claude and Berger in the Los Angeles production of the hit play happening at the newly named Aquarius Theater, formerly the Hullabaloo and previously the Moulin Rouge. (Hello, Bobby Darin!)

It was a legit offer, and it was for both of us. The proposition certainly deserved consideration. So we considered it. And decided that, right or wrong, this would definitely be the one move that would end our careers in the saddest possible way. No way, Jose. Neither one of us wanted to be Teddy Neeley—no offense.

Sigh. More depression. More time locked into that fetal position.

Oh, yeah. There was something else in that call from Volman: a reminder that, weeks before, the two of us had made plans to attend a Frank Zappa concert at UCLA's Pauley Pavilion. Frank had located his original bunch of ragtag Mothers of Invention from the Garrick Theatre days and combined them with Zubin Mehta and the Los Angeles Philharmonic for a one-time-only event.

We brought our wives and took one car. Mark drove, as always. The show was great. We got to hear "Call Any Vegetable" and "Concentration Moon"—all of our old faves from Frank's doo-wop beginnings—and, as an added bonus, Zappa previewed his latest orchestral piece and an early clue as to his new direction, "200 Motels." And, for serious music, I remember liking it. So afterward, the girls kept our seats warm while Mark and I went backstage to give our kudos to Don Preston, Motorhead Sherwood, Buzz and Bunk Gardner, and the rest of the motliest band that was ever assembled. And there was the maestro himself, leaning against the wall, cigarette dangling from his mouth and his ever-present thermos cup of coffee in hand, speaking volumes of truths to a group of drooling reporters. We walked over to shake the Man's hand and congratulate him on a perfect show.

"So I hear the Turtles broke up. What are you boys going to do now?"

We confessed that we didn't have a clue, but I did like being referred to as a "boy." It felt paternal somehow.

"Listen," he continued, "I'm putting together a new Mothers of Invention—none of the original guys. We're going to go to Europe, play some festivals, maybe some TV. . . . What do ya think?"

We thought yes.

"I'm having a family barbecue this Sunday. Why don't you guys come on over. Bring your wives. Oh, yeah, and your saxophones. You do still play saxophone, don't you?"

Saxophone? What the hell did Frank want us to bring our saxes for? He had the incredible Ian Underwood in his band and my old Selmer hadn't seen a new reed in five years. Mark and I traded a look not unlike the one that passed between us at the draft board. Still, maybe Frank just wanted us to honk along with an old-school tune—that we could do.

Comes Sunday and the big pool party at Frank and his wife, Gail's, purple house on Woodrow Wilson Drive, not far from my Laurel Canyon home. Wives in bathing suits, getting the third degree, screaming naked children running around the chlorined lagoon, the all-American smell of burgers and hot dogs: suburbia at its least corrupted. We ate, we drank, we schmoozed. Then Zappa motioned the two of us downstairs to his legendary studio to hear what we could do. I had my old tenor. Mark had his old alto.

He placed sheet music before us on stands and counted us off. We did what we could. Then he put on a tape of a classic MOI song for us to blorp along with. We did what we could. And then he turned off the machine and told us to put our instruments away. My heart sank. I guess, deep down, I had somehow counted on this all-new life.

"Yeah, you guys won't be needing those. We've got two weeks of rehearsal before we leave for England. Got passports?"

Oh, hell, yes. Frank wanted singers. The Turtles had been broken up for all of two weeks and we had a great new gig.

❖ ❖ ❖

Rehearsals were held in the big, private studio behind the offices on Sunset Boulevard that Frank owned with my cousin Herb Cohen. We had no idea what to expect, musically. No one knew exactly what direction Zappa would be headed in; that was one of the most alluring parts about being asked to join this newly invented Mothers. Brimming with anticipation, Mark and I arrived super early. The studio doors were open and band equipment had already been set up. The standby lights were glowing. There wasn't a soul around except for this guy Mike, a hirsute hippie who lived on a mattress in the back of the room. He was otherwise occupied, I guess, so Mark and I reverted to our usual pre-anything ritual and lit up a fatty or three. We were in fine shape, indeed, when Mr. Zappa walked in with a briefcase and a thermos. He sniffed the air and instantly registered his disapproval.

"I don't know what you guys are used to, but around here we have rules."

Oh, shit!

"And one of our rules is, there is to be no marijuana smoking in this studio. If the police are lured here by the decibel level of the music going on inside these walls, for instance, who do you suppose is responsible once they get a whiff of your shit? Me, that's who. And I sure ain't going downtown for your ridiculous vices. Do I make myself clear?"

He had every right to be pissed off. It was his room. We were jerks.

The second day, Gail dropped Frank off at the rear parking lot as always, and there were Mark and I, hanging near Mark's blue and white VW bus and sending up aromatic smoke signals that no one could possibly ignore. Zappa was livid.

"I thought I told you guys that there was to be no smoking of that shit!"

"But you said, no smoking *inside* the studio, Frank. We're outside, see?"

Frank was not laughing.

"You're not in the Turtles anymore, wise guys. My music is serious. This tour is serious. We spent twelve hours here yesterday working our asses off and our first show is less than two weeks away. I can't afford to keep going over this intricate shit just because you guys got stoned and forgot it."

And we said, "Test us, Frank. Anything we learned yesterday. Go ahead. Test us anytime you want to. And if we fail the test, we'll stop the smoking—we promise."

It was not unlike my leaving-college ultimatum.

So Frank did test us. We went over the bizarre and difficult music that we had been taught the previous day, note for note, phrase by phrase. And, not to brag, but it was perfect. Thank you, Mister Wood. See, kids? The sight-reading really paid off here. And Zappa was a little flummoxed, I think. He hesitated to find the right words to say in front of his entire new band.

"Yeah, well, if I catch you guys smoking dope, I'll test you right then and there. And I'll never bail you out. You get caught at some border crossing, you're on your own; I don't know you. Get it?"

We got it.

The guys in the band were amazing players. And they all hated us. Before we even walked through the door, they hated everything about us. We were the Turtles and they were serious musicians. More than one of them was afraid that Frank had lost his mind, not to mention his credibility, by selecting these fat, AM radio pop singers to join what was to be, ostensibly, a heavy FM blues/jazz fusion group.

Aynsley Dunbar certainly didn't understand. Jeff Simmons laughed, but not in a good way. George Duke had never heard of us and didn't care, Don Preston was against vocals, period, and Ian Underwood was happy just to be getting paid.

Man, if our own band didn't get it, how the hell would Zappa's ultra-hard-core fans react?

But we dutifully learned the Zappa classics and a bunch of new stuff while Frank drank coffee, chain-smoked cigarettes, and tried to figure out what to do with me and Mark.

FIFTEEN

A Hint of Possible Ascension on the Hipness Scale

The legal crap was still going on every day. Fortunately, the worst of the lawsuits had taken an interesting and semi-calculated turn. During the Turtles' final days, we had had the legal advice of not only the questionable Rosalie Morton, but our own, more personal attorney, a young partner named Paul Almond. It had been Paul who had told us how stupid the two of us had been to break up the band without calling him first. That Martin-Phillips lawsuit was still in daily depositions, and now, with the rest of the Turtles literally out of the music business and Mark and I about to become more visible, the evil opposing lawyers threatened to keep Mark and me from going to Europe at all by scheduling court appearances to coincide with the five days ahead that we were to be spending in Amsterdam.

Oh no! Don't you bastards dare take Amsterdam away from me!

Interestingly enough, through all of the legal horrors that we were facing and would continue to encounter, even years later, it was cousin Herbie Cohen who got on the phone with these white-collar types, cut through the bullshit, and was the voice of reason. We never considered Herb to be our manager, ever, and neither did he. But he was certainly a strange and dark angel who looked over both Mark and me like family (which I guess I was), only better.

In those rehearsal days, Carlos Bernal, one of our roadies, would still come over to my Woodland Hills house, just to hang out. So would Dean Torrence. So would Danny Hutton. As would the Volmans—Mark's daughter Sarina was a well-behaved addition to the mix. We were doing a lot of tie-dyeing. Just weeks before, in our downtime, we had spent a few days with Rainbow Annie, the lady who sort of started the whole fashion movement, at John Sebastian's camp (yes, he actually lived in a tent on the property of Cyrus Farrar from the Modern Folk Quartet, a few prime acres in the hills just above the Warner Bros. studios).

In May, Emily turned one year old. White Whale released our 1965 recording of "Eve of Destruction" as a single. Seiter came over with copies and we laughed. Then, of course, the stupid thing actually charted, though barely cracking the Hot 100. It was a weird way to go out.

Rehearsals were difficult, but it was really fun and stimulating to hear the jaw-dropping soloing of Mr. Zappa, a longtime hero, inches away from my head. Just picture yourself in a similar situation: One day, you're a drooling Led Zeppelin fan and the next, you're the new Robert Plant and when Jimmy winds down his amazing solo on "Black Dog," he points to you. Yeah, it felt exactly like that.

The guys in the Mothers were beginning to come around. It helped that I had a car and was willing to take Jeff Simmons home after rehearsals. We learned the greatest hits: Some we learned right off of the record, and others we would mutate, such as "Who Are the Brain Police," or use in medleys, linking "Mom and Dad" up to "Concentration Moon," for example. Frank had new instrumentals for the group to tackle too, so it wasn't just about them sitting around and watching the newbies play catch-up. We learned some of Frank's soon-to-be-recorded pieces. Our first encounter as a band had been on June 1, and on the morning of June 11, I flew to San Antonio, where Frank and I did some FM radio interviews and hung out at a bar that was actually called Bwana Dik, a name that soon would go down in Zappa history and be the site of many folklore-inspired incidents that would be turned into songs by Frank for fun and—for him, at least—profit.

I was nervous as hell before the next night's auditorium concert, but the audience seemed to either know who we were, or only came to see Mr. Zappa and whomever he brought with him. Which, luckily, was the case nine out of ten times. At any rate, to much applause and with the support of our new onstage best friends, night one went off without a hitch. It was a little loose, but that was to have been expected. Afterward, Mark, our new smoking buddy, Jeff, and I stayed up to party and evaluate our night, 'cause the stakes were going up with every concert. Our next warm-up show was a giant rock festival the following night at Braves Stadium in Atlanta.

I only remember the size of the audience and the feeling of validation, at last, as I actually glimpsed a hint of possible ascension on the hipness scale. The following day, I flew to New York to hang out with my song-writing buddy Steve Duboff, and to get high with my old pal Soupy Sales. There was a carnival in the East Village and it was raining, of course. The city felt different somehow. It was still romantic to me, but not in a love-lorn way. I was the lone traveler now, collar to the wind, and about to embark on a Herculean journey.

❖ ❖ ❖

Sadly, that journey, as had the one three years earlier, began with a trans-oceanic flight on the dreaded Air India—a not-so-instant replay—followed by a switch to KLM at Heathrow and a speedy flight to Amsterdam. I was to share a room with George Duke, but after I returned from the Paradiso with a pocketful of hash, George decided that I deserved a single. Smart man. Beethovenstraat shopping and beautiful pubs with pigtailed blond waitresses, those fantastic canals and the allure of the smoky coffee bars where tourists could sit for hours ordering marijuana and hashish off the menu while Hendrix music blared into the narrow cobbled streets . . . It was fantastic.

I was totally wasted for the recording of the following afternoon's Dutch television special for the VPRO network. It was precisely the correct frame of mind for that appearance and it's still around to haunt me, constantly, on YouTube. Sometimes, you have to trust the drugs. Now *there's* advice your mom's not going to give you.

And already, there were girls. Maybe being around Aynsley helped. Of course it helped. Still, I remember going to the airport the next morning with Marilyn and Barb. And those are the memories that just won't go away. The girls dropped us at the airport and we flew back to London, this time to stay at the tony Kensington Palace. I knew exactly where I wanted to go for dinner that night. I took a taxi to the Speakeasy. I did not, however, have the spinach omelet.

The next afternoon, June 20, fell on a Saturday. Mark and I met after breakfast and decided to take a stroll down the famous Portobello Road, where the lane had been designated as a weekend walking street for the trendiest of Londoners. It was really hot outside. We took our time, browsing the colorful booths and storefronts with vendors hawking sweet rock fashions and handmade head shop items and jewelry. This was the coolest place to be in all of London, and we remembered what our coolest of London friends had told us just months before: "If you guys are ever in London, give us a shout-out on the Portobello Road. . . ."

That's what Bolan had said. And here we were. The chances were pretty damned slim, but what the hell? So we started yelling his name.

Two blocks down and two floors up on the left, the window opened and out poked the curly, elfin head of our new best friend, Marc.

"What the hell are you guys doing here?"

"We came to party!"

And party we did. We listened to music—mostly California surf stuff. Marc had a lot of our albums too. We smoked and had tea. June was a lovely hostess and I fell in love with her immediately. And with Marc, too. No secret there.

We exchanged information. We would see them both soon, but had a 10:30 P.M. interview back at the hotel before a midnight show, guess where?

Did you guess the Speakeasy? If yes, move your marker forward two squares and take a guzzle of your favorite beverage.

Frank booked a session the following night at Trident, one of the best rooms in town, and I recall Alice Cooper being there as well as our buddy Harry Nilsson. I think Jeff Beck was there too. On my birthday, Frank and Jeff Simmons had one helluva fight about musical direction, but I didn't think much about it at the time. Hmmm. A foreshadowing, perhaps?

We took a bus the next morning to a castle, a real fucking castle in Littlehampton to do a press conference for the upcoming Bath Music Festival with Led Zeppelin, Pink Floyd, Canned Heat, Dr. John and many others. There were many things to ingest and imbibe there, and Volman wound up spending the night while I took the bus back to

London alone to dine on Wimpy burgers and watch TV. Then, at 11 P.M. the phone rang. It was Bolan. Are you guys around and available? I'd sure like you to sing on this track. I hopped a taxi to Trident, where native New Yorker Tony Visconti was producing Tyrannosaurus Rex and I tripled my background vocals on a song called "Seagull Woman." It wasn't exactly rock 'n' roll—not yet. But I got to sing on my buddy's very English new record. And I felt pretty damned good.

❖ ❖ ❖

We played at the Bath Festival on Sunday, June 28. I hit the stage before 250,000 Brits with the added help of all I could smoke from Donovan and Jefferson Airplane. It was terrific. The Mothers of Invention sounded great.

The very next day, the entourage left London on yet another Air India flying tandoori oven and wound up in Chicago to play the first of a few domestic dates that would get us back to Los Angeles for a bit or normality before beginning the first rehearsals for *200 Motels*, whatever that was: Lots of acid, W. C. Fields, Mexican food and, of course, the ever-present Dr. Lax, the infamous Beverly Hills physician who refilled Placidyl prescriptions with no questions asked. There was still a FOR SALE sign on our Woodland Hills house, although the foot traffic had dwindled down to a few new agents but no clients. Didn't anyone want a house with a corral anymore?

Meanwhile, Mark and I began production meetings with, of all people, Freddy Cannon, he of "Palisades Park" fame. We had found some great songs for Freddy and we were all ready to go into the studio to mount his comeback. I know, right?

I guess we figured that if you spin enough plates . . .

Toward the end of the summer, the Mothers of Invention played a concert at the Santa Monica Civic Auditorium, home to some of our earliest successes as the Crossfires. It was really close to my parents' house in Westchester, close enough that they came to the show.

I've got to mention here that, back when I was eighteen or so and visiting the folks over a long holiday weekend, I brought home the *Freak Out!* album and blasted it as loud as their G.E. console stereo would go. When my father pounded on the door, demanding to know what the hell I was listening to, I showed him the album cover and he almost exploded. With laughter. He couldn't believe it. He had the proverbial cow. Tears rolled down his cheeks. Really. So much so that the mere mention of the name Frank Zappa would send him into sidesplitting convulsions. And then there was Frank's picture. And the one with the pigtails.

Now, four years later, this clown was my boss.

We hung out near the apron of the stage after the concert ended. Mark's parents, Bea and Joe, were there as well; we had eaten dinner at their house before the show. Sid and Sally approached the raised platform as they had done hundreds of times before, rooting on the Belvederes, the Nightriders, the Crossfires, and certainly the Turtles. My mother kept scrapbooks of everything I had done since kindergarten and I knew when I saw the tears in her eyes that she was proud of her little boy and what he had accomplished in his short life.

She looked up at me as only a mother could and said, "What the hell was that? You go from singing like an angel on *Ed Sullivan* to making this Zappa garbage? I can't tell my friends about this crap. I can't write about this in the local paper. What are you doing with your life?"

So that went well.

Into the studio when we weren't rehearsing. This would be *Chunga's Revenge*. The tracks were cut at Whitney Studios in Glendale during the day and the vocals were done by night at the Record Plant. A week later, the album was done and mixed and Cal Schenkel had already designed the album cover. Mark and I weren't allowed to use our names on the record at all because of the White Whale litigation, so Frank had pressured us to come up with *noms de plume*, aliases we could use to disguise our true identities.

We racked our brains to come up with something clever before we remembered that we had nicknamed Carlos "the Phlorescent Leech" because of his mooching ways and his colorful garb. Our other roadie, Dennis Jones, looked more like an "Eddie" to us than he did a Dennis, so we called him that. They were the original Phlorescent Leech and Eddie. When he heard that, Frank laughed hard enough to shoot warm coffee like a spit take and we knew that, at least for a little while, I would be the Phlorescent Leech and Mark would be Eddie. And a little bit of history was made.

SIXTEEN

As Good as It Gets

On November 14, 1970, I drove by my old neighborhood in Westchester, just to ruminate on my life's twists and turns and sadly watch as the giant destruction machines tore down Airport Junior High School to make way for a Hertz Rent a Car. The following afternoon, Mark and I sang with Linda Ronstadt on her new single before rehearsal, and the next day we were off again, this time to Spokane, Washington; Edmonton and Vancouver, Canada; and then Seattle.

Girls and drugs were ever-present. Being in the hippest group in America didn't hurt. After most rehearsals, I occupied my time with a lovely lady named Elizabeth who Frank and everyone else knew as Lixie. She was an adorable, petite groupie with long auburn hair and a body that could stop traffic. She hung out at Frank's rehearsal hall and had obviously spent a lot of time with him. But now, with his hands full of tour and musical details, the poor little thing looked so lost. And everyone else was so married. Hell, so was I, but I was never one to turn my back on a helpless waif. We made love everywhere. It wasn't easy in the back of a Volvo, but I was much more limber then. And, of course, I was an asshole.

Once in Seattle, safely checked into the famous Edgewater Inn, I knew that a) not only could I fish out of my window for mud sharks to be used in unimaginable groupie sex activities, but b) I'd be spending a lot of time with another wonderful lady by the name of Lin. Judge me if you like, but life was zooming by pretty quickly and I was far too young to be exposed to this buffet of females and not sample as many dishes as I could. Of course, I had spent countless nights during the preceding five years with any decent girl who would take the time, but the girls that were coming around now were pretty special.

Lin was amazing, and not just physically. It was all so new to me. I confess, especially as a resident of the area now, that Seattle held a great deal of mystery to me. It's a beautiful place of sounds and inlets and lakes—not unlike Stockholm, I was soon to learn. And to sweeten the deal, Lin's house was on Vashon Island, a remote locale accessible only by ferry and with no cars allowed. Being there was downright exotic, and waking up in the morning to the mist on my face and the aroma of homemade bread wafting up from the kitchen, Joni Mitchell coming from the old stereo, well, I was transported. I never wanted to leave. Worse, I felt no guilt whatsoever. What a creep.

❖ ❖ ❖

We were playing some great shows around this time. In September, we'd played a club called Pepperland north of San Francisco, with Tim Buckley opening. I loved Tim. He was the gentlest, most beautiful angel ever to grace a stage. His music floated over you like warm honey and there wasn't a woman in attendance at any Buckley concert who didn't fall in love with Tim. Men too, I think. We also got to know Jefferson Airplane and made lifelong friends. The shows were great and the after-show hangouts were even better. This was top tier, man. This was as good as it gets.

There was plenty of good old-fashioned perversion too. During our next little run of dates, Aynsley had some amorous and rather public displays of affection involving a comely lass and a very fizzy champagne bottle, vintage unknown. It was actually a lot more harmless than it sounds, except of course for the young lady participant, who actually seemed to be quite enjoying herself. We were all just voyeurs. Nothing wrong with that. The weird part was that afterward, I didn't call home. I called Lin.

And then I returned home and told Melita everything. I had no idea at all what I was doing. I was treading water at home. We bought a gorgeous Irish setter that we named Ralph and went out for fondue dinners and spent evenings with neighboring couples. There was trouble with our Laurel Canyon tenants: They were about three months late with the rent and nowhere to be found. I was able to find another renter just before Melita's panic set in. This was a gentleman named Velvert Turner, an actual friend of Jimi's, although I've learned since never to rent anything to anybody. You'll see.

❖ ❖ ❖

In the fall, White Whale released the Turtles' *Wooden Head* album posthumously. It was a rather depressing set of B-sides and incomplete tracks, but I ran by the Sunset Boulevard office to pick up a few copies in early November before the Mothers left to play at both Fillmores. Neither Lee nor Ted was around when I stopped by. It felt like going back to elementary school to pick up a misplaced book. I had grown past this.

We laughed about it backstage at the Santa Monica Civic, where we were hanging with the Kinks at their gig before heading back to Manhattan for the first of many shows at the Fillmore East. Bill Graham had become a real buddy since the Turtles' show at the original Fillmore. He loved this new incarnation of Frank's band. I think it spoke to the vaudevillian in the man. He laughed through the shows in San Francisco, standing at the side of the stage with his hands in his jeans pockets. And he jumped onboard instantly when Frank suggested adding some heavy friends to the shows in New York.

On Friday, November 13, I got up about 12:30 for a 2 P.M. sound check at the Fillmore East. Things went well. We actually had time to go back to the hotel at One Fifth Avenue before the concert. Mark and I met Joni Mitchell there and brought her up to Frank's room for introductions.

We'd known Joni for some time. On any given Friday night, Stephen Stills, David Crosby, Jackson Browne, Mark, and whoever would sit around Joni's living room in a circle and someone would play his newest heartbreaker. Everyone would comment on it and the guitar would be passed to the next writer. I was a happy witness to one such session. Mark and I previewed the songs that would become our first album as a duo there. It was an amazing time to be around all of this burgeoning talent and we all knew it. All of the guys there had an enormous crush on

Joni, and she was magic to be around. Joni wrote the song "Conversation" about the strange relationship she and Mark had.

That night at the Fillmore East, we played our first set with Sha Na Na opening and went back to the hotel to get Joni. All we knew was that she had prepared something for the show and, in the true spirit of the band, we'd hear it when she did it. We played our complete second show, which was stellar as usual. Then Frank nodded toward stage right and out walked this tall, blond vision to thunderous applause from a shocked audience.

You could have heard a pin drop. Not even the sound of a nervous cough broke the silence. And this was a Zappa crowd. Softly and slowly, Joni spoke to an enraptured crowd.

"Penelope wants to fuck the sky . . ." she began. Frank smiled from ear to ear as he lifted his arms to conduct the group. I don't recall the rest of the piece, but it brought down the house and afterward, Joni went with Mark and me for pizza. It rained. It was wonderful. The next night, Grace Slick strolled onstage at the beginning of one of the sets and the band jammed while she did mostly nothing. We hung with her till dawn, but it wasn't as transcendent as the previous night had been. We were just higher.

That same week, we played a concert at Massey Hall in Toronto. It's a cold, old theater with dressing rooms that resemble turn-of-the-century schoolrooms, replete with folding chairs and horrible glass transoms above the doors. We were in one of these industrial green rooms when we heard a commotion in the hall outside. Then we heard the glass breaking before we knew what had happened. From outside, a young male voice yelled, "I love you, Frank!" and crashing to the floor came the enormous severed head of an adult male pig. Fresh meat. Uncle Meat. It was supposed to be a loving gift. A bloody, wide-eyed loving pig. It was horrible. And I'm no vegetarian.

Mothers of Invention fans were a little bit different. Deep in his heart, this idiot fanboy was doing something memorable and heroic for his biggest idol. It wasn't supposed to gross us all out; I'm sure the kid thought Frank would probably bring the damned thing up onstage with him and make a hero out of this little Canuck to his classmates and his girlfriend (though, truth be told, none of the ladies who attended Zappa concerts were likely to have come to the show with him).

❖ ❖ ❖

At home, the sex had ceased since my sincere confessional, and Melita and I were civil to each other at best. But there wasn't a lot of time to worry about such trivialities. In a matter of days, the laundry got done, the bank was visited, the baby was adored, and I was out of there again.

For the first time and for no apparent reason, the Warner Bros. people were at every show of the new European tour. We had this amazing press agent named Barbara Scott (who later became Barbara DeWitt), who babysat all of us and made us feel a lot less stupid. There must have been some sort of buzz, because the shows were all sold out. We lived like kings in the capitals of the world as winter descended at the end of 1970. Back to London, like jet-setters. Only this time, while the band checked into the familiar Kensington Palace, Frank stayed at the Dorchester. Yikes! We all took a taxi over to his hotel for interviews on our second day in town.

We had Thanksgiving in Liverpool and got sick in Manchester, but we lived out of London. On Saturday, Mark went out to Stephen Stills's house in Surrey and I went with Marc and June Bolan to a T. Rex concert at the Roundhouse. Things had really changed for Marc. The girls were screaming now; he had switched his image to that of a glam rock god and the frenzy was only just beginning for Bolan. He was the self-proclaimed cosmic punk now, and he was laughing all the way to the bank. I sang with the band that night. It was amazing.

The itinerary read like *Around the World in 80 Days*. From Stockholm to Copenhagen to the Amsterdam Hilton—yeah, we were there too. We did press conferences daily before our sound checks, and then we had a fifty-fifty shot at getting back to the hotel before the concert. Up early the following morning, no matter how much international partying was being done, to fly, go through customs, meet the new agent and the new Warner's guy and get to the next, albeit four-star, hotel. I loved walking the streets of Wherever-We-Were. Truly at this time of year, with the falling snow and the tiny shops lining cobblestone avenues, clock towers chiming festive holiday carols and strange-tasting food from street vendors' carts, it was even more magical than Central Park had been. Even our European promoter, Fritz Rau, was a jolly old elf of a character who only added to the illusion.

Jean-Luc Ponty, the world-renowned jazz violinist, sat in with us at the Palais Gaumont in Paris for an extremely uncomfortable show of mostly instrumentals for a crowd of socialists, and then I hit London one more time to spend a sad-to-go evening with the Bolans before our Air India flight blew the fantasy right out of the water and once again plunged us into a curry-scented reality. Just like that.

Home to the duplicity. Home to Emily developing a rather serious cough. Evenings spent with Spanky and her husband, Charly Galvin. Or Jerry and Judy (Henske) Yester. Or Jeff and Brina Simmons. Or Ian and Ruth Underwood. Or the Volmans: anything to avoid having to confront the elephant in the Woodland Hills room. We really weren't getting along at all, and the more worldly I became (in my mind, at least), the more restless I became at home. The pace was just too slow. I found that I had only two settings—full-bore or disinterested. As 1970 came to an end, I couldn't stop my engines from revving. I was all dressed up with no place to go. And despite Frank's tantalizing hints of a *200 Motels* movie project, there was trouble brewing on the horizon of the Kaylan household.

A Car Shaped Like an Enormous Penis, Sounds Like Good, Clean Family Fun

For the time being, all the domestic stuff was moved to the back burner. As the first of the year came and went, our attorney Paul Almond was poring over the contracts for Frank's *200 Motels* movie. We hadn't read the script. Hell, there wasn't a script. There was only Frank's assurance that there would be a script by the time we arrived at Pinewood Studios, outside of London, to film what would now be a United Artists release.

It was back to London, courtesy of Air India, on January 14 of what was to become a seminal year. We got to Kensington Palace around 1:30 and I was unpacked and in bed an hour later. But I was ready to party when June Bolan phoned at 9:30. Off to the Speakeasy for dinner and cognac. I ate, I laughed, I puked. I love London.

We finally got our scripts on Saturday night, and by Sunday afternoon, Jeff Simmons had quit the band. He and his wife, Brina, had looked over Frank's words and she, in particular, was convinced that Jeff would be throwing his life away if he participated in the making of this travesty. In the script, the character of Jeff is contemplating leaving the Mothers of Invention based on Frank's desire to play comedy music. He expresses his contempt for the entire genre in a speech that both he and Brina had decided would make him look extremely bad.

"No way I'm going to play this comedy music, man. I didn't join this band to become a laughingstock. I want to play the blues, man. Zappa's old. He's almost thirty, for God's sake. He just doesn't get it. We should take up a collection and buy him a watch!"

That's how the script read.

Brina was even more insistent than Jeff had been. "Jeff's not going to say that stuff. It makes him sound like an idiot. He joined this band to be a musician, not a goddamned comedian. And he would never say anything like that. He's got more class than that!"

Frank was not amused. In fact, he was genuinely bewildered. He nodded toward Mark, who produced his own portable tape recorder and flipped it on. And we heard Jeff speaking in a taxi en route to the Dorchester last year.

"No way I'm going to play this comedy music, man. I want to play the blues. Zappa's old. . . ." It was all there. Brina turned red and stomped out of the room. From the hallway she yelled, "Are you coming, Jeff? Let's go home."

And he got up, said nothing, and followed her back to Seattle. Now we were all trapped in England without a major player in a movie that was to start shooting in just a few days. Without him, there would be no movie. How could that bastard do this to us? We were up Shit Creek and Simmons hadn't even left us a paddle. He was intentionally sinking the entire ship because he didn't want his handful of Northwest friends to see the blues boy compromised within the confines of a comedy band. What a jerk! And now there would be no movie. Thanks for nothing, asshole.

However, the sadness I felt was nothing compared to the emotions running rampant in Mr. Zappa. This was the shot at mainstream success that he and Herb and even Frank's wife, Gail, had awaited for almost a decade, and the damned bass player was putting the kibosh on the entire affair. Zappa, after momentary paralysis, calmly devised a plan. He was not going to give up on his feature motion picture debut without a fight. We had Ringo Starr signed and ready to go, Keith Moon was onboard, the London Philharmonic was about to start rehearsing, the massive sound stages at Pinewood had been booked, and the sets had been built and assembled. All we needed to do was to find another "Jeff."

Time wasn't on our side, either. Frank soon realized that, no matter how quickly we shot the picture, we would never have time to shoot the elaborate ending he had written.

❖ ❖ ❖

This would be a good time to explain the genesis of that missing scene and the construction of *200 Motels* itself.

Many months before, traveling in some anonymous bus or train on the way to some foreign destination with Frank, I had told him about one particular groupie adventure that I had lived through back in the Turtle days. Back then, I had gotten to third base with some faceless fan who literally crossed her legs on our evening of lust and stopped the passion at a most crucial time. When I blustered out my frustration, she told me that she would go no farther unless I sang her my big hit record. What? Now? But . . .

So there I had been, pants down at my ankles, and just about to do the nasty. And she was going to make me sing?

That bitch!

I could never demean myself like that. How could she expect me to lower myself like that?

But she was so pretty. And I was so ready. "Imagine me and you. I do . . ." I wasn't proud. But I did get laid, damn it.

As I told the story to Frank that afternoon, I could almost hear the wheels turning inside the Master's brain. The ultimate groupie story. Now Frank had an ending for his movie. And the entire plot was shaping up based on my little groupie adventure.

The Mothers were to travel to Centerville—a real nice place to raise your kids—and meet a bunch of amorous groupie types for motel adventures while Jeff threatened to quit and Don Preston, one of the original Mothers, brewed up mystical potions that turned ordinary cigarettes into mystery roaches that, when smoked, turned the movie into animated nightmares for the Jeff character and gave the rest of the band time to get ready for the teenage nightclub. There, my character was to run into the girl of his dreams, who was actually Mark in full drag, and take her back to my cheesy motel room in a car shaped like an enormous penis. Sounds like good, clean family fun, doesn't it?

But there was no movie without Jeff. Or someone to play Jeff. Quickly! And so the search was on. We found some very unusual casting choices. It certainly would have been a different film. The first suggestion came from Ringo. What if Wilfrid Brambell, Paul's clean old grandfather from *A Hard Day's Night*, played the part of Jeff? It was ridiculous, but it was nuts enough to work. So the following morning, Wilfrid Brambell arrived at Pinewood in an ill-fitting tweed suit, ready to become Jeff Simmons.

We had a week to get it together. That meant everything. The acting, the music, the blocking, and the shooting. And shortly, Frank realized that we would never have enough time to shoot the ending of the movie as it had been written. We had only been given five days to shoot the entire movie, and there was no way in hell that we'd get to the tinsel-cock car and the fruition of the groupie saga. So Frank got to work immediately on a finale number that would wrap the entire story up in a song. He barely had time to write it and we were given even less time to learn it.

❖ ❖ ❖

During that week, nights were spent with the Bolans or Janet and Lucy, Frank's groupie actresses, dining out or clothes shopping at Biba. Keith appeared, ready to work or to play, he didn't care which. That changed the dynamic a bit. Supergroupie Miss Pamela had flown in to do a small part in the film and wound up spending her off-hours in Keith's company, which made me vaguely jealous for reasons I couldn't yet understand. Things were chaotic. Frank was having heated meetings with Tony Palmer, the video director hired to bring Frank's vision to the big screen. But Frank thought that the directing duties were to be split up: Frank would direct the musicians and the actors, even the dancers, and Tony would call the camera shots and be responsible for the look of the film. The entire movie was to be shot on videotape and later transferred to film—a never-before-used technique for a major studio production. But Tony wanted to direct the actors, and that was us. And we belonged to Frank. So Tony Palmer quit too.

Now United Artists was faced with a decision. Would they let Zappa keep running up exorbitant studio charges with a dubious cast and no director, or would they just shut down the project and swallow their losses?

If I had taken the time to care, I would have been a basket case. So I didn't. I just enjoyed England. We sang on three T. Rex tracks on Friday, January 22—one of the songs was called "Hot Love"—and on Saturday, Frank announced that he had just hired a new "Jeff" and it was Noel Redding from the Jimi Hendrix Experience. He could certainly play the bass parts. He just couldn't act. We rehearsed in the suite at the Kensington Palace and Frank looked crestfallen. This was not going to work. Maybe if Wilfrid did the acting and Noel did the bass parts—two Jeffs. Why not?

Rehearsals, such as they were, were over and it was time for us to leave our London digs and move to the Windsor Castle Hotel nearer to Pinewood. When we arrived at Pinewood on Monday morning, we discovered that Wilfrid Brambell had spent the entire weekend drinking himself into a stupor, not understanding the obscenities he had been hired to say, and that, regretfully, he had quit the film also. Apparently, this was one dream that was about to self-destruct. Frank joined the rest of us in Ringo's dressing room to speculate on our futures. Things were bad and there was no sugarcoating the situation. We were screwed. We had no ideas between us. We were resigned to going home. Then Frank said, "How about this? The next person who walks through that dressing room door gets the part of Jeff. Period. Whoever it is."

It was a risky statement, but we all took it seriously, whether Frank had meant it or not. No one spoke for the longest time. It felt like a spaghetti western in there. All of us watched the door for signs of movement. And then, it happened. There was a cursory knock, the door opened a crack, and in walked Ringo's chauffeur, Martin Lickert, a twenty-something, longhaired hippie type with a psychedelic sweater and a Beatle accent. He was perfect!

"Can you act?" Zappa asked the petrified kid as we closed the dressing room door behind him. "I dunno. I never tried," came the shaky answer. "Do you play an instrument?" Frank queried. "Um, yessir," came the answer back. "Just a bit of bass guitar."

Unbelievable. Some higher power really wanted us to make this movie.

So Martin Lickert was signed to play the role of Jeff, we all breathed a sigh of relief, and *200 Motels* was back on track.

❖ ❖ ❖

The week was a blur of cognac, no sleep, Pamela and Keith, and the orchestra recording their pieces on tape and then behaving like schoolboys between takes because they considered the entire project to be a joke.

And then there was Theodore Bikel. The world-renowned folksinger and actor had been signed to play the role of Rance Muhammitz, the sinister liaison tasked with acquiring Mr. Volman's signature in exchange for his soul and some mystery burgers.

In one scene, Frank had him acting as a game show host spinning a big wheel to determine the fate of Larry the Dwarf, played by Ringo. The entire scene was written to be done in a single shot with the orchestra, the King's Singers—who were our chorus—and Mark, Janet, Lucy, and I reciting our lines onstage along with Theo. But Theo's lines were filthy—at least, in his opinion—and he flat-out refused to say them. Frank followed him back to his dressing room, begging him to reconsider. Finally, after two hours of dead time, Bikel agreed to say the lines, but only if he wasn't on camera for them. If he saw a red light on one of those video cams, he'd be gone.

Comes the rehearsal, the cameraman doesn't get the memo and the red light goes off right in front of Theo's face. And he walks, yelling the entire way to his dressing room. What a pro! I think, at that point, Frank told him that it had only been a rehearsal and that the footage would never be used. He lied.

Making *200 Motels* was one of the greatest experiences of my life. I took to it like a duck to water. I dug the stupid early mornings and the urgency in our abbreviated time frame. I loved being called to the set and spending off moments walking the 007 stages in the adjacent studio. I thought to myself, "I could get very used to this!"

I hung out with Linda Ronstadt, who flew in with her new producer, John Boylan, and ate lunch in the commissary with Tony Curtis. These were strange times of sealed tuna sandwiches and torchlight parades. New songs like "Penis Dimension" and "Shove It Right In." On Friday, February 5, *200 Motels* wrapped shooting and Keith held the cast party, which continued into the wee hours of the morn. On Sunday, we were back at Kensington Palace and the newspapers were already talking about the protesters in front of the Royal Albert Hall.

It seems that someone had gotten a hold of the movie script and Her Majesty's powers that be were planning to block the Mothers' performance of *200 Motels* with the Royal Philharmonic at that stately venue scheduled for the very next week. The concert was sold out. There was only one thing drastically wrong with this picture: There had been no rehearsals for a concert at the Royal Albert Hall. At all. None. We never even talked about it.

So it was not without reservations that we found ourselves in a taxi on the way to Albert Hall to confront the protesters and reporters. In fact, as Herb and Frank organized the band's response to the questions of the frantic newspeople outside of the amazing building, it occurred to all of us that, despite the headlines, it was *never* intended for us to perform at that concert. It had all been an elaborate publicity stunt. Herb knew that the British government wouldn't let us perform the obscenities that were in *200 Motels* in such a hallowed hall. Frank knew it too. The only people who didn't know it were us. We were on a need-to-know basis, and it was determined that we didn't. Need to know, that is. Herb was a genius. We made headlines all over Europe for a concert that was never to have happened in the first place. It was brilliant.

❖ ❖ ❖

I flew home to L.A. on February 9, the same day a major earthquake hit Southern California. Perfect. Velvert Turner's credit was proving to be a problem at the Laurel Canyon rental, so his producer, Tom Wilson, a great guy and former Dylan recordist, cosigned his lease and made me breathe a momentary sigh of relief. Melita relaxed, but we still weren't communicating. I called Lin for a bit of encouragement but got very little. Then I called Pamela. She had spent all this time with Moon during the movie, but she knew that I had fallen for her—big-time. And now she was the only girl I could really talk to. So we spoke. A lot. She was there for me. I appreciated her immensely.

Melita and Emily busied themselves. Bolan called to tell me that "Hot Love" had become his biggest hit ever in the UK, and Jerry Good, the producer of *200 Motels*, wanted to meet with me and Mark about some other project. We met with Elliot Roberts, who managed Joni and Neil Young, listened to Judee Sill's album, watched the Mothers' Dutch documentary, and spent time fixing up the Woodland Hills house. Realtors were still around, taking pictures and adjusting our home's price constantly as we prayed for a speedy sale. We were going underwater and no amount of Zappa money was going to save us.

We overdubbed the movie soundtrack, adding vocal layers and doing the voices for the animated section still to be completed. And still, there were the depositions. We were still in court with the Martin-Phillips case. I was getting $500 advances from Herb and spending half of it on elaborate dinners out or champagne and caviar from our local Chalet Gourmet. I was used to this lifestyle and was not about to give it up.

In April, Bolan came to town and phoned one afternoon after I had met with Frankie Avalon about production(!) and had gone to the Ice House with Russ Giguere of the Association and Paul Williams to see Jerry Yester's new band, Rosebud, featuring John Seiter on drums. Bolan was in L.A. specifically to put Mark and me on some new rock tracks he had recorded. Marc had just signed with Reprise in the States; they had just released "Hot Love" as a single and had flown Bolan and Tony Visconti to Hollywood to finish up their new titles.

On February 17, the whole lot of us went into Wally Heider's studio in Hollywood, armed with cognac, champagne, and copious quantities of Aztec Marching Powder to sing "Bang a Gong (Get It On)" and two other tunes. The little curly Brit was about to become a rock 'n' roll legend. And therefore, by proxy, so were we.

EIGHTEEN

Anybody Got Any Dope?

So many things were going on simultaneously that I should have been a lot more successful than I really was. During the day, I slept until 11 or so unless given a reason to rise earlier. Melita usually took Emily with her while running errands, or, when a hellacious fight was brewing, she would take her and spend days at a time with Helen in West L.A. So I would make my phone calls, secure my daily drugs, and make the necessary visits to the lawyers or to Herb's office in an attempt to somehow get the cash to get through the month. Realtors kept bringing prospective buyers through at all hours, and Emily grew and cried and as we finished the overdubs on the *200 Motels* album. We were also talking serious management with Herb.

At least, he was serious. Don Preston announced his intention to leave the group—perhaps prompted by his very limited on-screen participation in the movie, but he also wanted to play even stranger music—and the film's producer, Jerry Good, wanted Mark and me to consider doing an animated feature for his company. It appeared that things were winding down for this bunch of Mothers, but when we least expected progress, Frank gave us all copies of his latest opus, "Billy the Mountain."

Without Jeff Simmons in the group, Frank asked the boys in the band to come up with suggestions for an actual replacement bass player. So it was welcome to the Mothers of Invention for our dear friend and fellow Turtle Jim Pons. The fact that he had been my best man didn't enter into the equation. There were tons of bass overdubs to do on the movie soundtrack, since Martin Lickert's live performances were not exactly Zappa-level stuff. Plus, Jim's low voice was a real asset, for the background harmonies as well as in the animated sequence. Now there were three Turtles in the new Mothers, and we needed a keyboard guy to replace Don. We'd had no keyboards in the Turtles, but Judee Sill's husband and the coproducer of "Lady-O," Bob Harris, was available. Frank gave him an audition and he was instantly in the band as well. Things were damned comfortable. At work.

❖ ❖ ❖

At home, Melita and I fought throughout Emily's birthday, so I got high at Paul Williams's house so I wouldn't have to deal with the shitstorm. The next day, I drove Pons to Las Vegas and we caught George Jones and Tammy Wynette—don't tell *me* I don't love country music! The mini vacation did me a world of good. Exactly one week later, I picked up Jim, Bob, and Frank and drove out to Claremont to debut the new lineup at Pomona College. Both Lixie and Pamela were there. I should have anticipated trouble.

We began the next tour in late May and oh, how we did party on that tour! I look back at my daily diaries (which I have kept since 1968 and which have been invaluable in the preparation of this book) and I am astounded at the substances, legal and otherwise, that my toxic little body has absorbed in pursuit of the perfect truth. Or just to get loaded. And I am blown away by not only the amount and frequency of my forays into the hallucinogenic, but the circumstances under which I allowed myself to function.

I think that it hits me hardest while reliving the Zappa years, on account of Frank's famous anti-drug stance. It would be naive of me to think that the brilliant Mr. Z didn't know what was going on. He was a man of his word, however, and I was allowed to live in my polluted little world as long as Frank's much larger one wasn't affected. The cocaine and the marijuana guaranteed that I was, at least in my mind, living the life I had always dreamed about—one of sex and drugs and rock 'n' roll. I didn't realize that I was searching to fill a huge void in my life. But I sure didn't have to wait for long.

There wasn't a lot of sleep to be had. Given the choice between sleep and all of the other post-concert options that were open to us, the decision was obvious. We plowed through the Midwest: Illinois, Ohio, Michigan, Wisconsin. We'd fly to most shows and take a regular seated charter bus to the closer ones. After the shows, it was always the women and/or the impromptu jam sessions that lasted until dawn. We were lucky to average four hours of sleep a night. Frank, ever the father figure, would stop in almost nightly to see how his lads were doing, but his visits were brief and he never participated in our antics. Not yet.

❖ ❖ ❖

On Saturday, May 29, 1971, I met a girl.

It began as a causal encounter, sort of. The concert was in Rochester, Michigan, at a beautiful outdoor venue, the Baldwin Pavilion at Oakland University. Livingston Taylor opened the show. In attendance that evening were the members of an alternative-lifestyle group that lived and loved together. They grew food on their land and set up kitchens to feed the hungry hippies who lived only for music. They called themselves the Rainbow People's Party and lived in Ann Arbor at a residence they referred to as Hill House. One girl, in particular, caught my eye and changed my life. Her name was Dianne MacKellar and she had the bluest eyes I had ever seen. Long brown hair and a smoky, squeaky voice that stole my heart. I took the freethinking lady back to my room, spoke passionately about her politics, made mad love to her, and watched her pass out. Normally, that would have been considered the perfect evening. But I hadn't wanted her to pass out. Something in me snapped.

I had no idea that there were girls like this in real life. There certainly hadn't been in my previous world. Dianne was the embodiment of hippie freedom. Oh, she shaved her armpits; that's not what I mean. But she had bigger plans than I had. I only wanted to make music—Dianne wanted to change the world. She didn't care where she lived or even who she was with. She was a gypsy and she dressed appropriately. A vision in her see-through white shirt, ropes of obligatory ceramic beads, ground-hugging mirrored skirt, large hoop earrings, and an all-over tan that said, "Come sunbathing with me," she had me before I had even heard her sweet honey voice. I was in love.

But there was work to do. Aysnsley's new wife, Olivia, flew in to hang for a while and we did amazing shows. And then it was back to my old stomping grounds: New York City and the One Fifth Avenue hotel. I was a bit nervous, understandably, and, as usual when a big show loomed on the horizon, my voice was raspy. We were to do four shows over two nights in early June at the Fillmore East, our first shows there since the previous fall and the first with the new lineup including Jim Pons. It would be another trial by fire, where we'd be judged by an audience of the ultra-chic. We would be auditioning all over again, but Frank had a plan. The last time we'd played there, Joni and Grace had turned up. This time the invited guests would send massive shock waves throughout the building.

❧ ❧ ❧

On Saturday afternoon, I walked solo through the Village during the Feast of San Gennaro, treated myself to a sausage and pepper sandwich, and bought a new, round, flat, clay hash pipe. Then I walked over to the Fillmore, did two shows—which went very well, according to my diary—and walked back by 4 A.M. The following morning I awoke to a phone message, did some interviews courtesy of Barbara DeWitt, and then met Mark in Frank's room and waited for his afternoon visitors.

At about 2 P.M., John Lennon and Yoko Ono arrived. Frank really didn't know John very well and none of us had ever met Yoko before, so things felt a bit stilted and formal at first, like everyone was waiting for a second shoe to drop. John remembered the Turtles' encounter at the Speakeasy, mumbled a quick but heartfelt apology, and at least broke the ice a little bit as Zappa started noodling on his unplugged Strat, searching for something that he and John could jam to at the show later that night. Yoko shifted uncomfortably in her overstuffed chair. John cleared his throat.

"Anybody got any dope?" the former Beatle asked innocently.

Frank was quick to reply. "I don't do that stuff, but these guys do." And with that, he motioned toward me and Mark. What the hell was he expecting me to do? I shot Zappa a look, but he answered with a reassuring, "It's okay. Go ahead."

"Really, Frank?" I was incredulous for a reason. "Be right back!"

I ran down to my room, fetched my new hash pipe and some pot, and was back in Frank's within a minute. My hands were shaking a little as I filled the virgin pipe and passed it and my lighter to John. He drew deeply and passed it to Yoko. She took a hit and held the pipe out to Frank, who politely declined. So the pipe returned to me for refilling, then to Mark and back to John.

I couldn't believe what was happening. Not only was I smoking weed with my hero, but Frank, my father figure, was watching me do it. And without even the famous Zappa raised eyebrow. I don't think I've ever been that high in my life. I was sailing.

The cycle continued as John was given an acoustic guitar to mess around with. He sang a blues song or two and Frank obliged him with lead guitar parts to complement John's verses. Yoko wailed a few times and Lennon actually told her to keep it down. We were in a hotel room, after all. Frank played some amazing licks that Lennon couldn't keep up with, and then John settled on a riff that would become the song "Scumbag." I ad-libbed the ridiculous lyrics. We smoked some more and talked some more and agreed to meet later at the theater. I put my pipe back in my suitcase and brought it home with me after the weekend. I still have that little pipe. It's one of my most treasured possessions.

If our first Fillmore show that evening was wonderful, our second was transcendent. When the concert ended and the audience stood, waiting for their encore, it felt as though a herd of elephants had entered the auditorium as the world's most famous couple walked onstage. The resulting jam was recorded by both Frank and the Fillmore and was released on two different albums. John released it as the fourth LP in his *Some Time in New York City* compilation on Apple, although he took writing credit on every song, including Frank's iconic "King Kong," which he renamed and tried to publish. Frank's lawyers had to sue John's lawyers to straighten the entire thing out, and it really wasn't all that great anyway, but at least I can say that I am among a handful of people, right alongside Paul McCartney, to ever share writing credits with the immortal John Lennon. So there.

NINETEEN

A Closely Guarded Secret

I smoked pot with Frank Zappa. Not once, not twice, but at least three times. It was a closely guarded secret, and no one in the Zappa family nor any of the chronicles of Frank's life have copped to it. Frank was famously anti-drugs and anti-liquor too. But when he was feeling particularly low or even fabulously good, the man would sometimes follow his famous nose to where the smell of Mary Jane took him. And that was generally my room or Mark's. I gotta admit, the first time it happened, I didn't know how to react.

Frank would often nurse a syrupy green concoction when the band went out on the town. It was crème de menthe or a grasshopper or something abysmally sweet. Generally, Frank would imbibe only when he was with a lady, which was pretty often. But later on, when the band actually started feeling like a band, it wasn't uncommon for Zappa to be one of the boys.

My first recollection of him smoking was when we were all in the same room, and we were all happy. It was me and Mark and Jim. We always checked with Frank before we did any substances in his presence, but after the John Lennon episode, our habits weren't as taboo as they once had been.

We were smoking a single joint between the three of us when Frank came over and asked if he could have a hit. We were in shock.

"Are you sure, Frank?"

"Why not?" was his reply, and he took the joint from me and inhaled deeply. Just the one toke. He exhaled a huge cloud of smoke.

"Tastes good." he said.

"More?" we asked.

"No, thanks," came the reply. "This shit gives me headaches. But don't let me stop you." And we didn't.

There were one or two group orgies where the green booze flowed and Zappa sought out a little combustible solace. He was often just trying to impress a young lady, which he certainly didn't have to do—he was fuckin' Frank Zappa, for Christ's sake! But in this new and more democratic Mothers of Invention, which Frank had shortened to the Mothers, all the old bets were off. We were a close-knit bunch of musicians on a common mission, and camaraderie was a huge part of our band dynamic.

◆ ◆ ◆

June 14, according to the good old daily entries, was the day that we signed the settlement with Martin-Phillips. It was ordered by the courts of the great state of California, that we—meaning the Turtles—owed this New York company the sum of $65,000. It was a good deal, our attorney Paul Almond assured us, and under the bizarre circumstances of the management confusion of the '60s, he was probably right. Of course, we didn't have $65,000 or even two sticks to rub together, but the Fillmore album was coming out and someone at Warner's must have heard some street buzz, because on that same afternoon, we picked up checks for $10,000 each from Herb's office. Even better, Herb told both of us not to worry about the money that we owed or anything else. Enjoy, he advised.

So I celebrated. The now elusive marriage bed was visited and I schlepped down the hill to Chalet Gourmet, the amazing upscale grocers, for champagne, caviar, and lobster to go with the extra hits of blow we'd consume that night. Even in the dark times, we lived large, but it sure felt better when you knew that you could actually pay for it. Four days later, we finally got an offer on our Woodland Hills house. Things, it seemed, were rapidly turning around.

Frank had hired a language instructor for Mark and me. Her name was Lu, and we had met her in Germany. Now she was currently living in

Frank's basement or guesthouse; I really don't know which. He had an idea for our next, post-"Billy" opus and it all seemed to depend on our progress in the Germanic language arts. Frank was thinking, at least, three steps ahead. We weren't singing in German yet.

On June 29, we left for the summer tour and Frank felt, I think, that we were truly a band for the very first time. In Quebec City, after a boys' night out, I hung with him and Aynsley until dawn, and the next night the two of us went to a rancid discotheque and spoke philosophy until the wee hours. We were almost like buddies. I kept my distance; I think I knew my place, but I was being myself. It wasn't like I felt like I was on my best behavior around my boss. There wasn't anything about me that Frank didn't know. I believe that part of the man's genius was to get inside his players' heads and bring out the best or the weirdest or the most perverted part of them to amplify and turn into a piece of theater. I was certainly ripe fodder in 1971.

On July 5, in Frank's hotel room in Montreal, Zappa played a happy new guitar lick while the band jammed along and, unbeknownst to all, I hastily scribbled out the absolutely obscene lyrics to "Magdalena." They grossed out even me! But in the spirit of the Mothers and madness of that band and that city, they seemed perfectly and disgustingly appropriate. Even more than that, they made Frank laugh. Really laugh. Like, sit down on the bed and wipe his eyes laugh. I have never felt so good. It was parental approval for this kid.

I felt like telling the world, but it was 3:30 in the morning, and the only person I felt like talking to was Lin in Seattle. I was very confused. Confused enough to actually pass up a now-famous Zappa-era orgy in Winnipeg. I don't feel bad about missing it now, but at the time, especially knowing all of the girls as I did, it was sort of like *not* being the guy who walked on the moon to earn his ranger's badge. In fact, Mark, Jim, and Frank developed an actual salute that I also adopted, although never earned: full, military right hand on the heart, then lifted skyward to the chant of "Rangers, ho!" I never got to be an actual Winnipeg ranger, but I still think of one of those girls, Enid Finnbogason, every once in a while. I think I saw her in a soft-core porno thing a few years ago and she was looking good. Hi, Enid. Rangers, ho!

❖ ❖ ❖

I don't remember what story I made up to tell Melita, but I didn't come home when the rest of the band did. I went, instead, to Seattle, took the ferry to Vashon Island, rented a bicycle, and pedaled to Lin's house for an amazing week, off the books. I needed every minute of it. It was amazingly romantic in that nonpermanent and safe way: the misty island, the beautiful girl with the long brown hair. We went to a beach party together at her mother's house, also on Vashon, and woke up together spooning beneath her always open bedroom window with the gauze curtains brushing against my newly grown Zappa-era beard. She smelled of vanilla. It was wonderful. For the first time, I knew clearly what I had to do.

It wasn't Lin or the thought of Lin. Actually, it had been Dianne and the thought of Dianne. It was personal and very selfish, but as I returned to my home in Woodland Hills with our marriage's inevitable collapse ahead and my young daughter literally in her mother's arms, I drunkenly walked through my front door, suitcase in hand, and announced my departure. There was an ocean of wonderful and new women out there for the taking, and none of them nagged me or told me that I was lazy or held their hands out for a check at the end of the month. Of course, that was a little something called responsibility and I certainly hadn't learned anything about that. Fuck, man, I was a rock star.

So I helped Melita and her mom move out of our classy McMansion and into much more modest digs and I found a little non-family-friendly place on Treasure Trail to begin the first of a great many crises, midlife and otherwise. I felt nothing—no remorse—and shed not one single tear. This would only affect my daughter for the best. She certainly didn't need to be around two parents constantly screaming, I justified.

We were still learning German and rehearsing in the evenings, and Frank was supervising the animated section of *200 Motels* at the offices of Murakami-Wolf, the production company that had coproduced the movie with Zappa and Herb. It was there that Jerry Good handed Mark and me the script for a new animated feature that one of his animators had written especially for us. It was something about a weasely little insurance salesman and his foulmouthed friend, a six-foot duck. You bet, pal. Anything if the check clears.

❖ ❖ ❖

Two houses now, one for each of us. And I've got to talk to somebody. I hate to be truly alone. So I spent hours on the phone—only landlines in those days—to Lin and to Dianne, and when I finally really needed a shoulder to cry on, I found it in a very unlikely place. After rehearsals, it fell to me as a Canyon dweller to transport Frank home after rehearsals. Frank and Gail had two children at the time, Moon Unit and Dweezil, and had hired a most nontraditional nanny, the lovely Pamela Miller, she of *200 Motels* and GTOs fame. I would drop Frank at his front door and then circle around with my headlights off to park behind his guesthouse, wherein dwelt the lovely Miss Pamela. I was pushing the envelope now and certainly should have known better, but look at whom we're talking about here. Excess R us.

On August 7, the Mothers sold out the very same Pauley Pavilion at UCLA, the old alma mater, where I had gone to congratulate the old Mothers less than a year before. Frank recorded the entire concert on his portable Uher reel-to-reel machine and it would soon be released as an album, without a single overdub or studio sweetening, as *Just Another Band from L.A.*, but that was a long way off in Zappa time.

Pamela and I partied, hung with Danny Hutton of Three Dog Night, saw our buddies Cheech and Chong at the Troubadour, and went to Disneyland. I was talking to Dianne for hours in the daytime and then doing my wash with Pamela at the Zappas' and running around naked in the middle of the night, as the entire household did. Except I wasn't part of the Zappa household. I was a naked employee who was drinking milk out of the carton while being framed in the nude by the refrigerator light. Not cool.

Dweezil was still in diapers. It sounds weird to say after all these years have passed—I recently worked with Dweezil's band—but life is full of surprises.

My relationship with Miss Pamela wasn't exactly normal either. There were no secrets here. Not really. Pamela sort of knew about Dianne, although not the total picture, and I was obviously aware of Pamela's famously promiscuous past and, indeed, present. One evening, while we were relaxing in the guesthouse, a long black stretch limousine pulled up in front of the little house, the back door opened, and Pamela rushed by me dressed in diaphanous scarves and made up for an evening of play. She said that she was sorry but she had forgotten to mention that Led

Zeppelin were in town and she had this standing arrangement with Jimmy Page—she knew I would understand, which I did. I was just as guilty, or innocent, as she was. It was a time to be free.

But hey, was it phenomenal!

❖ ❖ ❖

On Monday, August 21, the Mothers' white-covered *Fillmore East—June 1971* album entered the *Billboard* charts. Four days later, we played a long show as a favor for our good friend Bill Graham at the Berkeley Community Theatre. We met a lady friend of Jim's whom he had flown in from the Midwest and ate a lovely dinner. After an uneventful concert, I was in my room when a call came in: orgy in Frank's room!

There were these Eastern Airlines stewardesses there that we had encountered earlier in the day, and by the time I arrived they were both naked, each on one of the two double beds in this particular chamber. A living room separated this room from Frank's king-size master.

And they weren't alone. The entire band was there, as were the crew and a now-infamous groupie named Nigey Lennon (no relation to you-know-who). This girl actually spent several years in Frank's company and proudly wrote a book about this night and her ongoing affair with the maestro. But on this particular evening, she focused her attention on one of Frank's shoes. That's right, a large, well-worn purple saddle shoe. She wanted to put on a show for us all, this considerate lady. And the only condition was that we all get naked. Well, hell, no problem.

So we disrobed, and Nigey began to put on her show. All of us—except for Frank, that is—wore bemused smiles as he watched her writhing on the double bed. He puffed his cigarette and drank his disgustingly foul green drink as her captive audience watched and she reached her climax. It was intense. Masturbation, insertion, groaning, and coming. When she finished, she wiped the sweat from her brow, tossed aside the object of her desire, and asked, "Who's first?" She was obliged by one of Graham's roadies, but that's all it took to begin the free-for-all.

Bodies were everywhere. The stewardesses were more than courteous and accommodated three or four guys at a time. No coffee or tea was served. There was something sad about seeing Jim's little Midwest friend, Miss Prim and Proper, get hauled into the fracas, only to be happily ravaged by Aynsley and everybody else for hours. It was great fun, and although after a while even orgies get old, it felt like we were a club now. We had, for better or worse, a shared secret, and nothing brings a band closer than a shared secret. Ask Fleetwood Mac. I had shot my wad, so to speak, and was happy to return to my room. There, I called Lin and made plans for one last trip to Vashon Island.

We took psilocybin cuddling in a blanket, watching the sun come up over Seattle and talking of the pompatus of love. We were terrific together. It was great fun, but it was just one of those things, as the song says. Three days later, I flew to San Francisco, where Dianne met me at the airport in her VW bus with her dog, Trucker, and all of her belongings. We drove to Los Angeles to begin our new lives together.

TWENTY

A Pony Harness Dipped in Enchilada Sauce

On August 14, I did a brief interview in the old Woodland Hills house. That wasn't unusual. Reporters and music writers would frequently get their best stories going to the interviewees' domiciles. Comfort meant letting your guard down. The surprise was that the article came out in *Rolling Stone*. Six years of supposed show-business success and now, at last, I was deemed hip enough to be interviewed by the only validating newsprint vehicle of my generation. It wasn't a huge article, but it allowed me to breathe a massive sigh of life relief. And by the way, it was written by a young freelance writer from L.A. named Harold Bronson. Some of you more astute record collector types will recognize Harold as one of the future owners of Rhino Records, which would reissue all of the Turtles' albums and release a lot of other stuff Mark and I did.

Harold started his article by putting my life at the time into proper perspective. He wrote, "Working in the Turtles, working in the Mothers, it's all the same, Howard Kaylan says. But he has undergone a transition nevertheless. Gone is the superstar showbiz Woodland Hills suburban dwelling complete with wife and pool in favor of a small, unimpressive wooden house north of the Hollywood Bowl. 'I went from a Mercedes to a Volkswagen,' he puts it, 'but I didn't understand why until now.'"

Dianne and I were living in the new little house on Treasure Trail, struggling to keep cool during one of the hottest, un-air-conditioned summers in memory. On Labor Day, Bolan called from the Chateau Marmont, and Dianne and I picked him up in her camper van. We got plowed and listened to his new album, particularly the amazing background vocals, and the two of us made love with Marc passed out in a cognac stupor. It was perverse and very cool. I think he was passed out. If not, what the hell? We were brothers.

It was a busy week. Mark, Jim, Frank, and I went into the studio on Tuesday to record the voices for the trailer and movie commercial. June Bolan phoned the following morning, way too early. Marc was already in the studio and she was bored, dahling. We walked the expensive boutiques on Sunset Plaza, dined and champagned at the Old World restaurant, and wound up back at their suite. Then both Dianne and June decided that it was time for me to be officially welcomed into the world of hip. With enough room service champagne and the assistance of June's little stash bottle, I was deemed sufficiently numb enough to have my left ear pierced by these two well-meaning alcoholics.

June didn't know what the hell she was doing. Dianne didn't either. I was wasted and they wouldn't let me see. I only heard, "Oops!" and that was enough to make me blanch a bit.

"Oh, shit. Oh, shit. It's okay. We can fix it." Not what you want to hear. "Sit still, my angel," says June. Only by now the damage had been done. I had an earring in my left ear all right—at the bottom of a very long and bloody gash. Rock 'n' roll! What are you going to do? I didn't go nuts about it then, and I don't regret it even now. An earring still dangles from the bottom of that scar. Call it a souvenir of the best era in my life. Of course, this is a judgment made more than forty years after the fact.

❖ ❖ ❖

That night, the Mothers had a photo shoot with Henry Diltz for the press kit that would accompany the movie premiere, but the next evening I had set time aside to have a very important dinner. I picked up Pamela at her mother's house and we went out to dinner at the Chart House in Marina del Rey, one of my favorite haunts. It was a serious and unhappy meal. I told Pamela about Dianne. She had known her name, but had no idea that I had intended to fly her in from Detroit to live with me. I had only just separated from my wife and child—how did this happen so quickly? I didn't have an answer that made any sense to her except that I had fallen in love. But didn't we also have love? It wasn't the same, I told her. The lady cried. Even though what we had was far from exclusive. Even though she has admitted, even in her own best-seller, *I'm with the Band*, that I was never really her type, we had something.

Several years later, Pamela married musician Michael Des Barres. They were happy for many years and remain close. I'm still close to Pamela too. She's that kind of wonderful girl.

But I was so in love with Dianne. We took an amazing drive up to Yosemite, picking up hitchhikers, camping on the river, and making love at every opportunity, whether mobile or stationary. We hiked to Vernal Falls and skinny-dipped with like-minded new acquaintances. Then it was back through San Francisco, with the Grateful Dead's *American Beauty* and *Workingman's Dead* as our soundtrack. We laughed in the bars of North Beach and then drove south and meditated at Nepenthe in Big Sur. We loved each other. I had never felt anything like it.

It wasn't all smooth sailing. Dianne was jealous too. While I rehearsed with the Mothers or worked with Frank's studio engineer, Barry Keene, on a posthumous Turtles album at Whitney Studios in Glendale, Dianne was amusing herself by going to see James Taylor and the Moody Blues. The Mothers had shows to play, and already I was getting the "other girls" lecture. Dianne wasn't cut out to be a housewife. Of course, no one wants to wait around for their better half, especially when he's singing his filthy hit album to audiences of screaming groupies all over the world. To this day, she remains the only important lady in my life who *didn't* know who or what I was when the relationship began, because even at my meager level of success, the fame attracted people. It still does. But it was never about fame with Dianne. Quite the opposite. She needn't have worried, though. I was totally smitten.

❖ ❖ ❖

Another week, another tour. This one was a doozy. We were in Virginia Beach to do a show at the Dome. The sound check was fine; the show was great, as usual, although certainly not a standout. So it was with wide-eyed innocence that Mark and I followed Frank off the stage after our traditional instrumental encore, only for both of us to get handcuffed and led away by the city's finest. We were under arrest for obscenity. They threw the two of us into the back of a waiting cherry-top and carted us off to the hoosegow. They booked us, took mug shots of us, fingerprinted us, and locked us up as the band looked on.

Our bail was paid, fortunately, by our tour manager, Dick Barber, at Herb's request. I had only been singing and speaking the scripted words that were put before me. Both Mark and I were employees, for God's sake. We were contracted to perform those supposed pieces of art and, whether or not they were to be judged as filth in the future, on this particular evening, we were free to go. They weren't our words, after all: They had been Frank's. A few hours in the Graybar Hotel and then back to the actual hotel, where Zappa took us into his room to put a positive spin on the night. No press was bad press and this was going to be huge! Herb and our publicist, Barbara DeWitt, would have a field day with this story. Frank's legend would only grow.

Indeed, the following day, a huge press conference was held in Boston, and the hotel conference room was packed with foreign journalists and television cameras. Barbara flew in from L.A. to monitor the proceedings. Was this a case of First Amendment constitutional rights? Did we feel like the American government was trying to censor the arts? Had Zappa gone too far with his brand of off-putting smut comedy? After all, Jane Fonda had walked out on our concert at the Santa Monica Civic: She couldn't handle the pony harness dipped in enchilada sauce and shoved into a donkey's ass, I suppose. To each her own. We were national news. One week later, Frank Zappa and the Mothers of Invention were booked to play for the first time at Manhattan's legendary Carnegie Hall. The concert instantly sold out.

It was Columbus Day, October 11, and, due to my late hours the night before, walking the Village in the rain, turning my collar to the wind and feeling very much like a Tom Rush album cover, I was hoarse and quite a bit the worse for wear. I had also spent a small fortune calling Dianne, and our multiple calls hadn't ceased until 3 A.M. I nearly blacked out during the 2 P.M. sound check, but kept it together as news crews filmed us doing "The Mud Shark" up and down the hallowed halls of the renowned showplace. Both shows were fantastic. Carnegie Hall did not disappoint.

The holy stage felt like home, and we didn't repeat any material at all as we ad-libbed our way through every song in our impressive repertoire. Truthfully, we were terrific. Alice Cooper was there. More impressive, Bob Dylan was there. Bob fucking Dylan. He certainly wasn't falling asleep in his pasta on this night. He laughed. He got it. The Zappa Family Trust, aka Gail, finally released the recordings in 2011. I'm so glad.

There were press screenings of *200 Motels* the following afternoon; more questions and more photographs. There was a farewell party for us at Sardi's, of all places, and then we were back on the road, in Toronto again, at Massey Hall, home of the pig's head incident, and drinking at the bar with Enid Finnbogason. Rangers, ho! But not for this guy. Not tonight. This guy is totally monogamous—it's just an ever-changing monogamy.

Frank liked it best when we could do just a few big dates at a time in the States and call it a tour. Those little dates just whizzed by, each one featuring a different opening act: Lee Michaels, It's a Beautiful Day, Milwaukee with Fleetwood Mac. In Kansas City the familiar girls were waiting for us, but I was having none of that. I still had my Placidyls. I could still go right to sleep.

We got our copies of the *200 Motels* soundtrack album on October 26 and we all attended the L.A. premiere at the Doheny Plaza, a classy little art palace in West Hollywood. My parents came to see it. They were totally confused, as was most of the audience, but they supported their son, and it was great to know that they were still proud of my career. Sort of.

❖ ❖ ❖

Something new and very dark was about to enter the picture. Dianne's friends from the commune in Michigan began sending her care packages. About every two weeks, we would receive a shipment from Ann Arbor in a plain brown wrapper. It was an enormous quantity of synthetic THC, the active ingredient in weed. Holy shit! This crap was amazing. Why bother clogging your lungs with smoke when you could snort a little bit of this magic powder and be buzzed all day long? It wasn't like coke. It was more like a small acid trip, one that would actually wear off after a couple of hours. Of course, it was hell on the old nasal passages, but it seemed to be worth it at the time. Dianne and I didn't even think about it. We had so much of it that it just became normal to walk over to the table, do some THC, and continue doing whatever was on our schedule for the day.

We dined out every night, and every month it still fell on me to collect the Hollywood Hills rent from Velvert Turner. In November, he didn't have it. There were wax drippings over all of the carpeting and neon paint upon the walls. My place had turned into a rather infamous L.A. party house. I felt like a hooker, chasing the rent money, but I needed every cent. We were paid by the show. Touring came whenever Frank needed it. In Zappa's world, cash was never the motivator, but then again, he never walked a mile in my Nikes.

On November 11, the Mothers left again for New York City to tape *The Dick Cavett Show*. We stayed again at the fabulous One Fifth Avenue. The next day was the show. We got there early to rehearse. The sound was a little weird and we had to stay at ABC Studios all day with no food, but we did have drugs, and the 6 P.M. taping went wonderfully well. Cavett was a most immaculate gentleman, and being a part of this elite broadcast was a historic feather in our collective caps.

The following day, the band, plus Dianne, flew to London on—you guessed it—Air India. We checked in to the Royal Garden Hotel and the two of us immediately started to fight. I don't know why. Perhaps it was the singular lack of substances or the horrible transatlantic flight, but something in our chemistry shifted for a minute. Despite the strangeness, I had things to do and no time to get into this domestic shit. We went to the Speakeasy in the rain, but the band that was playing was no good and the magic was gone. Of all places, too. I had so wanted Dianne to experience this. Marc and June had promised to come around but were having problems of their own and never showed up, so Dianne and I walked the streets of Kensington, getting more depressed with every raindrop that fell. It was about girls and long-distance loving and being the "old lady" waiting at home. I couldn't reassure her enough. She saw the groupies; she sat in on the interviews; she felt disposable.

❖ ❖ ❖

200 Motels opened at the Pavilion in London to huge crowds and rave reviews. Go figure. There was a huge party afterward at the then-new Hard Rock Cafe, where I was allowed to become fantastically drunk on single-malt scotch with Roman Polanski. He told me that women had no place on the road. Now *there's* some sage advice from a master of relationships. Back to the hotel to talk and cry until morning. This wasn't going to work. Dianne couldn't handle the road. Hangover time, noon the next day: We were checking out of the Royal Garden and they had no room for Dianne, so I phoned the Kensington Palace, which could accommodate her until she could find a flight out, and met the Mothers at the airport to continue our tour in Stockholm. I felt like hammered shit. It was pouring.

No sooner did we land in Sweden than we were spirited off to a press reception on some floating boat/club thing, but I needed to punk out early and wound up cabbing it back to our hotel with Don Preston, who had returned to the band after Bob Harris's brief stay. I needed real room service food. I needed to call Dianne, and she sounded great when I did. I needed to stop being so scared.

Little things humble a man. Dianne called to wake me in the morning about 8:30. I didn't mind feeling sleepy; her voice was a panacea for me. I walked the streets, shopping for pornography, until the band traveled by bus and ferry through Copenhagen to the town of Odense. As I said, the *band* traveled—the equipment truck didn't. The damned thing broke down. On the second date of this sold-out European run, we had to refund all of the crowd's money. But Frank was far too nice a guy to walk away and we had all traveled so darned far anyway. . . .

So we did the show with acoustic guitars, with Aynsley playing on table-tops and ashtrays. It lasted an hour and a half and we were all, including Frank, drinking Carlsberg Elephant beer throughout the performance. Great stuff, but try sleeping after downing a few, with one eye open and on the alarm clock and a mind somewhere between Michigan and Denmark. I sure couldn't.

But it didn't matter. I was really happy. Dianne and I had identified the problem and eliminated it. It was just that simple. Easy to play two shows that day in Copenhagen; I'll sleep when I'm dead. Besides, this tour was just getting started. Our printed itineraries were pages long. It was freezing, and I cursed the asshole who had stolen my coat from backstage, but there were other coats to be had and other adventures on the horizon.

TWENTY-ONE

Smoke on the Water

What possible perversions would a band of scruffy American musicians participate in during an overnight train ride to Dusseldorf? The answer is: board games. Specifically, Speed Circuit, an auto-racing spinner thing. It was way more macho than Win, Place & Show, the horse-racing game that we played at home with our significant others. Zappa thought we were all nuts. Perhaps so, sir. Perhaps so.

Lu, our German teacher, was along on the trip in some unofficial capacity, and the two of us went clubbing after the concerts there. Frank had told us to be careful in Germany; things were interpreted differently here. Frank was an antiestablishment hero, and therefore everything he said or did must certainly carry social significance. They didn't get it. When Frank wrote about cars and girls, it wasn't a veiled metaphor about the rising of the proletariat, it was generally about cars and girls. Germans, Frank cautioned, were not known for their sense of humor, and I remembered his words as I made friends in the local taverns. I didn't mention World War II either.

It took a lot of nerve to actually perform Frank's "Holiday in Berlin" in Berlin, but despite all of the warnings and our walking-on-eggs attitude, the show there went down without a problem. The crowd was amazing. I walked the city, went to the Berlin Wall and the Brandenburg Gate, and bought Dianne a beautiful handbag for her upcoming birthday.

We were playing at the same glorious theaters that we had visited the year before: old-world opera houses and concert halls originally built for the resonance of a string section or a single pianist. Now we were assaulting Europe, finding gigantic pipe organs in classic halls and practically blowing out the ancient instruments by banging out "Louie Louie" for a throng of stomping Aryans.

And then there were the girls. I wasn't dead. I partied hearty in Hamburg. An interview with a stranger didn't end up so strangely. But I knew that it didn't count. I was just having fun.

Amsterdam next, at the greatest Howard Johnson hotel in the universe: a seventeenth-century manor on a canal, replete with more wonderful dope than I could handle. I knew exactly where I was in this town. I could find my way in and out of the red-light district—just looking, of course—and to the museums, the restaurants, and each and every coffee shop in town. That's where the legal weed and hash was sold, consumed, and treated with respect. I tripped down to the Paradiso just because I could.

❖ ❖ ❖

Sandwiches and beer on the bus ride to Rotterdam and Frank was now in the company of somebody new called Karen. This one was really lovely and very nice. Some were not. Frank had an amazing thing going at home and here's how it worked.

When Frank found a pretty young thing out on the road, he would often travel with her, treat her like a lady while she was in his company, and sometimes even bring her back with him to his home in Laurel Canyon to live in his basement or the guesthouse until he didn't need her around anymore. Gail and her family were devout Catholics, as were Frank's parents. The word *divorce* was not in their vocabulary. Frank knew it and took full advantage of the religion that he publicly ridiculed. Gail would never leave Frank, not even if she had to make tea or breakfast for this week's *belle de jour*. It might have appeared awkward, but this lady wasn't going anywhere, boyo. She knew it and she flaunted it.

Now, years after Frank's death, it's Gail who administers the music that Frank spent his entire life producing. She can decide to publicize it and make it available to the waiting fans or to somewhat bury it and comfortably live on the money that Frank left her after leasing his master recordings to Rykodisc. So far, she has mostly chosen the latter (although a large chunk of the catalogue was recently reissued), and many kids only know Zappa from his pictures. It's a dirty shame.

Turnabout is fair play, I guess. Gail had been a groupie too when Frank met and married her. She knew what she'd be getting herself into. Now it's her turn. My advice? Never cross Gail Zappa.

❖ ❖ ❖

KLM to Frankfurt and the InterContinental Hotel. Two more amazing shows. Lufthansa to Munich, one of my favorite cities. We checked into a Holiday Inn and promoter Fritz Rau treated us to an amazing dinner after an equally amazing show at the Circus Krone. Afterward, the fun continued as we all got thrown out of the Yellow Submarine nightclub for obscene dancing. Just like the Chunky Club in the Crossfires days.

I got frisked by German police on my way out of the country, but much to my (and Frank's) relief, there was nothing on me to discover. I was much more clever than that. Familiar faces greeted me in Vienna and I smoked hash in Barbara DeWitt's room, drank beautiful black beer, and watched the skaters on the rink below me. The hotel maid sewed a pair of pants for me and I got high with some friends. By the time I called home, it was 4 A.M. and by the time I read myself to sleep, it was after 5.

So I was completely disoriented when Dick Barber called my room to wake me eleven hours later. It was pitch-black outside and I truly didn't know if it was day or night. But I showered, had room service food, and got high in Volman's room before leaving at 7 for a great, long show at the Konzerthaus up the street. Too much sleep is very often a lot worse than too little, and that was the case on this occasion. I was so wired after the show that it took me hours to get to sleep, and even then, it was a fitful night with too many thoughts.

The next morning, an early wakeup call and all ten of us flew Austrian Airlines through Zurich and into Geneva. Then it was a James Bond–style bus ride through the incredible Alps and into Montreux. The hotel was fantastic. I soaked in the tub before we ate and took a slippery bus ride followed by a perilous hike to an even more obscure restaurant.

There was smoke in Barbara's room and the last of a Vonnegut book I had read three times already. I slept like a baby, never expecting that, in a few hours, everything would change.

❖ ❖ ❖

I woke about ten, walked the cobblestone streets of the gorgeous village, purchased a replacement suitcase, and walked back. Then, at noon, I walked over to the casino. The Montreux Casino was quite a famous place. It was the home of the Montreux Jazz Festival, of which we were a part, and the all the great jazz legends had played this beautiful room. On the floor below us, there was a recording studio where the British band Deep Purple was in the process of recording their new album. The performance space itself was on the second floor of the lakeside structure. The small stage sat against the far wall as the audience entered, and we performed with our backs to the plate-glass windows that framed fabulous Lake Geneva.

The motif was strictly Pier 1: A bamboo ceiling hung suspended over the audience for ambiance and a bit of sound control. The stairway that led to the ballroom was the only way in or out of the place.

Our show was at 2:30 in the afternoon, which was already a bit unusual. We were appropriately casual and had a really good set. It was during one of our final encores, "King Kong," and Don Preston's bizarre synthe-sizer solo, that—as Deep Purple famously sang in their classic song "Smoke on the Water"—"some stupid with a flare gun burned the place to the ground." He really did. A joker in the back of the crowd wanted to show his appreciation for the show with a bang and sent a flare straight up and into the bamboo ceiling, which ignited like tinder. Someone in the crowd yelled out, "Fire!" and, to be funny, I announced into the micro-phone, "Arthur Brown, ladies and gentlemen!" It wasn't funny. Frank didn't laugh. The audience panicked.

Zappa did the responsible thing and quietly advised the crowd to remain calm. Then he threw his guitar on the ground and ran to get the hell out of there. The kids were now throwing our amplifiers out of the windows behind the stage in order to jump the two stories to the ground below. There were pushing and shoving bodies everywhere and, as you can imagine, a great many injuries. We escaped by running through the kitchen and then down the side stairway, just in the nick of time. The entire building burned to ashes. Fortunately, nobody died.

We were taken, by bus, back to our hotel across the lake, and stood there, looking out of the scenic lobby at the Alpine view of a column of flame and smoke reaching to the sky. The whole band was there together. We sipped brandy and watched our equipment vaporize. Despite the severity of the situation, it was Frank who spoke first with a logical conclusion.

"Well, that's it for me. Somebody's trying to tell me something. Tour's over. I'm going home."

What? Hell, no, Frank! Please. Remember, we get paid by the show. And we had a lot of European dates left to play on the continent before a sold-out, two-week run in the British Isles. That's a lot of shows and a lot of lost income. We needed the work. We needed a plan. We begged, pleaded, and cajoled. Finally, we got Frank to concede. A few calls were placed and, within a couple of hours and after an atypical band meal, a decision was made.

Later that night, Aynsley and I were the last ones standing and he was, uncharacteristically, in my room inhaling the tars of India when we heard a single knock on my door—the knock of an insider, so we knew it wasn't hotel security. I answered and Zappa walked in.

"Mind if I hang for a while?"

"Shit no, man. Come on in. We were just contemplating our futures."

"Me too," said the Man.

And the three of us just sat there, passing the dreaded reefer and watching our equipment fry across the lake. It was a spectacular sight. After about twenty minutes, Frank got up from his easy chair and started making his way to the door.

"That's it for me, boys. Bedtime."

"What are we gonna do, Frank?"

"I don't know, man. I've got a lot of thinking to do." He went back to his room and we never had the chance to smoke with him again. But it was great while it lasted. We were finally a band after all this time. And I suppose that some things just weren't meant to be.

We would, regrettably, have to cancel a few shows, notably Brussels, Paris, and Lyon, France. That was a damned shame. But we could borrow equipment from the Who and Led Zeppelin, neither of whom was working at the time, and at least complete the ten shows or so that we had scheduled for the UK. It was better than going home.

The next day, December 5, I walked around Lake Geneva to the scene of the crime. The ruins of the once-famous music hall were still smoldering. Every single guitar and amplifier was destroyed. A single microphone stand stood ominously where I had been, on what used to be the stage. Mark was there too, combing through the rubble. He found an old cowbell that we used to use during "Call Any Vegetable." It was charred and smoky, but it hadn't melted. It sounded like shit, but we had to have it. It remains our only souvenir of the big Swiss fire. It felt like Dresden.

On the following day, we all trekked back to London and our familiar digs at the Kensington Palace. Everybody ran out to get their pictures developed. Then a bunch of us went to this amazing Mexican restaurant and got ridiculously buzzed back in the room. Hash and tequila—dinner of champions.

The next morning, I ordered this fantastic skirt for Dianne at Kensington Market and bought some tasty tops at Biba, a supertrendy boutique. Bolan came over about 7 and we went up to his place for cognac and cocaine, but shortly after we arrived, he and June started arguing and things got really ugly. Bolan was acting his character now, 24/7. He had become the Cosmic Warrior and June's traditional ways seemed to slow his roll. He was antsy and it wasn't just the coke. I got extremely uncomfortable and had to leave. I cabbed it to the Speakeasy and got drunk, bumped into Mickey Finn of T. Rex, who had some blow, and stayed up until 8:30 in the morning, talking to Dianne.

I slept through the next day, not opening my eyes until 3 P.M. The band guys went over to the Rainbow Theatre to try out the newly borrowed gear, but I certainly wasn't needed. To my surprise, Danny Hutton appeared at the hotel that afternoon with copious quantities of inhalables. Between him and Miranda, our UK rep, we kept ourselves amused with food, and Mickey Finn always seemed to be lurking about with the other stuff when we slowed down. I called Dianne late but happy.

Up at noon on Friday, but I didn't leave the hotel until 2 P.M. Something felt wrong—it really did. There was a very uncomfortable sound check at the Rainbow and I was bombarded with ticket requests for a show that had been sold out for months. It was a bullshit day punctuated by a cheap Greek dinner. The first of the Rainbow shows was at 7.

❖ ❖ ❖

Again, it was the encore—something about that damned encore.

We had finished our first set, which went amazingly well, considering the alien guitars and drums we were forced to use. The audience loved it and I did too. We had already taken our group bow and I was happily leaving the stage, feeling fulfilled and exonerated. As I reached the wings, I heard the audience suddenly stop applauding and gasp as one. There was a shocked silence in the Rainbow. I ran back to the stage, but I couldn't see anybody. Band and roadies were standing on the apron at the edge of the platform and gazing down into the darkness of the orchestra pit below. I ran over to see what the lack of commotion was all about. It sure didn't sound good.

There, at the bottom of the pit, lay Frank Zappa. He was unconscious and silent, his twisted body fallen below in the shape of some anatomical swastika. His arms and legs were bent at bizarre angles and I couldn't tell if he was breathing or not. Humans aren't supposed to bend like that. There was no reason to believe that Frank Zappa was still alive.

This had been a very deliberate act. It seems that an audience member named Trevor Howell, who was very, very high indeed either a) didn't feel as if he had gotten his money's worth or b), more likely, was responding to his girlfriend articulating her crush on Frank at the end of the concert. For whatever reason, this maniac jumped onto the stage just as Frank, his back to the audience, was placing his guitar in its stand. He pushed Frank in such a way that he first hit his head on the wall of the orchestra pit before falling to its bottom. We all thought Frank was dead.

Howell tried to get away, but the audience restrained him and brought him to the front of the theater. Here, official accounts vary. But I was there, and I know. Before Howell was delivered to the local authorities, Herb Cohen personally beat the shit out of him. Newspaper stories through the years have attributed this beating to angry roadies, but in fact, it was Cousin Herb who took control of an out-of-control situation. We were ushered out of the theater and back to the hotel before anyone with authority could tell us anything. Sure, why tell the band anything?

Trevor was sentenced to a year in jail. Me, I didn't know what to do. I called Dianne, but sympathy didn't go very far. I didn't want to be alone, so Danny Hutton came over. So did Mickey Finn and David Byron from

Uriah Heep. Many drugs were consumed. Many condolences were offered. It looked like I was out of work again.

I walked around Kensington the following morning before we had to meet with the Scotland Yard detectives in the hotel's banquet room. Everyone was somber. It was all over. Mark and I went to a double feature to take our minds off of reality: *Where's Poppa?* and *Bananas*. If you can't forget your troubles after those two, then your problems must be real.

And oh, they were.

I was pissed off the following day when we again weren't allowed to see Frank, or to even get an update on his health. Harry Nilsson came over and Danny returned. Brothers of the Road are always around to help another musician in need.

Monday arrived with still no word about Frank, so we all packed up and made arrangements to get to the airport. Only, remember, we flew Air India, and they decided not to honor our return tickets, which were for the following week. So we all sat in our rooms, our suitcases packed, trying as hard as we could to smoke all of our accumulated hash before departure. Finally, we got the word: Frank had just undergone a leg operation, was still broken and confused, but had asked to see us before we all returned to the States without him.

The guys in the band were let in to visit with Frank one or two at a time. Mark and I went first. Frank looked like death warmed over in that hospital bed. He was pale and fragile. His eyes were druggy from all of the medications he was on and his voice was raspy from the tubes that had been stuck down his throat. He was still hooked up to several IVs and it appeared difficult for him to turn his head to see us as Mark and I walked into his room. Neither one of us knew what to say, but Frank was the one who wound up breaking the ice.

His eyes opened about halfway, he sort of lifted his arm as if to conduct us and said, "All right. 'Peaches en Regalia' . . . One, two, three, four . . ."

That was the way we used to open the show. We knew then that Frank was okay. The three of us spoke briefly and then our time was over.

Our Air India flight was three hours late, so of course I missed my connection to Detroit and wound up crashing for a few hours at a Ramada Inn in New York. I cabbed to LaGuardia at 4:30 in the morning but my plane malfunctioned and returned to the gate. I was losing it. An hour later, I fell asleep on my flight into Detroit. Dianne picked me up and drove me to her parents' house in Troy. I met her father. I made love to her throughout the afternoon, and later, we shared a family-style dinner. Then, we went drinking, ate at the good old American Burger King, and danced until I collapsed in Dianne's arms and sobbed myself to sleep.

TWENTY-TWO

Air Supply Is a Better Name Than the Phlorescent Leech and Eddie!

I shortly discovered that the only true cure for melancholia is an acid-laced bota of wine and a Grateful Dead concert. Which are what Dianne and I enjoyed on the very next night in December '71. I was served something called cheese biscuits for breakfast, roast beef and Yorkshire pudding for dinner, and still had time to go to the Hill House in Ann Arbor to pick up the tickets. The Dead were amazing; they really were. The New Riders of the Purple Sage opened the show. Truthfully, I didn't know who the hell was up there on that stage, and I doubt I was alone in that sentiment that night. There was a wonderful feeling of rebellion in the little Hill Auditorium at the University of Michigan, like the revolution played there last week and it worked. The two of us stayed in and around Detroit for the rest of the week and flew back to L.A. six days before Christmas.

Every year since 1967, when I married Melita and Mark married Pat, the four of us, plus progeny, got together at the Volmans' house on Lookout Mountain, just up the hill from our original Canyon home, on the occasion of Christmas Eve. It wasn't a big deal, just an informal annual gathering that gave the girls a chance to catch up. We would eat popcorn, play Win, Place & Show, and listen to each other's most bizarre new vinyl acquisitions. I was determined that this year would be no exception. Pat, of course, had only recently met Dianne and had come to know and confess her secrets to Melita, who would never be around again. Melita and Pat had their children together. Now, somebody else was sitting in Melita's chair. It was an awkward evening, to say the least, made a bit easier with the inclusion of Jim Pons, solo, to act as master of ceremonies.

Christmas Day was even stranger. I picked Emily up at Melita's mom's and did my best to serve her the turkey, give her the presents, and offer up the normality that I thought she needed. There were no presents or trips to Disneyland that could make up for a lack of parenthood, but I needn't have worried: Melita already had multiple extra daddies waiting in the wings. It is truly sad that the poor girl never exactly knew who to call Poppa at any given time, but at least there were always a few of us around and still are. You'll always be fine, kid.

We tried to be a normal couple. Dianne got a sewing machine at Sears to have something to do during the day besides THC. Jim came over for dinner and brought his date, Enid Finnbogason! I nearly shit. We started going to hockey games: the L.A. Kings at the Fabulous Forum. It was a great natural rush. We flushed the horrible THC and told the guys in Ann Arbor not to send us any more.

Herb's brother, Martin (aka Mutt), held his annual New Year's party at his incredible house at the top of the Canyon, replete with wine dungeons and wandering goats, and I got to introduce Dianne to everyone there. There were the odd whispers, of course, but no one had really known Melita anyway, and this was Hollywood, after all, and Mutt was working on wife number six or so at the time, so I wasn't exactly a pariah. Eric Burdon was there. Mutt was his lawyer. I spent a long time talking to Don Schmitzerle, who headed up Reprise Records, the Warner's company that distributed Frank and Herb's labels, Bizarre and Straight. You never know, right?

I probably should have known better than to invite Lin over. She and a friend had hitched to L.A. for the holidays and Dianne, ever the open-minded partner, had nudged me into inviting them to the house to share some cheer. I almost shared my cheer with Lin and a bottle of champagne while parked at the top of Appian Way on the way to drop her off at the Holiday Inn. Happy New Year. Almost. Dianne was one resolution I didn't intend to break.

We made the sweet, sweet love everywhere in my zip code. January 3, 1972, on the beach, and the next day and the next. Not having that lethal synthetic crap around certainly proved to be a change for the better. I could actually carry on a conversation again, although while lunching with Paul Williams, a guy didn't need to talk much.

❖ ❖ ❖

And then, just like that, on January 5, I was back in depositions again. But this time, I was going to court with Melita. Ouch. Still, I was feeling pretty good, considering. The only elephant that was missing from the center of the room was Frank.

We had no idea at all where our next meal was coming from. None of us. Mark and I spoke, but not really about business stuff—there was no business stuff. My VW van kept blowing up, and we didn't have the five hundred in cash to rebuild the engine, so both of us would hitchhike to the bottom of the hill for milk or laundry. I sure didn't feel much like a rock star. Mark and I met with Herb about management, which was an early clue as to Frank's future, but we were all understandably wary, and Velvert Turner just up and disappeared one day, leaving me with a dozen garbage bags full of toxic undeterminables. I stayed up all night picking up after the well-connected rocker. His then-producer, Tom Wilson, who had done the first Zappa records, told me not to worry. He lied. It was my second shady experience as a landlord.

At the end of the third week of 1972, I got a call from Paul Almond at Mutt's office. I never knew what to expect when that office called: This could have either pertained to my career or my divorce. I braced for the worst. Instead, it seemed that Johny Barbata and Jim Tucker had hired a lawyer together. Johny hadn't been in the band for over a year, but he knew that his contributions had been worth something. Tucko left in 1967, but in such a litigious time, did we really want to be saddled with his ass? The Turtles had been a big band back in the '60s, but those days were over, and since Mark and I had obviously moved on, John and Jim wanted a lump sum of cash to just go away. It wasn't like the Turtles' name was worth anything. We would be in court for years and then what? Our time had come and gone. Corporation or not, give them some money and they'd both sign on the line and disappear.

We weren't sure why and we never really talked about it, but both of us knew instinctively that this would be the best bargain we ever made. We were absolutely certain that the Turtles weren't dead yet. People needed their memories and we had been part of a historical time, already gone. We wound up borrowing the money from Cousin Herb and paid them each a few thousand dollars. They signed.

While we were in management talks with Herb, we were also weighing his traditional management techniques against what, we were certain, was a new way for us to actually have some artistic control over our future as performers. We had made the acquaintance of a soft-spoken and well-meaning dude by the name of Larry Heller, who had been on the periphery of the business, in publishing or accounting or something. A nice smile, a hearty handshake, and a really good beard weighted the scales heavily toward his side. Larry offered the following intriguing proposition: Mark and I would start our own corporation, just the two of us. Well, three, actually: Larry would need to have a small piece of the pie. Then we would basically manage ourselves. We'd rent a nice office, wait for the phone to ring, sign these big record deals, and laugh at the traditional ways of old Hollywood.

Now, evenings were spent either in the company of Larry and his wife, Barbara, or at the home of our dear friend, Allan MacDougal, a most excellent Scot whose acquaintance we made while in England but who now worked down the hall from our buddy Paul Williams at A&M. These guys made me feel like I was still sort of in show business. I wasn't. I was collecting unemployment for the first time in my life. Hey, aren't you the guy I just saw with Zappa? Nope. Sorry. I get that a lot.

❖ ❖ ❖

Mr. Zappa, meanwhile, had returned home and was contemplating his next move even as we went into the studio to master the *Just Another Band from L.A.* album. I was impressed with how good we sounded on the big studio speakers, considering that, once again, the entire project had been recorded on Frank's little two-track recorder with no overdubs at all. Frank was confined to his wheelchair and still didn't know if he'd ever tour again. But his spirits were relatively high and I realized how much I had missed him. At the same time, Mark and I met one last time with Herb about management, but we had new ideas in our heads again, and if history was about to repeat itself, we weren't yet done riding our wave of bad decisions. We told Herb thanks but no thanks. Despite everything. I had a drink at the bar next door with Herb's great secretary, Ona Sheleika, and returned to my chores.

I was actually painting. Without being able to afford an empty rental property in the Hollywood Hills, Dianne and I were fixing up the Canyon house, packing up the Treasure Trail rental, and preparing to move in. It was a big step back up the ladder of self-respect to be on top of the hill again: swimming pools, movie stars. We were living there by the time Marc Bolan returned to L.A. in mid-February, and I was glad that he never had to see me in that rental, at the bottom. He crashed on our comfy couch a couple nights in a row. T. Rex played a great show at the Palladium and afterward, it was party time again with Micky Dolenz and Harry Nilsson. It was always a party with those guys.

Ona had landlord problems. Well, of course you can live with us. We've got a guest room. What could possibly go wrong? It was a lot easier getting the work done with six hands instead of four. We made hanging curtain rods a project. It was fun. We all got along great.

Mark and I needed a record deal and we needed it yesterday. We brought Jim Pons into Ike Turner's little studio in Inglewood, where Frank's engineer, Barry Keene, often worked on side projects, and cut five demo recordings. Everything had been arranged, flights and all. Harry Nilsson called on Monday morning to make sure that we had our flight information. We took a 747 into New York, spent the evening at Barbara DeWitt's apartment with her husband, Tim, and her brother, the famous fashion photographer Bruce Weber, and crashed at the One Fifth. Bruce took some great pictures of us. I wonder where they are.

The next morning, we took our little tape to the ominous RCA building, where my father had proposed marriage to my mother twenty-six years before. RCA loved it. They bought us lunch. They talked big picture. They shook our hands. They flew us home. Barbara played the tape for everyone at United Artists. They loved it.

Paul Williams liked the songs too. He took us to see the higher-ups at A&M. They said they loved it. Dunhill loved it. We took a big United

Artists meeting. Things looked good. We still had no management. The two of us were, foolishly, representing ourselves.

❖ ❖ ❖

Ray Davies and the Kinks came to L.A. in March and we partied with the boys, of course. Dianne was apologetic for being loud and passing out, but that was her MO and I guess I was used to it. I made another tape copy for Don Schmitzerle at Reprise. When I went to see Joni Mitchell a few days later at the Dorothy Chandler Pavilion at the Music Center, the Warner's rep there told me that he had already listened to our stuff and that Don really liked it. There was a buzz.

Dianne got a Kelly Girl job at Western Union, but got wasted celebrating her first day and called in sick for her second. They let it slide. The bank was sending me repossession papers. Things happened fast. The bus blew up again, Ona got busted the night before her birthday and Dianne appeared to be avoiding life altogether. I needed to get her out of L.A. for a minute.

We went to Baja, the five of us. There was me, Dianne, Tim and Barbara, and Dianne's visiting Detroit friend, Kathleen, a stunning blonde who had been crashing with us for few weeks. It was the best week ever. No one got out of line. In fact, there were friendly faces everywhere. When we got back, Lixie and Kathleen were hanging out together. Marc and June Bolan came to town again and treated us to dinner at the Rainbow. Even Jeff Simmons called from out of the blue.

Some faces weren't so friendly. A Bank of America clown came to my door before 8 A.M. one day to threaten me about repossessing the bus—I should have let him just take the thing right then and there. That very afternoon, Volman and I met Marc and Tony Visconti at Elektra Studios on La Cienega. Mark and I then drank champagne, sniffed a bit of magic powder, and sang on eight new T. Rex songs.

Larry Heller put the deal together. We signed to Reprise, the label that I had always dreamed of. Shit, Hendrix was on Reprise. Joni, too, and Neil. And even Soupy! It was Sinatra's company that he had sold to Warner Bros., but it still had the class of its founder. Ring-a-ding-ding! Sinatra always pronounced the word "Re-preese" and so did the people who worked there. So do I.

Everything was falling into place. We had meetings with Henry Diltz about the album cover and Gary Burden about the art direction. Barry Keene was going to engineer the project, Mark and I would produce ourselves, and we made a deal with Ike Turner to cut the entire record at his Bolic Sound Studio in Inglewood. The Zappa years had been but a momentary distraction. Now we could get back to the sophisticated Laurel Canyon acoustic rock that we had been born to play. We could pick up exactly where the Turtles had left off.

◆ ◆ ◆

By May, we had received a large advance from Warner's, had paid off all of our bills, and were cutting basic tracks at Ike's. The deal that Larry and Mutt put together with Mo Ostin was pretty amazing. Not only were all of our wishes granted, but as part of the deal, we received four season passes to the L.A. Kings home games, right behind the goal. In fact, Gordie Howe and Ralph Backstrom joined Mark and me on the ice to take the press release photographs. It was amazing. We also each got to choose one electric and one acoustic guitar from the Guitar Center on Sunset Boulevard. I picked a Gibson D50 to write songs on and a gorgeous blond hollow-body Telecaster. I might not be a great player, but I knew a great guitar when I saw one.

The Kaylan-Volman project, or whatever it was going to be called, was now a band. None of the Mothers of Invention had been contacted by Herb's office or even called on the phone by their pal Frank. Silence. No one returned their calls. Zappa didn't yet know what he wanted to do. But Mark and I had an album to do. And a deal to be signed. Which it was, on May 9.

A word about Ike's. Upon our arrival there at 6 P.M. on the previous Monday, we couldn't help but notice what appeared to be a gigantic Fabergé egg sitting on the mixing console. It begged opening. It was filled to the tip with cocaine. When Ike heard us come in, he joined us from his suite behind the studio. "Welcome to Bolic Sound, boys. Enjoy yourselves!" Then he scooped a mighty fingernail into the egg, inhaled its bounty deeply, and walked back to his office. We were in that studio for two weeks of heavy indulgence. That damned egg was never empty.

And Dianne, the wild child from the heart of Middle America, sat in Laurel Canyon, crocheting and making dinners. When we finally had the album playback party on the night of May 19, she had driven home from the studio, annoyed and frustrated, and was the only "lady" not in attendance. She was on her way to clear her head somewhere in San Francisco.

Weekends were always reserved for Emily, although God knows what the kid made of my relationship with Dianne or what her mother had told her about me. Excursions to Busch Gardens or Disneyland weren't exactly the same as parenting.

Zappa was recording again, and I stopped in one night to watch George Duke lay down some tracks. He never said a word about the guys in our band. We were invited up to Warner Bros. to meet with Schmitzerle. It was a drug fest. We felt right at home. Larry found an office. It was a fantastic Victorian mansion on Sunset, corner of Stanley, a huge space we'd eventually wind up subletting to Chrysalis Records for their headquarters. We named our company Dharma. Can't you just feel the shit about to hit the fan?

And what of our professional name? We certainly weren't Turtles anymore. And Volman and Kaylan, or the other way around, sounded like either lawyers or butchers. Reprise suggested that we had built a huge following with Zappa who knew exactly who we were and who would be waiting voraciously to snap this record up. These were the people that we needed to reach, the people who knew us as the Phlorescent Leech and Eddie. The music didn't fit the name, but they didn't care. And since they weren't 100 percent sure that they had been correct, the credits would have our real names too. It would be foolproof and we'd draw from all of our diverse audiences.

Henry took the photos in Mark's backyard. I wore a terribly British shirt with cute baby ducklings on it and Mark had a bright yellow cowboy shirt made for him at Nudie's in North Hollywood. It was a great picture. But Warner Bros. printed it the wrong way. Now Mark was on my right instead of my left. It was all backward, but it was too damned late. Despite all the planning, all the care and all of the professionals involved, Mark was now the Phlorescent Leech and I was Eddie. We could have stopped the release, I suppose, but since no one knew who we were anyway, it seemed like a dumb thing to do.

The entire name was a dumb thing to do. Anyone in their right mind, anyone who really intended on having a career in the music business, would eschew such a moniker in a heartbeat. I mean, Air Supply is a better name than the Phlorescent Leech and Eddie! But the die had been cast and fate had decreed that, for the rest of our career as a duo, the two of us would never be able to shake that moronic handle. Without it, we coulda been a contender.

TWENTY-THREE

Perception Is Everything

The album came out. It was produced by me and Mark, supervised by our manager, Larry Heller, engineered by Barry Keene and recorded at Ike Turner's Bolic Sound. It had a matte-finish cover, like the albums by real L.A. singer-songwriters had, and had handwritten, sensitive, lady-of-the-Canyon calligraphy printed on a recycled brown paper sleeve. Aynsley played his ass off, but the songs really didn't call for his level of expertise. Don Preston, as well, was playing in the band to pick up a check, although he was a monster on the road. Mark and I had no time to do much writing, so most of the album was composed of material that would have been included on the next Turtles album, had there been such a thing. It was all Joni-approved. We tried to retain a little of the Zappa insanity, but there wasn't much humor in those acoustic songs.

At home, it was me, Dianne, and Ona, and our Volkswagens. We befriended a weird Topanga couple named Allen and Saudi, and before we knew it, Dianne and I were swingers and heroin snorters. We went together to a famous naturist camp, and our naked bodies intertwined in the so-called meditation rooms in a junkie stupor. I screwed a couple of people I hope were girls. Preston was having domestic problems and moved in, briefly, across the hall from Ona. Shit, he never wore clothes either. He just floated in the pool all day.

Our very first show was at a tiny rock club in San Diego called the Funky Quarters, and it was a harbinger of things to come. Flo and Eddie were an unknown band without a hit record or even a local following. For the first times in our lives, we were, literally, starting at the bottom. From Carnegie Hall to the dumpiest dives in America—I had made my commitment to show business and this is where my decision had brought me. I was touring on a level that I hadn't thought about since 1965. I knew the bubble was going to burst eventually. Hell, this wouldn't be so bad.

❖ ❖ ❖

On July 7, Mark and I sang on a demo record for our pals Donald Fagen and Walter Becker at some little studio in San Diego before saying goodbye to Tom Ross, our agent, and our lady friends and heading off to Davenport, Iowa, for parts truly unknown. We played at armories, ballrooms, and shit clubs. We had a road manager named Larry, a real piece of work, who used to crush and snort phenobarbitals.

Warner Bros. decided to release "Feel Older Now," an autobiographical rocker of mine, as a single. We also mastered "Nikki Hoi," a silly Hawaiian riff that we had written the year before with Jeff Simmons, as the B-side. Reprise had no idea at all what to do with us.

But the reports from the road were amazing. Aysnsley's drum solos alone were bringing audiences to their feet. We killed opening for the Morrisonless Doors and for Dr. John and got standing ovations at Milwaukee's Summerfest. So we were pretty damned cocky going into the Hollywood Bowl to open for the Allman Brothers on August 6, 1972. We looked good, we were well rehearsed, and we were road buddies by now. How were we to know that the lines of coke on that table weren't coke at all but heroin? Someone thought they were doing us a favor. The entire band indulged. I felt like I was trying to sing in an ocean of honey. Every note seemed to take hours. I've never had to concentrate so hard in my life, and throughout the whole concert, the little voice in my head was screaming, "You're not going to get away with this. Everyone's going to know. Your career is over. "

We escaped with our lives. No one knew anything at all. Bill Graham was there and hired us to do some shows. That Bowl concert exists on the Internet and I've seen it many times over the years. We were great. Perception is everything.

❖ ❖ ❖

Speaking of Bill Graham, I loved the guy. Rock promoters are notoriously shady guys, but every hundred years or so, a true gentleman emerges from the ooze and such a man was Bill. If you played straight with Bill, he'd play straight with you. Of course, if you didn't, I'm sure that you'd walk with a cane for the rest of your life. And he loved the Turtles. He had been there for every show of ours that he booked, standing in the wings and laughing his ass off.

Regardng our brand-new Phlorescent Leech and Eddie incarnation, all Bill knew was that we were funny and, having just left Zappa, probably dirty. And that's what he was looking for, something with a little edge to open the show he'd booked just before Halloween of 1972 in San Francisco's Winterland for this new Brit sensation, David Bowie.

I had just begun hearing this guy's songs on L.A. radio. RCA was giving him an unprecedented push, promoting both the previous year's *Hunky Dory* and the new *Ziggy Stardust* simultaneously. He was androgynous and, evidently, so were we. We would open and Sylvester and His Hot Band would go on before Bowie. Sylvester was a full-on drag queen. We felt a bit out of place.

Also, Winterland was dark and weird and more than a few of the hippies in attendance were in outrageous femme couture. The stage was high and so were we. We hung backstage with Bowie's band, the Spiders from Mars, specifically Mick Ronson, the genius guitar player. Then it was showtime. The intro, the first song started: It was "Thoughts Have Turned" from the Reprise album.

I sang. I looked to my right and the Phlorescent Leech was gone. He had fallen off of the stage chasing his tambourine yet again. I'm sure that it was funny, but people were helping him now. Mark was wrapping his hand in something and security rushed him into the kitchen, presumably to procure some ice.

But he didn't come back. And the show must go on. And so it did. All forty minutes of it. With just the band.

AND EDDIE.

Somehow, I remembered enough lyrics to get me through the set, albeit without the planned jokes and the Hippo Limbo, a stupid circus trick that went nowhere but used to make Zappa laugh.

During the final song of our set, Mark returned from a local emergency room with his broken arm in a cast. The crowd let out an enormous cheer, the set was done, and we walked off to the approval of applause.

Backstage, we laughed it off with Ronson and Bowie. What else could we do? Bowie was a gentleman and his show was unbelievable. We watched the future of rock music. Again. It would be a few years before we would cross paths with David again. It was another auspicious beginning but by now I was getting used to it.

❖ ❖ ❖

Dianne and I took a road trip up to Canada that featured an extended stop at Lin's house on Vashon Island. Hmmm, in hindsight, I'd have to say that one was a mistake. It didn't make us any closer.

The shows were doing great. The album, not so much. Warner's talked Shep Gordon into throwing us out on tour with Alice Cooper, with whom we soon became the closest of friends. Alice's producer, Bob Ezrin, came out to see one of the shows in Connecticut and was suitably impressed with us, I guess, as he signed on to produce our next album. The next morning, Larry Heller informed us that we'd be doing the entire School's Out European tour. It was going to be a monster. Dumb luck one more time.

On October 3, I spent the day in divorce court for the first time. Martin Cohen was my attorney. It didn't matter. I was going to lose more than half of everything. Fuck it! Two days later, Dianne had some sort of massive seizure and we spent the day in ambulances and hospitals. Stress, they said.

We toured on, sandwiching in a Toronto meeting with Bob Ezrin and his partner in Nimbus 9 Productions, the legendary Jack Richardson. It was at Bob's house that Dianne reached me by phone to announce that she was pregnant! "Yay," I wrote in my diary. But, inside, I don't think I was saying "Yay." I loved her to death, but I wasn't feeling anything. One month later, I returned from a brief tour to find her at Valley Presbyterian Hospital, having miscarried. The next day, I left for London on the Alice Cooper jet, beginning the coolest tour of all time.

Top: Smoke on the Water. Taken from the Mothers' hotel across Lake Geneva from the burning Montreux Casino, December 4, 1971.

Center: After the fire. The next day, this is what was left of the Casino. The band saved exactly one cowbell.

Bottom: Sitting in the hotel lobby, Montreux, Switzerland. Dazed and confused, with no direction home.

Girlfriend Dianne MacKellar on one of many camping excursions she and Howard took in a VW bus, 1971. Howard calls Dianne "the one who got away."

Diana Kaylan, Howard's second wife, splurging on lunch with Howard's daughter Emily (from his first marriage), at the Kaylans' house in Laurel Canyon, 1973.

Left: Onstage with T. Rex at the Roundhouse, London, 1972. Howard and Marc Bolan. Marc later signed the photo: "To Howard with all my soul and deepest love as a friend, Marc Bolan."

Bottom: Chaos on the Radio. Sunday night at KROQ (aka K-Rock) in Pasadena, California. Rodney Bingenheimer (left, with glasses), Ringo Starr, Mark, Keith Moon, and Howard, surrounded by Rodney's Glitter People from his club on Sunset Boulevard, 1973.

Flo and Eddie on *The Midnight Special*, NBC Television, mid-'70s.

Hundred Dollar Babies: Onboard one of a million flights—this one, commercial. Mark, Howard, and Alice Cooper.

Top: Kaylan, Stills, Volman, and Young? Howard, Mark, and Neil Young surprised the audience by turning up for the encore of Stephen Stills' solo concert at the L.A. Forum in 1975.

Left: Instant family—Howard and his third wife Nancy Kaylan with her kids Justin and Rebekah. Laurel Canyon, California, circa 1974.

Wife number four—Howard and Susan Kaylan, 1986.

What you talkin' 'bout, Alex? With daughter Alexandra, St. Louis, Missouri, 1996.

Generations. Howard, daughter Emily, grandson Max, daughter Alex, son-in-law Lyle. Bellevue, Washington, 1997.

On the set of *Mystery Science Theater 3000*: longtime drummer Joe Stefko and Howard, 2000.

Top: Beam me up, Minister. Getting married for the fifth time. On the bridge of the Starship Enterprise, Hilton Hotel, Las Vegas, March 24, 2005. Left to right: Starship Captain Minister, brother-in-law Mark Dibble, Howard, Michelle Dibble Kaylan, her mom Carole Young, Howard's daughter Alex, and unknown Klingon.

Right: Happy Together. Howard and Michelle Kaylan, 2006.

TWENTY-FOUR

Spinning in Some Hippie Delirium

This time, the flight to London wasn't on Air India. Instead, Mark and I flew TWA business class and over the pole into Heathrow, where we were met by Warner's people, who drove us to the comfort of the Portobello Hotel. There were receptions for us—meaning the Alice tour—at the label and then at the BBC. We were presented with stickers that the label had created to announce our European swing. They said MARK VOLMAN AND HOWARD KAYLAN, FLO AND EDDIE, with a tiny Reprise logo, and were round and white, and predominantly featured a photo of a single human hand flipping the bird.

What? This was to be our new image? What happened to the sensitive singer-songwriters? Once again, no one knew what to do with us, least of all ourselves. We had FUCK YOU T-shirts too. Nice. Good will abroad.

Happily, Marc Bolan had been invited to the reception, as had Harry Nilsson, so I was surrounded by my closest pals and lots of drugs. I was adjusting well. They went with us to Radio London, where we recorded shows on radio and one for BBC television called *The Old Grey Whistle Test*. After the show, Shep Gordon had booked Morgan Studios for a recording free-for-all. Keith Moon showed up: Alice and Marc and Keith and Harry and Mark and me. Bob Ezrin recorded it. I have no idea what we did in there that night, but Ezrin has the tapes. One day, I expect to be blackmailed by the boy.

◆ ◆ ◆

In Glasgow, for the first but not the last time, we drank our breakfast with Alice and got a glimpse into his slightly addled world. In Munich, after the concert, Shep rented out a sex club called the Tiffany, where bouncers with German shepherds straining at their leashes stood watching us while we watched the show onstage. It was a live sex show and our drugs and liquor gave us the lack of inhibition needed to interact, whether inappropriately or not. When a pretty blond stripper tried to persuade Alice to join her onstage, he reflexively punched her in the face. This didn't sit well with the club owners or the growling dogs, so Shep paid some cash, made some excuses, and quickly escorted us out of the club and into waiting cars before somebody called the cops.

Alice was doing amazing stunts onstage: the decapitation, the hanging, blood squibs, and violent effects. These were all under the supervision of one James Randi, aka the Amazing Randi, a world-renowned magician and debunker of all fakes and flimflam artists. Randi deals in illusions, not lies. He traveled with us throughout both the European and U.S. segments of the tour and now works closely with my friends Penn and Teller in Las Vegas. The tricks were spectacular onstage, and Randi's card tricks and close-up sleights of hand kept us amused during the long rides and the backstage waiting.

I was calling home twice a day, more for my sake than for Dianne's, and in the decades before cell phones, this was a very expensive proposition. I kept telling myself that it was all worth it. This, after all, was the fragile woman I loved.

The shows were going great and the cities whizzed by. We weren't playing the classic, golden-age theaters that we had visited with Frank. These were modern auditoriums and only in world capitals. Europe was beginning to lose its charm for me the longer I was away from home. I spent Thanksgiving in Dusseldorf and Lixie flew in to supplement our hash supply. Perfect timing, as we had to fly into Berlin the following morning. In 1972, that meant flying into East Berlin and then driving into the Western Sector through Checkpoint Charlie. We bought souvenirs.

Lixie joined me in Frankfurt, too. We sat up and rapped through the night. I spoke a lot about Dianne instead of doing what we usually did, and she sort of left me alone and confused at about two in the morning. I'm not sure which one of us was more fucked-up. She did stay the night, but she cried in the morning. I realized that she was Lixie no more. She was, once more, Elizabeth to me.

In Zurich, Gary Rowles, our guitar player, learned that he had become a new dad. We celebrated with champagne and went on to London again. Alice and the band had returned home for the moment, and the Flo and Eddie band had one more booking at Imperial College, where I scored two encores and a journalism major who was adorable and spent the night.

Getting home wasn't easy either. TWA canceled our flight and booked me on a 2:30 Pan Am that left at 4:30 and then ran out of fuel in San Francisco, prompting a stop en route to L.A., where Dianne had been waiting for hours. She'd gotten a job at the May Company department store, just so she could feel like she was contributing, so I would wake with her at 8:30 to drop her off on Wilshire Boulevard an hour later. Then, later, I would pick her up and we'd head out to the Forum to see the Kings play, do our drugs, have a great dinner, and head back to Laurel Canyon. As I write this, it all sounds wonderful to me. I suppose, at the time, it was. Earlier days are always happier days.

Nine days later, we were on the road again. I had barely enough time to see Emily, discuss the band's future with Larry Heller, do laundry, and try to convince Aynsley to return from England in time to do these recently added shows. Our roadie Michael Moss waited for Dunbar at the airport, while the rest of us held a band meeting to discuss phase two. It was a lot like *Spinal Tap*.

❖ ❖ ❖

Under pressure, Dianne and I somehow decided on an actual marriage date: January 27, 1973. Dianne's folks were happy to be a part of the planning for the big day. But for now, I was still on tour. On December 13, I flew to Detroit to do a sold-out show at Ford Auditorium, where we had seen the Dead perform. This time, the hip crowd was there for us. Well, for us and Mott the Hoople, but it felt like the show was ours. Next, it was into New York and One Fifth Avenue—Alice brought the incredible Orson Bean with him the next day when we played at the Capitol Theatre in Passaic, New Jersey. I was thrilled.

Home yet again, and this time I was meeting with my lawyer, Paul Almond, on prenuptial agreements. Dianne and I spent Christmas with Emily and Ona, unwrapping gifts beneath our communal tree.

Mark and I were busy assembling cassettes of possible songs to record with Bob Ezrin when Don Preston unexpectedly quit the band. We kind of expected it. Musically, we had nothing challenging to offer to Donnie. We didn't even know what we were doing next.

As the year changed over, I was spinning in some hippie delirium. Professionally, we had been fortunate enough to drag ourselves out of the urine-smelling dives for a minute, but we harbored no illusions. Ezrin or not, we were hanging by a thread. The competition was fierce out there, and we had no real management—it was just us, as always, looking after ourselves. We did have Warner Bros. though, and that was great.

Besides, I had always romanticized the notion of the starving singer-songwriter as the hero of the new American dream. My adult life had been too easy, with success handed to me on a silver platter, if you will. Now, like John Sebastian or Seals and Crofts, I was the lonely troubadour making my way through the countryside with naught but a crust of bread in my pocket and a song in my heart. But I had Mark and he had me, and there was no way in hell that this was going to fail.

TWENTY-FIVE

Officially Bipolar

During the second week of January 1973, Mark and I flew first class, Air Canada, to Toronto to meet with Bob Ezrin about the new Reprise album. Warner Bros. figured that they could actually save money by supporting the entire Alice tour, including us, rather than trying to figure out where the Phlorescent Leech and Eddie actually stood in their contemporary lineup. Bob listened briefly to our first, self-produced effort before lifting the needle off of the album.

"You know what I'm hearing here?" he asked.

"Um . . . songs?"

"Exactly. Nobody wants to hear songs and chords and harmonies. I've never made an album yet that wasn't driven by power licks. You've got to have a guitar lead going through each and every song. That's how I do Alice. Every cut has to be an anthem."

Honestly, coming from the Jackson Browne school of songwriting, we didn't know what he was talking about. And we really didn't have that many power-driven songs. We played Bob our demo of "Afterglow," which he loved. And Ray Davies' amazing "Days," which we hoped we could bring our own flavor to. Nice. But when we got to "Another Pop Star's Life," he stood up and cheered. This, plus Mark's magnificent "Just Another Town," would make a mini opera. At the last minute, I poorly sang and miserably played my long, acoustic and autobiographical opus, "Marmendy Mill." I expected laughter, but what I got was approval.

"A full symphony!" Bob exclaimed. "And we'll do it live, like a Broadway show!" This was going to be great.

❖ ❖ ❖

Now, home again to wild lovemaking and even wilder arguments, both fueled by copious quantities of drugs. The pendulum was swinging far too wildly to control now. Dianne and I were officially bipolar. When we were good, we were very, very good, but when we were bad, we were beyond horrid. It was very Hollywood.

We recorded at the Record Plant studios in both L.A. and New York. Ezrin loved this old album Mark and I had committed to memory in the tenth grade about the death of the bullfighter Manolete, and we turned the dialogue from it into "Carlos and the Bull." Which made us laugh. Which is what we needed after a shaky start. Now we were up and running—the recording went great.

The album wasn't even done yet, but Bob had mixed "Afterglow" as a single—he worked through the nights with little but chemical assistance as the two of us bounced in and out.

We were really working around Alice's schedule now. The American leg of the Billion Dollar Babies tour kicked off in early March and we played many sold-out shows: At the Philadelphia Spectrum, with more than 20,000 in attendance, the kids broke the barriers down. Cops were moved in to protect us. Us! Now, this was more like it. Our road manager, John's brother, Jim Seiter, who had worked for Spanky, the Byrds, and others, provided the needed link to our past as the tour rolled on for months.

We were traveling now in Alice's rented jet, a full-blown 727, complete with stewardesses. Coop had appropriated the back of the jet, not for his own private bedroom—he never slept anyway—but for use as a poker lounge. I can't recall what I was paid on that tour, but I'll bet that I lost most of it back to Alice in the rear of that damned plane. Still, it was wonderful waking daily, whenever, and taking a limo to the plane and another car to the hotel and still another to and from the shows. Better than two station wagons.

❖ ❖ ❖

On March 24, my world shifted again. Big-time. There was a Warner Bros. executive flying with us on the Cooper jet. Her name was Diana Balocca. She was a vice president. She was amazingly hot. Her body was to die for. She wore see-through blouses and not much else. I was determined and I was vocal about it. I told Mark, "I will have her!" He laughed. Much like he had when I had lusted over Nita Garfield. But I showed him, boy.

The plane was a nonstop orgy of one kind or another. On April 1, our stewardesses were both fired for partying too hearty and we were assigned new Amish attendants. Dianne came to visit in Detroit a few days later. We spent time with her friends, drinking and dancing at her local stop, the Roostertail, with John Sinclair, the radical who'd recently been freed from prison after John Lennon did a benefit concert for him. Dianne passed out. On to Chicago and St. Louis. She passed out. There were so many fights. There was so much cocaine. Alice's road manager was in charge of Alice's stash; the rest of us were on our own.

Meanwhile, the shows were breaking records. James Randi hyped us on *The Tonight Show* and Alice quoted us in *Rolling Stone*. Ms. Balocca and I were talking a lot and sitting together on the plane, having eschewed the poker lounge in search of a more attainable quest.

On April 26, while in New Orleans, I received an uncharacteristically angry call from Marc and June Bolan. Seems they heard "Another Pop Star's Life" and instantly realized that it had been written about them. Despite all my claims to the contrary—that the protagonist of the tune had been an amalgam of every Brit rock star that we had ever met—Bolan wasn't buying it. He was pissed. He was betrayed. He was gone. I had lost one of my closest friends in the world for the sake of a song to throw on a disposable album. What an asshole. And I wasn't done yet.

On May 11, we played the Forum in Los Angeles to a monster sell-out crowd, followed by one of those parties that you only read about. It took place at the Rainbow on Sunset and continued in Alice's suite at the Beverly Hilton. Diana Balocca was on my arm and whispers could be heard. The following Tuesday, there was a meeting at Don Schmitzerle's office at Reprise, where Larry Heller and I shared celebratory champagne with the two execs. Larry eventually split and Diana started feeling a bit woozy, so Prince Charming volunteered to take her home. And that was it. The inevitable happened. I knew where I was. I knew what was going to take place. I owned my deeds, but that didn't make me any better. And I had to leave in two days. There wasn't even any time to discuss things. I went to Denver and hung out with Pons in a strip club.

Needless to say, it's not easy to repair a relationship over the phone. Especially one that is far past the fix-it stage. Dianne and I had known each other exactly two years. I should have had more alone time.

❖ ❖ ❖

The A.C. 1, as we called the plane, landed in New York on June 1, 1973. All of us were sick. Pons, Volman, and I left the One Fifth to walk the Village and lucked into a performance of the *National Lampoon's* new play, *Lemmings*, directed by Tony Hendra, a Brit who we'd met years ago when he and his partner, Nick Ullett, performed with us on *The Ed Sullivan Show*. The play was astounding. It starred unknowns Chevy Chase, Christopher Guest, and a portly genius we could totally relate to, named John Belushi. John was the funniest, most honest human I had ever met. He also had drugs. He followed us over to the One Fifth and stayed all night.

I went back with Diana to see *Lemmings* on the next night and solo the night after that, following our concert at Madison Square Garden. Belushi and his wife, Judy, spent the next night with me. Tuesday was Nassau Coliseum, and John was waiting when I got back to my room. We stayed up all night, obviously. There was a party at Mary Jennifer Mitchell's loft in the village—she of the sexy hippie parts in the play—and I stayed the night with her. Not for love, you understand, just companionship. And great sex.

The tour ended on June 7, and there was plenty of welcome-home lovemaking there as well. But I wasn't keeping score. Things were just moving far too quickly. We met with Chuck Swenson, the *200 Motels* animator who had written the script for his new X-rated film, *Cheap*, with Mark and me in mind. Dianne decided to do some camping, she said, and took the bus up to Lake Tahoe. I loaned Ona my car and was stranded until John and Catherine Sebastian picked me up and took me to Diana's. Poor Ona—the kid had loyalties to both of us, wanted to be nice to everybody, and found herself stuck right in the middle of my domestic troubles, just trying to cover all the bases. Ona and I drove through the hills, higher than kites, talking things through. I should have been talking to Dianne, but it was already too late. My dick had already done all my talking for me. She was gone. I helped her load her boxes into her VW bus. There was nothing left to say.

❖ ❖ ❖

We were recording the music for *Cheap* at Cherokee Studios with our good friends, the Robbs, so we were indeed productive, but we hadn't sold records for Reprise, and with Diana privy to all the poop coming from Warner's, we knew that our days there were numbered. Damn! We had our major label shot and blew it. And even schtupping the vice president wasn't going to help.

I have to say that if it hadn't been for my great friend Allan MacDougal at A&M, who gave us support, as well as background work on Hoyt Axton's album, I might not have made it. Between him and my ever-present buddy songwriter Steve Duboff, I got to talk through my shortcomings and avoided a rather dark fate. Larry Heller and Tim and Barbara DeWitt were my other saviors. I was still living at the house in Laurel Canyon along with Ona, though I wasn't spending a lot of time there. I was at Diana's every night. I was starting to wonder where my next meal was coming from. Then one night I went to a record release party at the Continental Hyatt House on Sunset Boulevard, where the rock bands stay, and who should I run into but Clive Davis's new head of A&R at Columbia Records: Ladies and gentlemen, meet Ted Feigin—the very same Ted Feigin from my White Whale days.

Diana met my parents and brother, but none of us knew that just eighteen days later, the two of us would marry at the Abbey Wedding Palor near the L.A. County Courthouse. The next night, Mark and I left for another tour. We fished for mud sharks at the Edgewater Inn in Seattle, but for the first time, I didn't call Lin. We weren't stars anymore. We were just Flo and Eddie. I called my parents to tell them that I had gotten married. They seemed elated. I think they had given up on me by then.

Lots of drugs in Seattle. Tim Buckley was there. Jeff Simmons was there. Lee Michaels was there. We played Vancouver for the first time and did shows in Denver at a club called Ebbets Field with Sopwith Camel. We were getting to be a pretty decent club band with Gary Rowles on guitar and Andy Cahan now on keyboards. We had no illusions of grandeur. Impossible when you're playing places called Humpin' Hannah's and the Smiling Dog Saloon.

❖ ❖ ❖

Back in Manhattan, we were, at least, in our element. A taxi to the One Fifth, calls to Mary Jennifer and Belushi, and all of us out to eat, drink, and make . . . Mary. The new *Lemmings* road company was now doing that show in the Village. I walked down to see them, but it just wasn't the same. In September we opened in Providence for King Crimson and in Amherst with Ike and Tina. We did a week in Atlanta at a club called Richards, where I burned my eyebrows off investigating a misfiring flash pot and thought, for a few hours, that I had gone blind. At the end of that month, with the tour finished and Diana having moved her stuff over in my absence, I carried the second Mrs. Kaylan over the threshold of our house on Hollywood Hills Road. I could barely afford it, but we were living high on the hog . . . again.

As for my new wife, she had made a significant move: She had abandoned her cushy gig at Warner's to take a job as the new head of A&R at Capricorn, the Atlanta-based Warner's subsidiary run by Phil Walden, a Southern legend. It was the era of Southern rock and the Allman Brothers, Wet Willie, Lynyrd Skynyrd, and a few others were burning up the airwaves. Plus, Capricorn had Martin Mull on their roster and lots and lots of money. Also, famously, lots and lots of drugs.

I had to borrow a thousand bucks from Shep Gordon just to get through the month. Where was the money really coming from? Well, we had started writing articles for *Creem* magazine out of Detroit for our friends, Barry and Connie Kramer. They sent a photographer to take naked photos of us that they published as a foldout *Creem* Dream. Sure. *Phonograph Record Magazine* hired us to do a Blind Date column with the music journalist Ken Barnes, who still remains a great friend. Ken would play records for us and not tell us who we were listening to, and we would give our two cents, sometimes rudely.

Warner's wouldn't give us our release yet, but Paul Almond kept telling us that the White Whale situation was cooling down—they'd settled with us in 1971, and the case was dismissed in '72—so Mark and I began structuring a double-album Turtles hits release. I was on unemployment again.

A&M passed on Flo and Eddie and Allan MacDougal had to break the news to us. Only an advance from BMI revitalized my Christmas. Emily hated Diana; that made life weird. Enid Finnbogason was still around. Lixie was around too. As was Pamela. And now, somehow, it was okay to be friends with all of them. I should have known right there that something was wrong.

TWENTY-SIX

Lobster, Caviar, and Cocaine

Mark and I spent one Sunday evening crammed into a tiny broadcasting studio with a stack of our personal records and our pal Alice Cooper. The program was sent out live via a fledgling cable network in L.A. called the Z Channel. It was great fun, a ridiculously good time, and casual to the point of anarchy. We never made it through an entire record: We'd leave our mics on to comment over the tracks and when we got tired of it, we'd put on another one. The tracks ran together into little five-minute sets, and then we'd come out talking to Alice about anything *but* show business. A really fun night.

But, lucky us, Shadoe Stevens, program director of L.A.'s rebel radio station, KROQ, heard it. He asked us to come in for a meeting, and exactly one month later, the very first Flo and Eddie radio show hit the airwaves at 9 P.M. All of our celebrity friends phoned in. Alice promised to come in for the entire three hours the following week. We had lots of sponsors and the show was an underground hit.

To the casual observer, it must have appeared as though Mark and I had hit the jackpot. We would now do our column, Blind Date, for *Phonograph Record Magazine*—the very same format that Lulu had used to lambast us back in '67—record spots at the radio station on Fridays, and then do the show live on Sundays. It might have looked like success, but I was still on unemployment. Of course, Diana wasn't, so it was still lobster, caviar, and cocaine. There were other perks connected with her job as well. We spent a week at the Acapulco Princess hotel on Warner's and went to red-carpet screenings and A-list parties where I'd nurse a cocktail as Diana flirted—for business, you understand.

By that time Ona had realized that she was a third wheel, and she'd moved out, so Diana and I were allowed to become, for better or worse, a couple. Unless, of course, Capricorn had an emergency requiring Diana to stay up all night, working, naturally, at Phil Walden's bungalow at the Beverly Hills Hotel.

❖ ❖ ❖

Larry Heller had quit the management business and somehow Mark and I wound up with two new clowns running the show, Mike Kagen and John DeMarco. I really don't know how it happened. They were mostly in the business of handling comics and dangled a lot of potential script and movie work in our faces. But they liked us and there really weren't a lot of people in L.A. who seemed to like us.

Herb still did. We would still go down to watch Frank rehearse, now with Jeff, Ruth Underwood, and George Duke. It was really friendly. Plus, the Casting Office, a terrific seedy bar, was right next door, where we could share a few beers with Tom Waits.

I don't think I could have made it through this post-Reprise era were it not for the radio show. I looked forward to it all week long. During our early weeks, when lining up guests was a daunting task, we'd save the show by doing Fondue Week or Mexican Night or Surfin' Safaris, where all of the emphasis was placed on the most absurd of musical selections, listener call-ins, and irrelevant facts. On other nights, our cup runneth over; our third show featured Bobby Goldsboro, Richie Furay, Paul Williams, and Iggy Pop. The show's appeal to celebrities was obvious. They weren't being asked to sell anything. It was just for fun. The stars would bring their own favorite records to play, preparing for our insults and the irrelevant frivolity to follow. On Easter Sunday, we invited Rodney Bingenheimer, the unofficial mayor of the Sunset Strip, along with about a dozen glam kids from his English Disco and our old pal, Keith Moon. We didn't really expect Keith to show up—he very often didn't—but on this night he did, albeit a bit late. Our nine-to-midnight show was about an hour away from its frenetic conclusion when Keith stormed in with

Ringo on his arm. KROQ stayed on the air long after its FCC-ordained midnight sign-off that night. The broadcast became legendary and its recording cemented our show's inclusion on quite a few syndicated stations.

❖ ❖ ❖

Diana was smart. She foresaw the potential of these boys' nights out and forced me to buy a professional Pioneer reel-to-reel tape recorder. Beginning with Alice, we taped every single program, which I later edited down to roughly seventy-two minutes to syndicate across the country as a ninety-minute weekly feature. The three of us—Mark, Diana, and I—formed a company, Earfull Productions, to make and sell the shows, which, when all was said and done, amounted to around two and a half years of Sunday nights. Still, her late evenings out continued and she'd get this faraway look sometimes.

We were fearless on the air. We had Albert Brooks and Suzi Quatro on the same show, Suzi trying to teach Albert how to be glam. We did a California night where we invited both Dean Torrence and Todd Rundgren to jam with us, brought on Joan Baez for Mother's Day, and famously asked all of the feuding members of the original ELO to join us, without telling the other guys. When Jeff Lynne and Bev Bevan saw Roy Wood and Rick Price, bodyguards from both camps jumped to their feet, but by the end of the show, the lads were all singing bawdy English music hall songs together.

Meanwhile, Mike and John were actually doing something. They were meeting with Clive Davis at Columbia and Seymour Stein at Sire Records. The *Cheap* movie, now renamed *Dirty Duck*, was just finishing up and I was editing and mailing out tapes to the stations that Diana had signed up to receive *Flo and Eddie by the Fireside*. And then the FCC pulled the plug on KROQ. We'd had such a great thing going. Not one to lose any momentum, Shadoe proposed an interesting plan: We would form a company, Big Bucks Corporation, or BBC, and produce our own shows. We drew up and signed the papers. We leased a studio on the corner of Sunset and Doheny, an expensive but beautiful space that Shadoe filled with state-of-the-art equipment. We would do our shows from there. Shadoe and his wife, Linda, could record commercials and radio plays from there and the shows would pay the rent.

So, in July, with the White Whale lawsuit behind us—we eventually bought out all of the other members' interest in the Turtles too—Flo and Eddie signed with Columbia Records and *Billboard* magazine ran a photo of the two of us with Ted Feigin. We also leased the Turtles' catalog to Seymour and the double-disc *Happy Together Again! The Turtles' Greatest Hits* was put into motion. Simultaneously, we inked with a company called the Wartoke Concern for public relations. Shadoe became the program director of L.A.'s heaviest rock station, KMET, the Mighty Met. It was a different sort of success, but we loved it. Our show started running weekly on KMET just before Dr. Demento's on Sundays at 9, our original time slot. The first installment was our interview with Harry Nilsson. It never got better than that.

❖ ❖ ❖

We didn't have a band anymore, so when we found a song that we really needed to record, we called Aynsley in San Francisco and asked him to join Danny Kortchmar and Leland Sklar from the Section to record tracks at Cherokee. We recorded Albert Hammond's "Rebecca" and our original Turtlesque "Let Me Make Love to You," as well as a comedic B-side called "Youth in Asia." Our original was picked for the single and Clive enlisted Joe Wissert to produce us. We were churning out "Happy Togethers" right and left. We were a hit machine. It would be like the Turtles were back and on a major label.

The *Midnight Special* people loved us. We would get a shot on this national music TV program. This, at last, would be it. Again. I flew into the shot on wires and covered in glitter as we did our glam opening on tape at NBC. It took me three days to get it off my face.

In August, we flew to New York to speak at the *Billboard* Radio Convention. Our panel, besides us, featured Clive Davis, Bobby Vee, Willie Mitchell, Bobby Colomby of Blood, Sweat & Tears, Peter Noone, and Eddie Kendricks of the Temptations. My nights were filled with Belushi.

For a minute, we were hot. Norman Seeff, the brilliant celebrity photographer, took our portraits for his book *Hot Shots*, and I bought a new VW bus. Diana and I celebrated our one-year anniversary. Flo and Eddie began a raunchy Advice to the Lovelorn column for the prestigious *L.A. Free Press*, which had the great nerve to place our joke column next to the works of such luminaries as Harlan Ellison and Charles Bukowski.

❖ ❖ ❖

By the mid-'70s we were gaining quite a reputation as background singers. David Cassidy made a fantastic album called *The Higher They Climb, The Harder They Fall* for RCA and we were there. We sang on Hoyt Axton's *Life Machine* album along with Ronstadt and on Roger McGuinn's *Peace on You*. But one record stands out from the pack.

We wound up recording Keith Moon's 1975 solo LP, *Two Sides of the Moon*—twice: both times at the Record Plant in Los Angeles and both times the exact same songs. The first time we went in with Keith, Mal Evans, the Beatles' former road manager, produced. It was great. Mal was such a wonderful man: a big ol' gentle protective bear who looked after Keith as if he were a son. Keith sang the Beach Boys' "Don't Worry Baby" and the Beatles' "In My Life" and you just wanted to cry.

Then MCA Records heard the raw, emotional record and threw Mal under the bus. Oh, they loved Keith and they loved the songs, but something about the production just wasn't right. So they let Mal go—so sad—and the team of Skip Taylor and John Stronach was recruited to save the project. Same songs. Same drugs. I couldn't tell the difference blindfolded. MCA, however, with their superior powers of perception, thought it was amazing and finally released the album in a beautiful die-cut foldout sleeve. It tanked. The single was "Teenage Idol," the old Ricky Nelson hit. Go figure. I loved that wacky Brit. And we did many mad things together. That Record Plant will certainly never be the same. It was cocaine and caviar. First class, baby. Both times. Anywhere, anyhow, any way I choose.

There was a sadness to Keith though. Maybe that's why he and Mal worked so well together. He was truly of a different time—hell, maybe even a different planet—but he never fit in. Not with all the chicks and butlers and driving the Rolls into the pool. Not even with his own band. But you felt the genius coming off the boy like electricity. He almost crackled. It was an honor and a pleasure being around rock royalty. I pity the fool who could have had my opportunities in this life and not taken advantage of knowing that, at that very moment, you were making rock history. Go ahead. I dare ya. Build a time machine, go back to Hollywood with Moonie in his maddest days and tell me you wouldn't have partayed. Answer no and you're a pussy. Beat it.

◆ ◆ ◆

On December 1, we rode down Hollywood Boulevard in the Santa Claus Lane Parade in an armored personnel carrier, along with the other KMET DJs. It felt nice to belong. But on the following Tuesday, the skies got a lot brighter. We were in the middle of an interview with the *NME* when the phone call came in from MRI studios. It was Marc Bolan. We literally ran there. We made up. We hugged. I cried a little. Tony Visconti was on hand, as was Marc's new girlfriend, singer Gloria Jones. We sang on three of Marc's tracks for T. Rex's *Futuristic Dragon* LP including his classic "New York City," and on one song for Gloria as well.

CBS decided that we should hit the road to promote the single, so armed with a new guitarist, Phil Reed, we wound up snowed in near Christmas in Vail, Colorado—now *there's* a smart booking! Still, we needed the practice. We were to play over Christmas at the Troubadour in Hollywood, and while we had in many ways outgrown that venue, that particular club in that particular town was still a mighty big deal. It couldn't have gone better. In attendance that evening: Albert Brooks, Linda Ronstadt, Joni Mitchell, James Taylor, and Carly Simon, among others.

As the year came to an end, I nursed a missing voice, saw our nude photo appear in *Creem*, and left the austere offices of William Morris, the agency I'd signed with back in the White Whale days, the hypothetical assurance of CMA and a new deal. Life was good.

TWENTY-SEVEN

Skating on Thin Ice

It was a case of too much, too fast. On January 2, 1975, we had a meeting at Mutt Cohen's office. Mutt and Herb shared an office, but Mutt was all business, no management for him. He knew everything there was to know about the law and was a total nightmare to go up against in court. And while that didn't help in the case of my divorce, in the world of show business his name was revered and/or feared. We told him that we didn't like our current management and he said, and I'll never forget this, "Fuck 'em!"

Two days later, we shook hands on a management deal with our pal, Canned Heat manager Skip Taylor. Skip knew Diana, and Diana knew our new CMA agent, the guy who had repped Alice on the road, Johnny Podell. Plus, we had our weekly radio show going and columns in the *Freep* and *Phonograph Record*. Mondays would be for the lovelorn stuff; Wednesdays were usually spent at BBC with Shadoe, pretaping our Sunday KMET shows with whatever guests we could assemble; Thursdays were Blind Date days, when Ken Barnes would record our responses to his cross section of new releases.

We had great club dates, did three SRO nights at the Roxy, became critical darlings and friends with beautiful people like rock critic Lester Bangs, an early and vocal supporter. I thought I had finally gotten it right. On April 23, I tried to call home but got no answer. Curious. When I finally spoke to my wife, she apologized and reassured me that all was fine. Really?

But I was on the road. She knew that. I couldn't fly off to be by her side. It wasn't that I didn't care; I was just already used to a lot of drama in my life. And I had shows to do. But when the tour was done, it was Diana's turn to hit the road. She just had to get to Macon, Georgia, for important Capricorn meetings. When she did return to L.A., it was with Martin Mull, everybody's best friend. Martin was a well-known comedic musician and Renaissance man. A great wit and a burgeoning artist, Martin was big on the nightclub circuit and made records for Capricorn. But hey, I was a big boy. And I liked Martin a lot. Still do. He passed out in our guest room one night after the three of us had stayed up late drinking wine and playing board games. She went to *The Dinah Shore Show* taping with Marty and he played the Troubadour on the next night.

Just to sweeten the situation, Martin was given the chance to do his own PBS special, one whole hour of the Chicago-based *Soundstage* series. He got to choose his guest stars. He chose Flo and Eddie. The program was called *Sixty Minutes to Kill*. It was funny. You can still see it online. I met Greg Hawkes there. He's our current keyboard player and, of course, a founding member of the Cars. We had a great time. Everybody laughed a lot. When it was done, I flew to L.A. and checked into the Tropicana Motel on Santa Monica Boulevard, so I knew I couldn't fall any lower.

The next day, I did. I rented an apartment behind the Hollywood Ranch Market. The place was a one-bedroom dump right out of a James Ellroy crime scene. Two stories, stucco, twenty units around a pool. The VW bus stopped running, so I drove to KMET in a rental wreck to do a live Sunday night funfest. The show must go on.

❖ ❖ ❖

Meanwhile, Columbia had been shocked by the lack of success of "Let Me Make Love to You"—it should have been as big as "Happy Together." Perhaps the problem had been that our producer, Joe Wissert, hadn't seen our act live since the mid-'60s. When he finally did catch us, along with the other members of the L.A. CBS brain trust, he couldn't help but notice that we did comedy. Well, he hadn't expected that. Armed with this new information and seeing how amazing our audience responses were, it was decided that our Columbia debut album—and believe me, we were lucky to get one—was to be recorded live and to be funny. Kind of.

We recorded a few songs in the studio and of course they were the songs that got released as singles, but the majority of *Illegal, Immoral and Fattening* was done live at the Roxy on Sunset Boulevard. We made cocktail glasses for the audience with our new logo etched in, and gave everybody in the crowd free chichis. It helped. The record was full of celebrity slams; no one was safe. Joni thought hers was hilarious. It was Volman in a wig doing his best impression, speaking of screwing Stephen and Neil and Graham—and maybe you?

Some artists were not so amused. In our parody of the recent George Harrison concert tour during which he famously lost his voice, not only did we have to pay for the use of "My Sweet Lord," but we narrowly avoided being taken to court for libel and Harrison's office actually threatened to stop the album from being released. Fleetwood Mac laughed but got paid anyway. When all was said and done, including, "There's No Business Like Show Business," which also cost a fortune and almost stopped the record, CBS had a rather expensive album on its hands.

Back at the crappy apartment, I was in full bachelor mode. I was lonely and sad and mentally licking my wounds—real bottom-of-the-barrel shit. I didn't blame Diana, but ours was a true Hollywood marriage in all the worst ways and doomed to fail. Marty Fox was a kid right out of college when he became a junior partner in a huge Century City accounting firm. He was happy to handle the Flo and Eddie account, and together we'd prowl bars off Hollywood Boulevard or near his place at the Marina. I indulged my curiosity regarding the forbidden Asian woman and one or two ladies of color who wouldn't ordinarily stand in line for a Turtles concert. It was sad and dramatic.

I gave up my two-month deposit on the apartment and moved back into Hollywood Hills with Diana, based on our mutual fear of loneliness, but we both knew that we were skating on thin ice.

And, of course, I was still a tremendous asshole.

❖ ❖ ❖

Flo and Eddie had been invited to play the Diamond Head Crater Festival in Hawaii in July and we had a wonderful time there with the lovely promoter Ken Rosene and Fleetwood Mac and recreational drugs. And while there, who should I run into but Steve Duboff's adorable girlfriend Lynn. She looked spectacular in a green floral bikini. We spent three incredible nights together before the band left for our first trip to Australia.

Our promoter's name on that tour was Ian Riddington. We flew a Qantas 747, eleven hours with a stop in Fiji. We did radio and TV in Melbourne and Sydney. Then we flew to Brisbane and drove an hour and a half to the tiny village of Toowoomba for the first show of the tour. About a dozen locals sat in the seats of the school auditorium as we did our sound check. We let them stay. Then we went to dinner. When we returned for the concert, our audience was the same twelve people. I thought it was funny. We sounded great. Volman had a cow. He was freaking out.

We had a lot of dates on our itinerary. Of course, that meant nothing once we saw what we were dealing with. Ian had no money. No one was promoting these shows. CBS was literally invisible Down Under. They had a two-person office and no promotional staff whatsoever. Riddington took a meeting with us after shows in Brisbane, Gold Coast, and Sydney, where the only relief from reality at all was a chance encounter and a few glorious days spent with the hilarious Lou Reed. He sang with us and we sang with him.

Ian was blunt. No money was coming in. We had no tickets home and that was many thousands of dollars and half a world away. Then luck saved us one more time. We had made friends with an Australian band called Skyhooks. These guys were a phenomenon in the Southern Hemisphere, sounded a bit like Rush, and drew crowds like the Beatles. Their label was called Mushroom, which was owned by Ray Evans and Michael Gudinski, the two biggest concert promoters in Australia. They liked us. They bought our contract from the nonexistent CBS Australia, and we played huge and successful shows in Melbourne, Canberra, and Sydney.

We had to stop in Hawaii on our flight home, so I called Lynn and we spent the night together. She was flying to L.A. the next day, so I changed my flight to be with her. We shared a cab home and I got dropped off first. Diana saw us kiss goodbye and that really wasn't such a good start. But we were doomed anyway. It lasted a bit longer. Uncomfortable.

❖ ❖ ❖

We played a wonderful show at the Mississippi River Festival near St. Louis where Andy Cahan, the keyboard clown, latched onto a comely lass who reminded me a lot of Joni—big points in her favor—and I immediately began flirting with her despite the million reasons not to. She was married, with kids. And her husband? Oh, no problem there: He was in prison.

And she was Canadian! That was almost the deal breaker. Needless to say, that little voice in the back of my head started yelling at me instantly and I declared, once again, I Will Have Her!

The blond girl's name was Nancy Lauraine and she comforted me, long distance, once Diana found a house and moved out while I played a disastrous festival in Coos Bay, Oregon. The following week, Nancy met me at a show in Saskatoon. We went to her apartment in Toronto for a week; she made some babysitter arrangements, and flew into L.A. with me on September 12—I hate an empty house. She did have to return to Toronto eventually and I did have shows and career stuff to do, but we were together via the phone. I'd get updates about her husband's prison status and his good behavior. I even spoke to him while he was in there; it was weird. He had been busted with a rented boat full of cocaine. If his deal had worked, they'd have been rich. It didn't.

I proposed over the phone on October 6 after three nights at the Bottom Line in full Belushi mode. On the 10th, Nancy's husband was released from prison. Nancy and her children, Rebekah and Justin, moved to the United States. Of course they had to have a U.S. address and they did—mine. It was an instant family; the house would never be empty again.

Our concert career was flying high, pun intended. We were an opening act, but a really good one. And that's an admirable place to be. We alternated shows opening for Jefferson Starship and Stephen Stills, singing "Suite: Judy Blue Eyes" with the latter as the encore to every concert. The reviews were amazing. We played Pauley Pavilion again and sang the "Suite" with Neil Young on guitar.

We did *The Dinah Shore Show* on November 17. I loved Dinah—I had the biggest crush on that lady. We flirted too. I was sooo close.

We ate Thanksgiving dinner with Marc Bolan and Gloria Jones, which was a bit surreal. I was trying to pretend that everything was normal when I spent weekend time with Emily. I now had three kids but I barely felt like I had one kid. I just wasn't the daddy type—yet. Rebekah was enrolled at Wonderland School now and singing in the Christmas pageant side by side with Mark's daughter Sarina and it just felt wrong.

New Year's Eve found us in concert with the Tubes at Winterland in San Francisco. There was just enough time to pack a larger bag so that we could meet Stephen Stills and company at Jim Guercio's Caribou Ranch in Colorado for one of the weirdest recording sessions ever.

The album was called *Illegal Stills*, and man, it should have been. I've never seen so many drugs in my life. And this is *me*! I really enjoyed making that record, though it took hours to get even the simplest thing on tape. Plus, I got to listen to Stills's imaginary war stories and sit outside of Volman's room with Stephen and his huge vial and buck knife in hand. He was screaming as Mark was schtupping one of the studio managers: "It should be me in there, man. I'm the star here! It should be me!"

TWENTY-EIGHT

Moving Targets

For an L.A. minute, things were as normal as they could be on the domestic front. Skip was booking dates, albeit entry level, from time to time. But we didn't mind, really. It was great to be back in the bars, with at least something to look forward to. And every once in a while, we'd do the giant dates that proved, at least to us, that we were still members of a rather elite show-business community. Hell, we were in the studio daily. Columbia now wanted to produce a second studio version of "Elenore." They were certain that by making it part of the CBS catalog, the public connection would be complete and Flo and Eddie would be welcomed into America's heart. Full circle. We said sure. I bought an Audi and consciously went on a diet and lost a ton of weight. Of course, the drugs helped a little, but I was just an occasional user at this point. I bought a white three-piece suit.

Nancy loved being thrown into the limelight, though she would argue that now, I'm certain. She sure didn't mind when Bowie called and she got to party with Alice, Ringo, Rod Stewart, and Linda Ronstadt after David's show at the Forum. She got into an existential conversation with Ray Bradbury that she actually did write home about. We had babysitters.

We played at the CBS Records convention in San Diego. The label still loved us. We began recording the tracks to the *Moving Targets* album at the Record Plant in L.A. and finished up at the Plant in Sausalito. They charged us a fortune to block out all these weeks of studio time, which we charged to Columbia, which charged them all back to us on paper. It was decadent. It was catered. We lived large—Mark, me, Skip, and the amazing Ron Nevison, our engineer. There was no one looking over our shoulders.

There should have been a lot of hope connected with the project, but this was album four for us and the lyrics reflected our impatience and frustration with the music biz, no matter how optimistic we tried to be. My words to "Mama, Open Up" say it all: "Motel rooms and flying tombs / And food I couldn't chew / From the Fillmore to the White House chasing fame / But nobody buys my records and my roof is leaking too / After all these years my life appears in vain."[1]

❖ ❖ ❖

We were hanging up our rock 'n' roll shoes. It was clear that we weren't needed here. We felt sorry for ourselves and were going to take our balls and go home. Domestically, I was doing the same thing with Diana. We had spoken a lot over the months since our breakup, and on March 9, 1976, I drove down to the L.A. County Courthouse and filed divorce papers. It was strange and rather bittersweet, but of course I had mentally moved on. Now neither Diana nor Nancy would talk to me.

Bowie flew Mark and me into New York at the end of the month to meet about his screenplay. It was a first-class journey that wound up at his Madison Square Garden concert, backstage. Then we went to the Village for more of the same. Limos took us everywhere, although we got to see David for all of about ten minutes. Still, I don't think there were any complaints about the trip. Whatever Bowie wanted.

Meanwhile, over at CBS, Ethan Russell had been enlisted to take photos for the album and Dave McMacken, who'd illustrated the *200 Motels* cover, was hired to design this elaborate shooting gallery painting for the cover. Both of these guys were top tier. Money was being spent. I was really impressed. The record was finally finished. We enjoyed our toots with champagne at the opulent home of our guitarist, Phil Reed, whose wife had inherited her fortune from her father's interest in Daisy Air Rifles. Random, right? Those two had money to burn.

---

[1] Written by Kaylan and Volman. Published by High Concept Music, BMI.

There was a screening of *The Man Who Fell to Earth*, starring Bowie, at a theater in Westwood. David had sent us our invitations in a large cardboard box. What the hell? Ah, also enclosed were two copies, some 750 pages each, of David's screenplay notes for a feature film to be called *The Traveler*. The film was to deal with the very real alter ego that Bowie had created for himself, that of the Thin White Duke. Eschewing air travel, David would only travel to and from America via ocean liner where, once onboard, he would assume a disposable two-week identity where his lines between fact and fiction blurred and he regaled the other passengers with amazing tales of his conquests and heroics.

There was a lot to take and it offered a great many opportunities for fantasy and wordplay. I was excited. It took many hours to read this "outline," as David called it, and I finished it onboard a 747 en route to London one more time. On this occasion, CBS England was taking a chance on Flo and Eddie as producers of a very promising Byrds-inspired rock band called Starry Eyed and Laughing.

We checked into the Portobello but London was impossibly hot that summer, so there wasn't much sleep to be had, despite the familiar surroundings. Wandering down to the lobby on the morning of the Fourth of July, I bumped into fellow American and miscreant Harlan Ellison, the writer, always looking for an ear to complain to. I loved this guy. Still do. We ate what passes for lunch together there and Mark and I got busy on the record the next day. CBS surprised us by hooking up a huge stereo system in our living room and we were both suitably impressed. The next night, we went out to a lovely French dinner on the label and brought one of the execs, our friend Dan Loggins, back to the hotel to hear *Moving Targets*. Loud. And late.

Bang! Bang! Bang! The door almost rattled off of its hinges. "Open up! What the fuck is going on in there? Are you nuts?" It wasn't the cops or the hotel security. It was Harlan.

"Sorry, man. We didn't mean to wake you."

"You didn't wake me, you assholes. I'm trying to save your butts. They're about to call Scotland Yard downstairs!"

He was right. They almost did. We turned down the volume. We hid the pipes. Ellison never lets me forget. "Hey, Kaylan. Remember the night I saved your life?" Yessir, I do. Thanks again.

The records were great. The singles were called "Song on the Radio" and "Saturday." Try to find them. I dare you.

❖ ❖ ❖

From London, we flew directly to Australia, where the guys at Mushroom Records had a contract on us—literally. We were theirs in the land Down Under for the next entire month. The place was still a slave colony, evidently. But we owed those guys big-time and they were going to release *Moving Targets* a full thirty days before Columbia in the U.S. It was a crazy month, as you might imagine. You're a world away from the States and, in that separate reality, anything goes. I'm surprised that I survived. We made a video for "Mama, Open Up," did tons of radio and television, and had sellout concerts and happy groupies. We flew home from Auckland, New Zealand, with all involved pleased.

We played a great show with the Marshall Tucker Band at the Forum in Los Angeles, where, of course, Diana was, so a huge fight ensued. I had no time to worry about it. Meanwhile, WABC, the powerhouse New York City station, wanted to play "Keep It Warm" and Columbia wanted very much for that to happen. *But* the song was far too long and these verses about killing whales and smoking pot would have to go. Edits were done at the Record Plant and the song, for all intents and purposes was ruined. All the venom was removed.

We hosted a huge concert at Anaheim Stadium with our buddies Aerosmith, Jeff Beck, and Rick Derringer and on September 15, KLOS officially added our album to its rather tight playlist. Amazing. We were on FM radio at long last. The very same day, I stood across Sunset Boulevard with my camera in hand as the workers from Pacific Outdoor erected the humongous *Moving Targets* billboard, complete with moving neon centerpiece, in the lot next to Tower Records. It felt like we were actually going somewhere.

Back to the Roxy for three nights of star-studded sellout shows. I remember Grace Slick and Al Kooper and riding around in Stills's Rolls-Royce after the shows. Alice was there and Bernie Taupin. The reviews were fantastic. This time, when we went to New York, the label put us up at the tony Warwick and I spent October 6 with Belushi at his NBC office, hanging with the writers and doing many naughty, un-network things.

The whole next week was spent in the company of a Dutch film crew from VPRO, the same government broadcasters that had done our Zappa concert footage when we had first signed on in 1970. We took them on a tour of Flo and Eddie's Hollywood, which consisted of a Jack in the Box burger purchase, the SIR rehearsal studios, and the iconic Hollywood sign. On October 22, we left to begin a coast-to-coast tour with the Doobie Brothers. The first stop was Salt Lake City—15,000 kids and a pretty good show, despite the lack of sound-check time. We had a couple of days off. Mark accompanied the Doobs to the Caribou Ranch aboard their Doobieliner private jet, but I stayed behind with the lads on the night of October 24. I couldn't sleep.

❖ ❖ ❖

The police called at 5:30 in the morning. I called Bob Truax, our road manager, to let him know. Then I phoned around Boulder until I located Mark. And then I called the band. Phil Reed, our guitarist, had been found on the sidewalk outside of the Hilton after having either fallen or been pushed from his ninth floor balcony. There was a suspicious entry made from the adjoining balcony, an unoccupied room, and fingernail marks running down the side of the building, as if someone were trying to hold onto something, anything, for dear life. The police agreed: The clues made it look very much like foul play. Did Phil have any enemies? Did he do drugs?

I called Skip in Los Angeles. The previous night, he too had had visitors. He and his girlfriend were sitting at home when two armed men forced them to the floor and held guns to their heads. Skip was forced to empty his safe and warned to keep his nose clean, so to speak. If we can get to your biggest touring act, buddy, then we can certainly get to you.

While we scrambled to pull our shit together, the hotel had the decency to move us to another wing and to post security guards at our doors 24/7. Truax stayed with me. We bolted our doors. We stayed on a very low floor. The next morning, Detective Johnson assembled us all in our drummer Craig's room for a session of theories and possible suspects. Then, with barely enough cash to check out, we boarded a commercial jet and flew home. In our minds, the *Moving Targets* album had proven to be a self-fulfilling prophecy. It was over. Mama, open up. We're comin' back in. CBS, however, thought otherwise. They had paid for a tour and, by golly, they were going to get one.

On November 19, armed with our new guitarist, Billy Steele, we opened for Frank Zappa at Cobo Hall in Detroit and performed four encore songs with his band. Frank knew what we were going through. So did Belushi, who phoned about Frank's *Saturday Night Live* performance of the following evening. The entire rock community was very supportive and generous. I had always suspected as much, that when the chips were down, no real rocker would ever stand by and watch a brother in pain. I was correct.

In Toronto, Nancy's husband cornered me after our show at El Mocambo to speak to me, privately, of Nancy's infidelities. Why would I believe this con? Columbus, Boston, the Bottom Line once again, this time joined onstage by Dave Mason and Nicky Hopkins. And the next night, December 6, found us onstage in the Village with Mr. Zappa, himself, in the audience. He came up to do the encore with us, but our band knew none of his material, so that small part of history is, at least for me, disappointing in hindsight. I wish we had been more prepared.

TWENTY-NINE

Getting Spit On
by the Boss Himself!

On New Year's Eve of 1976–77, we headlined a concert at the Santa Monica Civic with Sparks—Ron and Russell Mael—and went to the Rose Bowl the next morning to see Nancy's Michigan lose. It had been one hell of a year.

Later that week, while up at the CBS offices to check on Starry Eyed, Don Ellis, our rep there, told us that Skip had lied about our cash advances and that our services were no longer needed. Screw 'em! They never got us anyway. They paid us some cash to go away, but we were crushed. We still had our weekly gig in Canada though.

One week in February, we were about to fly home from shooting the show in Toronto when we bumped into this weird, dreadlocked Caucasian kid who identified himself only as Natty Dreadlock. Sure, kid. Whatever. But this guy was a Springsteen roadie on his way to a gig in Cleveland and we had nothing better to do, so we went with him. By the time we got to the arena, the Boss was already onstage in the midst of one of his famous six-hour sound checks. Mark and I just hid in the audience, being as small as we could make ourselves. Ronnie Spector was there, onstage. We knew Ronnie. From the stage we heard, "Hey, Flo and Eddie! Are you guys out there? Come on up!"

Which we did. The Boss embraced us. Us! We rehearsed "Walking in the Rain," "Baby I Love You" and, of course, "Be My Baby." Singing on the mics with Miami Steve and getting spit on by the Boss himself—shit, I didn't even want to wipe the saliva off—was like a badge of honor. A great night. Bruce told us that we'd do it again soon. I was content with just this, but he was the one who was right.

The next week, we moved into Herb Cohen's office on Sunset Boulevard, wrote the spots for Alice Cooper's upcoming Anaheim concert, and spoke to our friend, TV producer Lorenzo Music, about doing a comedy pilot over at Universal. We had nothing to show him, really, that would demonstrate our comedy potential except for *200 Motels*. We had a screening of the film at Lorenzo's office and it was enough to get a development deal. Richard Lewis, my neurotic comedian friend, called me to offer his congratulations. News travels fast in Hollywood.

We were in the studio producing a group called the C. Y. Walkin' Band. We left town long enough to fly and then helicopter for the Sunfest in Lakeland, Florida, where we shared the stage with Orleans, Canned Heat, Richie Havens, the Atlanta Rhythm Section, Leon Redbone, Earl Scruggs, Jimmy Buffett, Jonathan Edwards, and Pure Prairie League. Nice.

We were still doing our Blind Date column and took about two weeks to do the soundtrack to an independent film called *Texas Detour* starring Patrick Wayne. Anything for a buck.

❖ ❖ ❖

Universal Studios, based on Lorenzo's recommendation, signed both Mark and me to a television development deal as he and his partner, Steve Pritzker, wrote our pilot episode. But hey, we couldn't act—funny is just something we were. Hence, the studio signed us up for an improv class with the great director and actor Howard Storm. It was fantastic. Some great actors were in that class. My pal Mackenzie Phillips was in there too, although she already had her own television series.

I was driving Nancy's '71 911 Porsche, which sucked money like a sieve, registering her daughter, Rebekah, at the pricy Immaculate Heart School, where Mary Tyler Moore famously attended classes, and hosting Alice Cooper's Anaheim show within the same week.

Nancy and I fought, and in June I wound up going solo to see the Doobie Brothers play a benefit concert at the Century Plaza Hotel. We sang the encore with them and I sat with Mackenzie, Candy Clark, Mo

Ostin, and Dinah Shore. I loved Dinah. I went to the theater twice that week, once to see a new movie called *Annie Hall* and a second time for a film called *Star Wars*. Not a bad season for new films at all.

On July 13, *Dirty Duck* opened citywide in Los Angeles to a resounding "So what?" but we were still taking classes, hosting concerts, and making ourselves feel useful on a daily basis, a practice that I still highly recommend. We wrote a song for Lorenzo and Steve called "Are You Ready," but they both hated it. I was depressed enough and then Elvis died on Tuesday, August 16. I had never met the man, but when reporters described the scene at Graceland that night, Elvis had been listening to records and our *Golden Hits* was one of them. Respect, Brother E.

ABC passed on us.

Polydor passed on us.

Groucho Marx died on Friday.

Not a good week.

We hosted again at Anaheim Stadium, this time with Lynyrd Skynyrd, Ted Nugent, Foreigner, and REO Speedwagon.

Lorenzo and Steve apologized for ragging on our song; there were hugs and words of encouragement and we kept on working for Universal and taking classes. That was the best part of my week. I loved doing the Viola Spolin space exercises and learning how to listen to other actors and still be funny.

Mark and I put together a charity bowling event with our graphic artist friends at Pacific Eye & Ear, who had done our last few album covers, and went on local television with our bowling pals, David Cassidy; his wife, Kay Lenz; and Marcia Strassman from *Welcome Back, Kotter* to promote it. The following week, Alice Cooper, David, and fifty-one other stars with whom we had been in phone contact made Rock 'n' Bowl a complete success.

◆ ◆ ◆

On Friday, September 16, the TV news announced the death of rock icon Marc Bolan and I cried for three solid days. I had never loved a man the way I loved Marc.

Herb Cohen officially became our manager in September, the same day as Nancy's final divorce papers came through. Lorenzo brought us down to CBS to meet Bud Grant and Bob Self, big cheeses in the TV department—we were moving ahead. The same week, we did our regular segment on *90 Minutes Live* for the Canadian Broadcasting Company. Our guest: the Amazing Randi. Strange, right?

We met our director, Doug Gordon, recorded the music for the pilot and shot *Happy Together*, the Flo and Eddie sitcom, along with our TV wives and families on October 6 at CBS Television City on Fairfax Avenue in Hollywood. Nancy and I celebrated with a fine Château Lafite Rothschild '64.

❖ ❖ ❖

Flo and Eddie were celebrities on Long Island. But still, we were somewhat shocked when we were contacted by somebody at Passport Records to produce local New York City heroes the Good Rats. They had released an album called *Tasty* on Warner Bros., so I sorta knew who they were. What they were, however, was astounding. The epitome of the band that doesn't sound the way they look, these guys, like us, were no poster boys. But their songs were fantastic and their lead singer, Peppi Marchello, was one of the best hard rock singers I'd ever heard. Brother Mickey played EBow feedback electric lead guitar, years before his time.

The label paired us up with engineer John Jansen, who proved to be magnificent, and, in a little studio on the Island, *From Rats to Riches* was recorded. "Taking It to Detroit," "Dear Sir," "Don't Hate the Ones Who Bring You Rock & Roll" . . . Truly a triumphant recording to this day. The band was great—really funny guys, that is, until the weed ran out. That's when the phone calls started. Eventually their "guy" came through, and in through the studio doors walked this Iggy Pop clone, complete with the requisite shoulder-length platinum Todd Rundgren hair.

"That's Joe Stefko," said Peppi Marchello, paying Joe for the pot. "He's a drummer."

Indeed.

Sadly, *From Rats to Riches*, which came out in 1978, never delivered on its promise. But for us, Joe Stefko did. We grabbed him up to play drums for us and he's still with us today.

❖ ❖ ❖

We were still recording with the Rats when we got the call from Lorenzo. Not only had CBS decided against picking up the pilot, they were going to recast the program and do it without us. Hey, that's showbiz. We really hadn't expected much more.

Back in New York, we checked into the swanky Drake Hotel on Park Avenue and walked over to the nearby Mayfair, where Bowie was waiting for us. Finally, that great long talk with David about the movie project. He explained his notes to us in greater detail. The movie was to be only a light exaggeration of David's real life: He eschewed flying around the globe. He was a man of taste and leisure and much preferred to spend two weeks sailing to America than the harrowing seven-hour flight from London. Once onboard, he would take on one of many secret identities—a prince, an author, a thin white duke—and stay in character for the entire cruise. It was these vignettes, his individual fantasies, that David wanted to share. We could help him. Obviously. We were the guys.

Volman borrowed a suit. We all went to Regine's, a legitimate NYC hot spot where we wouldn't have normally been allowed, but tonight we were cool. Tonight we were with Bowie.

We spent the next day with David as well. That night, we met David's assistant Coco Schwab and his friend King Crimson guitarist Robert Fripp and his wife, for a fantastic sushi feast.

The next afternoon, we met John Martin, our producer at CBC-TV, along with an entire remote crew, to film an exclusive interview in David's suite for our segment of *90 Minutes Live*. It was fantastic. It was long. It was perfect. We hugged, said our goodbyes, and limoed to Kennedy for our weekly Toronto flight. David never did finish the movie and we never heard another word about it. But if he called tomorrow and asked to take a meeting in Dubai, I'd be there. It's Bowie!!

❖ ❖ ❖

Nancy had flown to the Dominican Republic to file for a divorce from her husband and we got married on November 14, 1977, at Albertson's Chapel on Wilshire and La Brea. Instantly, the kids resented my presence, and I can't blame them. I wasn't Dad. And Nancy wasn't about to force the issue. But the rumblings of discontent were already sounding in the bedrooms down the hall.

THIRTY

Singers Don't Get Desks

The guys who had held a gun to Skip Taylor's head had shot a hole directly through the actual target on a copy of the *Moving Targets* album cover. They meant business. Together with Phil Reed's mysterious death, it was enough to make us give up the road for a good, long time. Luckily, the CBC was enamored of us as a comedy duo and gave us our own slot every Friday night on their *90 Minutes Live* program. It didn't pay a lot, but we got treated like stars and made new friends every week. We did a show with Harlan in Vancouver. The next week, it was Jay Leno and the following week, we brought up the Runaways and Kurt Vonnegut.

We took a new young comic named Robin Williams on his first limousine ride and the producers flew a crew to Los Angeles to film Mark and me chatting with Peter Noone, the Moody Blues' John Lodge, and the Beach Boys' Bruce Johnston. However, the icing on the cake was a long and soulful exchange with then bachelor and miscreant Tom Waits in his home in West Hollywood's infamous Tropicana Motel. Amidst the piles of rubble, Tom shakily spoke of his hard life and times and performed a ballad, accompanied only by his tuneless upright piano, that made me cry.

Meanwhile, NBC had been attempting to interview many of our friends for their *Midnight Special* Friday night show. However, they were having no luck securing the stars on their wish list who didn't feel like fake talk with a phony TV personality. So they negotiated a deal with us and the CBC. The first interview that aired was our Bowie conversation. Lou Reed watched it and insisted that only *we* be allowed to do his upcoming *Midnight Special* as well. Soon we were interviewing second-stringers and introducing rock videos and it got stupid.

But in Canada, we were still those Yanks on the telly every Friday.

❖ ❖ ❖

Martin Mull hosted the *Midnight Special* that taped on June 7 of '78 and his special guests were, guess who? Yep. Us again. We sang a great Australian hit song called "Natural Man" and did some memorable comedy shtick that still haunts me on YouTube. Still, I wonder to this day, why us? Guilt, I'm betting.

The band, such as it was, played a few really good shows at the Roxy and out at the Golden Bear in Huntington Beach, California. But best of all, Herb Cohen had given us an office to use however we saw fit, in his Moroccan-style complex on Sunset Boulevard, home to Frank's famous rehearsal studio. My former roommate Ona was our secretary and Herb's accountant, Dee, was helping with our finances, such as they were. Herb introduced us to his buddy Carl Gottlieb, who had cowritten the screenplay for *Jaws*. He had an idea for a script called *Roadies*, but had no time to actually write it, so he put us on a salary to sit in Herb's suite and construct a masterpiece. It was wonderful having an office. I had never had a day job before. Just having somewhere to be, somewhere where I wouldn't be underfoot at home, a desk and a parking space. It might not seem like much, but it imparted a false sense of importance to me. Singers don't get desks.

Things felt good. Then Melita got remarried and I had to sign a bunch of horrible papers. Emily wasn't a Kaylan anymore.

❖ ❖ ❖

Shortly after we finished the Good Rats project, Seymour Stein from Sire Records recruited us to produce a newly signed punk band from Boston called DMZ. We blindly accepted the challenge, being huge fans of the angry new genre. We booked a studio on Long Island and brought in our assistant engineer from the Good Rats project. This band, we were told, was hardcore. We didn't really know what that meant until the sessions got under way and the screaming began. The de facto leader of the band was their singer, Jeff "Monoman" Conolly. Amazingly true to the sound of the Pacific Northwest, circa 1967, this dude demanded no effects and no stereo bullshit, as he called it, and commanded absolutely no sales potential. His influences were the Sonics and the Wailers (the original '60s band, not the Bob Marley one), and if you didn't get it, he had no time for you.

On our third day in the studio, the biggest blizzard in twenty years hit the New York City area and we became snowed in to our subground studio. It was then that the band's drugs ran out. Things got bad fast. We slept under packing blankets, spread out in the studio and the control room. There was no food. No one wanted more coffee. The next day, Clay Hutchinson, the engineer, was able to shimmy out a window and bring back some greasy burgers. We tried to keep recording. On the song called "Cinderella," the drummer actually broke his hand. We left the sound of it happening on the album. It's a very short, angry record.

In the midst of the madness, something good *did* actually happen. We located those Chess Studios recordings that the Turtles had recorded way back in 1968 and that White Whale had shoved under some rug, never to see the light of day. And we took a meeting with our old Westchester High buddy Harold Bronson, who had graduated in my brother's class and gone on to co-own a very hip local music store called Rhino Records. Harold and fellow Rhino Richard Foos had corralled Larry "Wild Man" Fischer, a neighborhood schizophrenic who'd once made a record for Zappa, and had him record "Go to Rhino Records" back in 1975.

Harold, who had written about the Turtles for *Rolling Stone* and *NME*, knew exactly where these lost tunes fit into the history of the band and was anxious as hell to release them on his infant label, also called Rhino Records. Certainly, no one else cared. The best part was that this release was to be a picture disc—two beautiful photos of the band from back in the day pressed into the vinyl of the disc and packaged in a custom blue White Whale cardboard sleeve.

The fledgling label released the disc, which sold moderately, but more important, the pairing of the Turtles and Rhino Records was established and would shortly play an important part of our ongoing career. Destiny plans ahead.

Meanwhile, I was dropping Justin off at the Wagon Wheel, a school in Hollywood with approximately the same tuition as Harvard, and picking Rebekah up at Wonderland, fortunately a public school, but not for long.

Days were spent writing and holding court in the Bizarre offices and alternately listening to our latest obsessions, German electro pop and authentic Jamaican reggae music.

◆ ◆ ◆

Bowie asked us to do the radio ads for his latest album, so we worked on the copy, phoned our presentation to the RCA honchos in New York, went into tiny little Ascot Studios on Sunset, and had the resulting spots messengered to the city. *Lodger* was released the following Tuesday and our ads were national. It wasn't like making a record, but at least we were on the radio.

It was a stupid hot summer in 1979 but we had some giant shows booked on the East Coast in July. We appeared on Robert Klein's national radio show along with Tim Curry and Nick Lowe and hosted/opened for the Beach Boys at Monmouth Park Racetrack in New Jersey for 30,000 fans. On Saturday, July 14, we, the Beach Boys, the Cars, and Eddie Money played at the Yale Bowl for 50,000. On Sunday we split a bill with Hot Tuna's Jorma Kaukonen at Belmont Racetrack in the daytime and that evening found ourselves at that gross little club with squishy floors on Long Island called My Father's Place. Michael "Eppy" Epstein, the owner, had a reggae barbecue party before the gig at his house with the infamous scuzzy hot tub, and the next afternoon I met his secretary, Susan Olsen. Flags should have been raised, but they weren't.

◆ ◆ ◆

When we returned to L.A., we resumed our normal routine at Herb's. Ona on the intercom. A call for us? Chuck Swenson, the animator from *200 Motels*, was phoning from across the street at the Murakami-Wolf animation offices. Did the two of us have any interest in writing songs for a children's animated special? American Greeting Cards owned this little girl character and was looking to sell dolls and lunchboxes through a saturation television and marketing campaign. We didn't know what that meant, but if somebody needed a few songs and had cash in pocket, we were their guys.

We had Andy Cahan bring his portable keyboard into the office on Monday afternoon, and Mark and I knocked out the three most important songs of the new project. The following day, we played the songs for Chuck, and on Wednesday, we played the songs over the phone to the project's producer, Romeo Muller, in New York. He loved them too. Romeo had written the timeless Rankin/Bass TV classics *Rudolph the Red-Nosed Reindeer*, *Frosty the Snowman*, and others so this might actually work. We were writers for hire, but what the hell? Maybe this new character would take off.

As it turns out, *Strawberry Shortcake* was and continues to be huge. Our song "Smile a Sunny Morning," one of the three that we whipped off that afternoon, is still used in the Macy's Thanksgiving Day parade whenever the Strawberry float comes out of mothballs. We wrote and recorded the entire soundtrack for *The World of Strawberry Shortcake* and helped Chuck produce the voices, the amazing Russi Taylor as Strawberry and the hilarious Bob Ridgely as the Peculiar Purple Pieman. That first time, especially, was magical.

We kept getting requests to return to My Father's Place, the club with the squishy floors, but flying a band back and forth to New York seemed pretty impractical. Then a familiar figure stepped up to the plate: Joe Stefko, the guy who had brought weed to the Good Rats sessions. He had been all over the world playing drums for Meat Loaf on the *Bat Out of Hell* tour, worked with Mick Ronson and Ian Hunter, and even braved Europe with John Cale. Joe would put a band together for us. They'd learn the entire set and all we'd have to do is show up.

We arrived a few days early to rehearse and had to pass by the New York Jets' training facility between Joe's house and the rehearsal hall. Jim Pons was now working there, having persuaded the Jets that they needed a film department to shoot isolated players for review during the week ahead. All the teams were doing it. With his media experience, Jim was hired on the spot and remained with the Jets until he retired and handed his position to—wait for it—our ex-drummer John Seiter, who only recently retired.

❖ ❖ ❖

On September 4, 1979, we drove into New York and met Bruce Springsteen, Steve Van Zandt, and Bruce's manager, Jon Landau, at the Power Station to put backing vocals on a new song called "Hungry Heart." Jon sent the four of us into the studio to sing four-part harmonies, but when we listened back, something sounded terribly wrong.

"Somebody is really singing flat," came Landau's voice from the control room. So we listened back and heard it ourselves. He was right. It was wrong. Back out there to try it again.

"Nope. Still flat."

Shit. I prayed that it wasn't me. These guys were paying us to deliver a killer track for the Boss and somebody was letting him down.

"Um, Bruce, you wanna come in here for a second?"

Springsteen trotted to the booth. We couldn't hear the conversation, but Bruce was listening and nodding his head in agreement.

"Why don't you guys try this on your own?"

So the three of us did and it sounded great. It had been him. The Boss was singing flat. Then Landau had an idea. He asked Bruce to strap on his guitar.

"Try it now," he insisted.

And it was perfect. It was all about stance and attitude. With that axe slung over his shoulder, Bruce's Bossiness returned and he was in his element again. And the record tells the story. Mark and I overdubbed the harmonies a few times and listened to the all-important playback.

"I think we got it!" Landau said. It still didn't sound like a Springsteen hit to me, but I have never been so happy to be wrong.

Still, no one was sure if it would make the album or not—they were considering something like forty songs. It sure didn't *sound* like a Bruce record. There were no motorcycles, no Wendy in the night. It was more like a Top 40 single than an FM anthem. We left the studio without much hope for the song despite having had a great time, as always, just hanging around those guys.

The following year "Hungry Heart" became Springsteen's first Top Ten single.

❖ ❖ ❖

Back to L.A. to host the *Billboard* Awards (before they became such a big deal) at the Century Plaza hotel. The *Strawberry Shortcake* TV show was finished and all that remained was to come up with her theme. No problem. Who sleeps all night in a cake made of strawberries? Strawberry Shortcake, wouldn't you know.

The very next day, we met with *Laugh In*'s Chris Bearde about becoming head writers on his new pilot for Murray Langston, *The Unknown Comic*. We were hired. And hey, we'd be working with a guy we already knew from high school, our pal Phil Hartman. Phil's brother John was Poco's manager and Phil had designed their logo. Chris's office was on the Santa Monica Promenade, just down from the King's Head pub. I was about to spend a lot of time and many lunches at the old King's Head.

We shot the pilot at KCOP studios on Sunset and on the streets of L.A. It was corny, but funny in a vaudevillian way. We were satisfied and pretty well compensated. The day after the shoot, we flew, first class, to Chicago and drove to the Playboy Resort in Lake Geneva, Wisconsin, to produce a great midwestern band, Roadmaster, for Mercury Records. Together with our L.A. engineer extraordinaire, John Stronach, we had formed a company called I'm a Legend, You're a Legend specifically for this project. These guys were brilliant and never got their chance to go national. We hoped that with *Fortress*, they would have that shot. We realized that we were in trouble when Mercury refused the cover art, which showed a model being chased down by a semi. It was gorgeous. They said it was sexist. They put out the album in a yellow cover with an obelisk on the cover. What?

When I called my dad from Lake Geneva to wish him a happy birthday on November 15, my mother was in the hospital for tests. The '70s came to an end with a lot of doubt, too many spinning plates, and not enough income to justify the work and the angst.

THIRTY-ONE

Hey Ma, Look—I'm a Performance Artist!

They say it never rains in Southern California. Well, on February 16, 1980, it poured—man, it poured! The mountainside behind my little house at the top of Hollywood Hills Road came down and into my famous black-bottomed pool. The water overflowed, causing a torrent of mud to come cascading into my neighbor's yard and taking out his living room. The fire department came. There were sandbags. The community helped me shore up our little stucco box and I helped keep the storm drains open all night. The TreePeople laid out tarps and filled sandbags. The entire Canyon broke out from the poison oak that was ubiquitous. The kids were staying with friends when they could, but we were all contagious and at each other's throats. The fighting began.

In March, Suzanne Somers called—really—and we dressed like bunnies to sing "Elenore" and "Happy Together" on her big Easter Seals Telethon. The producers had passed on our initial offer to perform "Keep It Warm." Yeah, good call. And, during that very week, Rhino Records decided to release our bizarre Rhythm Butchers series of EPs—mostly fun hotel-room stuff recorded on cassette while winding down after gigs and during all-night drives or on the way to concerts—and our first *Strawberry Shortcake* TV special aired in L.A. We were broke, but you wouldn't know it. That, my friends, is the key to a successful show-business career.

Necessity being what it is, inspiration was now guiding us. It certainly wasn't an invisible bearded guy. We had an epiphany. We had always sung about being cheap little guys and now it was time to put that claim to the test. It was Howard and Mark and Andy Cahan, the keyboard guy and all-around verbal punching bag. Andy had graduated from driving down to Santa Anita with our bet money every day and was back playing keyboards. It wasn't exactly a three-man operation. We named it Flo and Eddie's 2½-Man Show. We're talking a lot of years before Charlie Sheen.

We flew down a road manager, an Englishman who was working for a sound company in Sacramento, named Mick Coles. We gathered our old tour slides together. We rented Don Preston's old drum machine. We bought a portable screen, projector, and professional reel-to-reel tape deck. We took the vocals off our hit records so that we could sing live over the tracks and we created new bits. Pink Floyd was huge with "The Wall," so we sped up their hit, unrolled a bamboo rug, and threw stuffed animals over the thing from behind as it transformed into Flo and Eddie's "The Fence." We opened the show in yellow plastic hazmat suits, coming out of a fog of incense being coughed out of two bee smokers charged with smoldering charcoal, to the strains of an original German-style tech recording. We did our bits. We sang our hits.

Our first test show was on April 8 at the Ice House in Pasadena. It was a sellout. It was over two hours long and it got us a standing ovation. This might actually work. We had created something brand-new. Hey Ma, look—I'm a performance artist!

❖ ❖ ❖

By the time we finished our first little tour of America and Canada and returned home to count our losses, Rebekah was hanging out on Hollywood Boulevard. Nancy blamed me and we weren't speaking. My White House photos had been taken off the walls and placed down in the flooded basement to be ruined: Nancy never liked American politics much, anyway. Melita, meanwhile, had given me a court order to sell and surrender her half of the house. Good times. The house sold instantly and I knew already that I'd be making my next move, as always, alone. On July 26, the family moved out. On the 27th, the SOLD sign went up in Laurel Canyon and I bought a tiny little shack with an enormous garden in Studio City. I'd just sit there. The only company I had was my accountant's secretary, Maggie Lawrence, who supplied the occasional flirtation. Empathy, at least.

Flo and Eddie made a deal with our pals at WLIR, a radio station on Long Island, to do a weekly specialty show for their Sunday night lineup. We would record the shows out in Fullerton in Orange County, and then send the shows, on tape, to New York and pretend to take phone calls, do local ads, and give the overall appearance that we were doing a local show. It was silly and it paid hardly anything, but it helped and we needed it badly. Every once in a while we'd actually have a gig on the East Coast and do a show live on the air. That helped the illusion.

We did the Bottom Line with the 2½-Man Show in early September and I went back to my hotel with Susan, the receptionist from My Father's Place. I still couldn't see the trouble clouds gathering offshore.

We were playing bars now: the Fast Lane, the Long Run, Toad's Place; Bill's Meadowbrook for our friends in the New York Jets organization.

I guess I fucked up again. I thought my marriage was over. One night, after we did a show at the Roxy, I took Maggie home, crashed into a center divider, and taxied to my new house. I was very confused. It was my first brush with therapy. My doctor told me that I was a fool to try to save my marriage. Her analogy was of returning a second time to a bottle of spoiled milk expecting the milk to be better. $250.

One night, Maggie made spaghetti as sort of a housewarming dinner. That same night, Nancy decided to see how I was doing, saw a voluptuous brunette serving me food, and threw a brick at us, smashing in the entire glass front of the house, and leaving us picking shards out of the carpet for weeks. Maggie held down the fort, so to speak (in fact, it *was* a little fort with walls facing the street and only my garden paths and gazebo visible from my living room), and I would fly off to Jamaica.

❖ ❖ ❖

Mark's and my obsession with reggae had gone so far that our national reputation as fans of the genre preceded us everywhere, and Michael "Eppy" Epstein of My Father's Place, also an aficionado, actually put up the cash and enlisted his buddy Warren Smith, of Epiphany Records, a niche label in San Francisco, to get us to make an authentic reggae record using the real players and the actual location. We flew into Kingston with Warren and his wife, stopped off in Trelawny Beach to score some native greenery and eventually found the tiny Indies hotel. There were no windows here. Just shutters.

The real pot was to be had at the studio itself. We were to record at Bob Marley's Tuff Gong Studio, which was pretty much his house. Earl "Chinna" Smith, the Jamaican guitarist who was coproducing the album with Errol Brown, Mark, and me, picked us up the first day just to sit around and play songs—we really didn't have an agenda at all; we were just dumbstruck being in this fantasy world. Before we even walked into the studio, Chinna made sure we stopped at Juicy's Hut. Juicy sold fruits and other sustainables to the island locals, about twenty feet away from the main house. And we bought tons of it, figuring that happy players guaranteed a happy album.

Things got a bit too happy, although the quality of musicians—Jamaican legends including Augustus Pablo, Carlton "Santa" Davis, Leslie "Professor" Butler, Aston "Family Man" Barrett, and the rest—was beyond world class. We all got wasted—again, what would *you* have done?—and we all had a great time. We recorded "Happy Together," roots style, which made the players smile. That song has become sort of an island standard now, I'm proud to say. We also cut my parents' favorite song, "Prisoner of Love," in a romantic island style. I was singing it for them. They hated what I was doing to my life and couldn't understand where they'd gone wrong.

❖ ❖ ❖

We got home to pick up checks from Maggie at Marty's office for the second *Strawberry Shortcake* special. The Boss came to town around Halloween and, hot on the heels of *The River*'s success, enlisted Mark and me to sing on as many live shows as we could to get a version of "Hungry Heart" that would sound good enough to use on his new live record. Limos took us to the L.A. Sports Arena and the event was star-studded, as one would imagine. And there he was—after all these years—backstage, just milling around, Bob fucking Dylan. I had to approach him.

"Mr. Dylan," I sputtered. "Hi. I'm Howard Kaylan from the Turtles. Thanks for writing our first hit."

"Was it any good?"

"Yeah, I think so."

"So we both made money then?"

"Yessir."

And he shook my hand. "Well then, I thank you. Let's do her again sometime."

And that was it. Four sentences in fifteen years.

Ronald Reagan was elected president the day after Bruce's final L.A. gig. Born in the USA, indeed.

Maggie quit her job at Marty Fox's office to become Jeff Conaway's personal assistant on the set of *Taxi*—see the trouble coming, kids?—and I finished up the reggae vocals at the Indigo Ranch in Malibu. Monday night, John Lennon was murdered and I cried all night for all of us.

Christmas wasn't about the kids, although I still saw Emily, of course, as well as Justin. Rebekah had been seen around town, but that was all.

Bruce flew us to New York for more live show recordings at Nassau Coliseum and we flew home on New Year's Eve. We ushered in 1981 on-stage at the Roxy and I've never been more befuddled about my life than I was right then.

THIRTY-TWO

Who the Hell Are These Fat Guys, and Why Are They Here?

I said goodbye to Maggie, flew to New York, played two nights at the Ritz with the 2½-Man Show to raves and great crowds and Susan Olsen from My Father's Place. Then Mark, Andy, Mick, and I flew the six and a half hours to London, completely bypassed customs, and were driven to the Virgin Records townhouse in Shepherd's Bush, where Richard Branson, the founder of the Virgin empire, made us eggs and gave us the toots and the scotch whiskey that sent us off to bed. He always liked us and helped out whenever he could. Some incredibly successful people deserve to be where they are and never forget their friends.

Jann, our tour promoter, lived in Denmark, so it was there that we went to see how this scaled-down attempt at performance art would fly. Shows in and around Copenhagen went well. The crowd was mostly college age and usually Zappa freaks and curiosity seekers. The show was relevant, artsy, and incredibly cheap, and to the European audience at large, that meant that you were making a social statement, whether you were or not. The phone calls home were costing as much as I was making, but sanity has no price. We returned to London, where they totally got it. In Amsterdam, Andy and I walked the red-light district and laughed our asses off. They got it there too. All over Germany, it worked. In Stockholm, we got to do a fifteen-minute segment of our live show in front of a national audience from the Studio Club. Our set there went really well too and that night, a new Irish band visited our dressing room for autographs and advice upon the release of their first album. We shook their hands. Adam, Larry, Bono, and the Edge. Good luck, kids.

❖ ❖ ❖

I got home to find Jeff Conaway in the hospital for advanced syphilis and gonorrhea. Maggie got a shot—just for protection. Andy Kaufman called. We traded VD jokes. He said I was a genius. I laughed my ass off.

In April, our second *Strawberry Shortcake* TV special aired while we were in New York meeting with the Strawberry team about doing the third one—at a reduced rate, of course—and we went back to Europe again. We should have stayed home. After a week of shows, our German booking agent had proven to be a flake, the tour got canceled, and all of our money was stolen from a hotel safe in Bonn. The next day, we joined Springsteen onstage in Amsterdam, but despite the after-show partying, we had nothing left to say to one another. Mark and I rode back to our hotel in uncomfortable silence.

In July, after being treated for any number of sexually retransmitted diseases, Maggie gave up making excuses and quietly left the little house on Landale Street. I saw my doctor. He said I was fine. I got vaccinated anyway. Always a great judge of human nature.

Our final WLIR radio show ran on July 5, 1981, and we were out of that business. Again, we did interviews with *Rolling Stone*, *NME*, and the *New York Times*, but basically, we were unemployed and unemployable. We did have some more live shows to record with Bruce in L.A., and our buddy Richard Lewis demanded to be introduced to his idol, the Boss. We were only too happy to oblige.

Mutt Cohen had a check for us from K-tel, the conglomerate that released anthology albums. He had made a deal to lease them "Happy Together" for use on a compilation. We didn't technically own the master—yet—but our attorney was taking a calculated risk here and not only did it pay off, but the cash was absolutely needed.

Then we got a life-altering call. It was Joe Stefko, the drummer who had helped us out a while back by putting a band together for us. He had seen Flo and Eddie's 2½-Man Show, but it really wasn't music, was it?

Why not, he suggested, let *him* come to the rescue again by putting together a band of the best players in New York and we could just fly in and do the shows? Why not, indeed. And that's how Joe wound up being the Turtles' drummer for the past thirty-two years and counting.

Our world tour consisted of shows at My Father's Place and the Bottom Line, but the band was fantastic and it felt amazing to front a group again instead of a tape machine or—no offense, Ange—a half-man. I spent those days with Susan. What the fuck!

❖ ❖ ❖

Herb moved out of the Zappa offices and pretty much hung up his manager's shoes, so Mark and I, fully aware of how important maintaining an office had become, moved in with our graphic design friends at Pacific Eye & Ear on La Cienega. We found things to do during the day, afternoons were often spent with Harry Nilsson at V.J.'s bar on Sunset, and my nights were reserved for the now-familiar two-hour coast-to-coast phone shenanigans.

Mark and I flew to Manhattan during the first week in October to sing with Jan and Dean onstage and with Steve Forbert in the studio. I spent my nights with Susan and ignored the incoming calls from the front desk all morning. Finally, my brother, Al, got through. My mother had suffered a heart attack and was in the hospital. Here I was, 3,000 miles away, fornicating like a crazed weasel, and life was begging me to pay attention.

Marriage? What marriage? Ring? What ring? Oh, the one that you and your mother already picked out! See the funny little clown. We took a taxi to the Garden City Exchange and, at my most vulnerable, I bought Susan the lock to my future.

Now that Mutt Cohen had opened the floodgates, requests were coming in for the Turtles' recordings from all over the world. We were getting TV offers. And we were singing in the studio with the Knack at night. On the first of November, with volume four of the Rhythm Butchers in release and exhausted from our Halloween concert at the Greek Theater, Maggie called from Las Vegas, where she had just gotten married. Congratulations to the groom, baby.

I was back at the Gramercy Park on December 20 as we started to map out the TV pilot for George Honchar, our mentor and producer at Imero

Fiorentino Associates. It was just another offer and just another meeting, but this one actually worked out. Our discussions led to three Flo and Eddie television specials (later edited down to two), which were syndicated by Metromedia and ran in New York City on CBS late Friday and Saturday night. We filmed street bits with the Guardian Angels and at the Fulton Fish Market at dawn. We interviewed Kiss and Mackenzie Phillips and introduced America to Twisted Sister and the Catholic Girls. We sat behind a desk. Our announcer was named Vince Manze: He went on to run the NBC Agency.

❖ ❖ ❖

As the year ended, we were onstage for the first of many years of sold-out holiday shows at the Bottom Line and I felt more New York than L.A. I was talking to Susan on the phone daily and waiting. Maggie would call in the middle of the night and I either indulged her briefly or ignored the incessant ringing. One night, someone shot the windshield out of my little car. You just gotta move on.

Sue came to live with me and my little cat, Ozzie, in the little Landale house in February 1982. Maggie kept calling and ruining the mood. Susan and I found solace, as a couple, with our NYC friends Steve Duboff (he of Soupy Sales fame) and his wife, Maureen. They had an amazing house on the beach at Malibu and enjoyed the same things that we did, which in 1982 meant cheesy horror movies and inhaling substances. After a few more movie nights, the Duboffs would volunteer their home for our upcoming nuptials.

In the real world, our third *Strawberry Shortcake* TV special was written and recorded, our fifth Rhythm Butchers EP was coming out, and Rhino had agreed to release a high-concept record that we hadn't even recorded yet. On February 24, the two of us and Andy went into Sun Swept Studio in Studio City, armed with only our toy Casio keyboards, to record our album *Checkpoint Charlie*, an unabashed Kraftwerk spoof. Songs included "Show Me the Way to Go Ohm" and "Charlie Does Surf." It took us six hours. Harold was so excited, he released the record on vinyl in a limited edition that only played from the inside out. That's right. You put the needle down next to the label and the disc played out toward the record's edge. It was hilarious. So were the graphics. Too bad the record wasn't better. Still, since we had our greatest hits out on Sire, Harold was the only guy who wanted to release all of the individual albums on their own. And with advice from Mutt and Herb, we entered into our first real deal with Rhino Records.

Another Easter, another telethon. We wore bunny suits and got to guest host a segment. And from Team Strawberry, a great new animated project, *Peter and the Magic Egg*. Basically, the purpose of this one was to hawk Easter egg dye from the Paas Company. And their lead character was a rabbit named Peter Paas. I'm not proud of it, but the coolest part of this one was working and writing for the cartoon's narrator, Ray Bolger, the scarecrow in *The Wizard of Oz*. The script was stupid, but we wrote a great song for Mr. Bolger, which he hated. Not bouncy enough. Give me a C—a bouncy C—for real. And he helped us rewrite the tune to fit his vaudevillian mentality. The script was still weak, but I got to sit on a piano bench next to the Scarecrow and teach him my little song, which he recorded. Nice.

Our TV shows aired in New York on April 9 and 10. We did great on Friday and of course got creamed by *SNL* the next night. Duh! I would never have predicted any other outcome. But it was going to be okay. Mutt and Herb were meeting with Harold about assigning the entire Turtles catalog to Rhino. We had a dozen offers. Big stuff. But Harold was hungry. Rhino had no real acts. We would become the first major act on the label and the first catalog act that would launch that label into the stratosphere as the premier classic rock label in the world.

❖ ❖ ❖

On April 18, Sue and I got married at Steve Duboff's house on Pacific Coast Highway. My parents were there. Her mom was on the phone. I got rip-roaring drunk and began serenading the cars on the busy coastal thoroughfare till the CHiPs made me stop.

Back to Manhattan, and up to Todd Rundgren's house to listen to his new project, the Psychedelic Furs from England. The infamous Butler brothers, Richard and Tim. We showed up at Todd's home studio the next day. Who the hell are these fat guys and why are they here? We don't want no poncey fairy voices! Even I could see their point. But they were wrong and Rundgren knew it. We sang on about half of *Forever Now*, even stayed a couple of nights in the guesthouse. We shook hands at the end and were about to fly home when Todd asked if we wanted to hear the Furs' single. Then he played "Love My Way" and Mark and I knew that we had to be a part of that record. What we added made it even more mysterious and weird than it was without us, and I'd like to think it was one reason for the song's international success. I'd like to think!

Things were popping now. Rhino released a turtle-shaped disc, we got copies of and a check from Strawberry, and we had taken a meeting with Westchester guy and fledgling director Allan Arkush, about his musical comedy spoof *Get Crazy*. Volman didn't like his role—he was to play a drummer in the Stones-ish band fronted by Malcolm McDowell—while I read for the part of Captain Cloud, the bearded hippie leader of a pack of bus-riding flower people. Typecasting. The day before the movie began principal photography, Mark walked and was replaced by John Densmore of the Doors.

It was, actually, a wonderful experience. And it earned me my SAG card, a commodity not easy to come by as a novice actor. My trailer(!) was next to Malcolm's. Daniel Stern was the romantic lead. Lou Reed was amazing. Ed Begley Jr. and Fabian and Bobby Rydell. Veteran Allen Goorwitz actually gave me notes. When I wasn't just hanging out backstage holding court, I was watching Allen do the setups and make movie magic. My scenes were few and far between, but Allen was a huge fan and wanted me to experience the world of cinema firsthand. I loved it.

I leased a spiffy new car. Mistake. When the picture wrapped and the money ran out, the spiffy new car went back to the dealership and I swallowed my pride and my payments. The movie never really had a major release either, but if you've never seen it, I highly recommend it. It really is a hilarious and smart rock movie.

In 1983, we were back at Elektra Studios with Roy Thomas Baker and a British band called Espionage. These were just kids who had made a demo for Roy that he really liked. He recorded their tracks for them with his amazing, portable 64-track, the machine responsible for the multiple tracks on Queen's "Bohemian Rhapsody"; took the band into the studio to do vocals; and then realized that they had recorded the entire project in a key far too high for the singer. In the olden times, before Pro Tools, when everything was recorded on wide strips of magnetic tape, there was no way to correct this error except to record all the tracks again. But the band was in England and Roy had no plans to return there in his foreseeable future. So Mark and I got to be Espionage and we sang the entire project. Gunslingers for hire.

And now we were making records for the Care Bears too, twelve fuzzy little fellas who lived in the clouds. They were all pastel colors and each wore their special emotions as symbols on their adorable tummies. American Greetings, the folks who gave us Strawberry Shortcake, were responsible for these guys too. There were no villains. There were no stories, just uplifting life lessons.

Wouldn't you turn to me for uplifting life lessons? No?

❖ ❖ ❖

The little Landale house was just too small, and with the eventual winning of the White Whale lawsuit, all of their remaining unspent assets, of which there were precious few, reverted to me and Mark. But we also won the rights to the Turtles' name and, perhaps most important, the two of us were awarded all of the band's master recordings and the rights to use our own names again. Check it out—you can count on one hand the number of bands from the '60s, '70s, or even now, who own their records. When you hear "Happy Together" used on *The Simpsons*, or in *Shrek* or *Adaptation* or the countless television commercials that have, thankfully, licensed our little master, remember that all of that booty is split between me and Mark.

Susan and I bought a house at the corner of Vantage and Hillslope in the Laurel Canyon foothills, with an Olympic pool and a badminton court. I was across the street from my *Cheers* friend, George Wendt, Ed Begley was three houses away, and Ed Asner often had to park in front of my place when his kids came to visit.

On Tuesday nights, at exactly midnight, George would sneak his old Beemer out of the garage, roll up to my house with his headlights off, and the two of us would get blotto on our way to this crowded little alt-rock club far to the east on Hollywood Boulevard. We'd stay until closing, around 3:30 or 4, and sneak back home with our wives never the wiser. I loved L.A. then. I was never going to leave.

THIRTY-THREE

Turtles Once Again

The drive from my Studio City home, over the Canyon, to our new office at Imero Fiorentino's new L.A. headquarters, took about fifteen minutes; the return, during rush hour, was twice as long. Our New York producer, George Honchar, was in charge of the West Coast operation. He knew that we needed an office, took pity on us, and gave us a space there for "development." The only caveat was that we were also to chaperone the young candidates for Miss USA, Miss Universe, and the Miss Teen pageants. Nice work if you can get it. We earned our keep. We were good boys too. We got very good at organizing large groups of young women. When we weren't writing stuff or accompanying the ladies to Las Vegas, we would still do shows as Flo and Eddie with the band from New York. The rest of our time was spent trying to be creative. We nicknamed our little operation Alternative Vocations and did pretty much anything for a buck while listening to German techno and our beloved reggae.

Melita decided that Los Angeles wasn't where she wanted to be, and with very little notice, she and Emily packed up and moved to Bellevue, Washington, a then-sleepy bedroom community less than ten miles from downtown Seattle. I wouldn't be seeing them any time soon. Emily Not-a-Kaylan didn't live here anymore.

The Turtles' catalog was doing a lot of our work for us. Mutt was licensing our hits all over the world and was leasing the use of our master recordings for soft drinks and automobiles. Then, one little phone call and everything changed yet again. It was from the offices of a Manhattan-based lawyer and promoter named David Fishof. He had an idea. He wanted to package a good old-fashioned rock 'n' roll tour, à la Dick Clark's original Caravan of Stars, and our name came up. Would we be interested? Because if we *were*, he intended to call the show the Happy Together tour. Well, this sounded pretty good to us. If the tour worked, we might be able to tour with this name forever—Turtles once again. The powers that be certainly couldn't do a tour called Happy Together without the Turtles.

It was a lucky day for all involved. We had tour buses and equipment trucks. There were light guys and sound guys and local radio tie-ins. As a band, we had decided that riding in the corporate tour bus was not for us, so we elected to get our own vehicle and follow behind.

The lineup was our old friends Spanky and Our Gang, who opened the concert, followed by Gary Puckett, who performed the entire tour in a red leather jumpsuit that he would air out on a hanger in the tour bus all night; then the Association, Laurel Canyon buddies; and we closed the show, followed by an all-hands-on-deck encore. It was great, and it worked. The following summer we did it all again with a slightly different lineup and this time, we were really organized and actually had a sponsor, Members Only. We all had matching black tour jackets with our names embroidered on the front.

Everyone was riding on the tour buses, but not us. We valued our privacy far too much. We found a big old RV that we could call our own. Stefko and I commandeered the back room, which sat directly over the rear tires, and turned it into Mary-Land with cutout photos of Mary Tyler Moore all over the walls and cabinets. We played obnoxiously loud classic oldies and bounced around so badly that my back *still* gives me grief. No one went back there but the two of us. And we worshipped Mary to an insane degree. It was mostly to keep our minds from the dreariness of travel, but we had a great time with our obsession.

❖ ❖ ❖

One night in Minneapolis, the two of us stole the motor home, grabbed a bunch of weed, and parked in front of the house that was used for the exteriors on the original *Mary Tyler Moore Show*. It took us hours to find it—the first time. We unfolded the tiny dining table and delicately sepa-rated the red and purple threads of the marijuana from the green ones. Then we would roll a joint of just the red ones. Then, just the green ones. It was stupid and it really didn't work. But it was a ritual and we needed religion. Afterward, we silently stole rocks and pebbles from the garden and drove back to our hotel like the thieves that we were. I still have my "Mary rocks." Years later, when we told this story to Mary, she looked rather disturbed but chalked it up to our being musicians. I think her response was, "Yeah, right."

These tours were long and grueling affairs. In 1985, we started off rehearsing at the Abbey in Lake Geneva, Wisconsin, on April 10 and stayed out on the road until the season ended in September. It was hard work: I figure that, when all is said and done, I get paid for all of the stupid travel associated with the road. That's what kills ya. I swear, after all of the pent-up angst following an all-night drive, I'd do the damned shows for nothing. But man, you had better be prepared to pay me for my travel time. And with every season spent on tour, my mind and body crave their own bed and that warm body to curl up next to, more than they ever did as a kid. I'm not one of those guys who intends to give up the ghost in some cheesy motel room a million miles from home. But you, dear reader, will know if I ever made it. It'll be too late for yours truly by then.

It was astounding to see the enormous and appreciative audiences that attended the first year of shows. There were the screaming girls again. Or their daughters. Or their granddaughters. We didn't care. What mattered was that here, in these huge arenas and at state fairs, three gen-erations of fans were all singing "Happy Together" as if one. It was an eye-opening and rewarding stage experience that continues to this day.

In '86, Fishof brought us out again with another lineup of classic artists. This year, VH1 sponsored the tour, so the network covered the event daily in its news. A big-time Hollywood movie called *Making Mr. Right* used "Happy Together" as its theme, so the two of us did a new video for the film. VH1 put the video into rotation and Mark and I wound up hosting their Top Ten countdown for the week. TV again. We were almost relevant.

It was another high-paying, hardworking summer, and we all thought that these seasonal tours would last forever. But we were wrong. The following year, Fishof picked up the Monkees for management as well as

Ringo Starr. Now he had bigger fish to fry than our little tour, so we were left on the sidelines, so to speak. Mark and I took a meeting with David to pitch our idea for a rock 'n' roll fantasy camp. He was fascinated by the concept, which had never crossed his mind and would take a certain amount of cash to launch. He still runs the Rock 'n' Roll Fantasy Camp. It's made him many millions of dollars and is franchised all over the world, but we never got a dime or any credit. He remains high on my list of show-business bastards.

With the Monkees tour out during the summer of 1987, we were flung back into the world of one-nighters. Fishof's partner in the tour operation, Howard Silverman, decided to leave his sleazy New York partner, moved west to Ojai, California, and started his own agency, Paradise Artists, with whom we still work today. In a world of dishonest creeps, we finally found a good guy. Based on the success of the Happy Together tours, it was decided that we would try to raise our concert price to be competitive in the very crowded music marketplace. Which we did, by about 250 percent. Supply and demand. It worked. We would never be the Beach Boys, but we could certainly, and finally, command a pretty decent dollar when it came to concert appearances.

❖ ❖ ❖

And we worked a lot. No tour buses or RVs for us now. John Hoier, our L.A. engineer, found an old Bluebird school bus that we painted white and nicknamed the Gullfire. It was old and had no shock absorbers to speak of. It broke down constantly and we finally gave up on it when we had to push it into the hotel parking lot in Minneapolis.

We were back to station wagons and a roadie or two in a Hertz truck. There were many lonely hours out there, and Joe and I decided to fill them by collecting fine, first-edition books. Most of these were by popular contemporary horror and fantasy authors such as Stephen King and Harlan Ellison. We spent thousands on books in an era when our peers were collecting drugs. We started attending conventions where these extraordinary people gathered. We attended the World Fantasy Convention in Providence, Rhode Island, and we were hooked. I began to explore the idea of writing fiction, and when the brilliant author Tim Powers attended one of our California shows, Joe asked him if he would be interested in releasing a limited edition of his latest volume called *The Stress of Her Regard*. It was an amazingly beautiful handmade volume that sold for hundreds of dollars and launched Joe's career as a publisher of fine and rare books. Powers would soon write *On Stranger Tides*, which was made into a Disney pirate movie twenty years later. And Joe continues his other job as the owner of the Charnel House publishing company.

As a band, we were doing so much flying from coast to coast it was getting cost-prohibitive to do shows in the West. That is, until we stumbled on the ultimate solution: We got Andy Cahan, our L.A. keyboard player, to assemble a band of superior musicians in Southern California. They would be our West Coast band. The division of work was simple. If the shows were east of the Rockies or the mighty Mississippi, depending on the costs involved, the New York band did the concerts. In the West, it was Andy's group. We saved thousands on each and every show. We still tour this way. I don't know why every band doesn't do the same thing.

The West Coast band played a party for the Super Bowl when it was played at the Rose Bowl. We were doing a lot of session work: the *Autoamerican* album with Blondie, three or four albums with Alice, Livingston Taylor, the Knack, one with the Guess Who's Burton Cummings. We did a great record with Roy Thomas Baker producing. It was an album called *Thunder* by Andy Taylor, the guitar hero from Duran Duran. We got to work with Steve Jones from the Sex Pistols, an idol of mine, who was producing with Roy's 64-track recorder. We stacked up so many vocals, only the skilled hand of a master producer could make it still resemble a rock album and not the Mormon Tabernacle Choir. You crank this sucker up and your walls will move. Life couldn't possibly have been better.

❖ ❖ ❖

During the summer of 1987, we were touring across America on the Happy Together tour. I was doing my laundry backstage in Memphis at the Mud Island Amphitheater when I got a phone call from my father. Panicking, I answered the phone tentatively. I expected the worst, but instead, my dad was actually happy. And that was rare. So, the reason for the call? My dad was at home when the doorbell rang and standing there, big as life, was my eighteen-year-old daughter Emily, who I hadn't seen or spoken to in a great many years. She and her mother, Melita, were still living in Seattle, but until she reached legal age, her mom refused to let Emily have anything to do with her birth father. Now she was in L.A. and I wasn't. But we spoke, for the first time in forever, and made plans to get together as soon as the tour was over. I was floating. I was on cloud nine. My life had come full circle. I was together again with my daughter and we've never been out of touch since. There was a lot of catching up to do, and I suspect that once she reads this book, there will be more talks to come. What can I say? Honesty has its price.

A few months earlier though, on March 4, 1987, there had been other family news of a less joyous nature. My mother checked into the Kaiser Permanente hospital in downtown Los Angeles for a back operation, contracted some bizarre infection, and never came out of her anesthesia. I had never known loss like that in my life. The only music I could listen to was *White Winds* by Andreas Vollenweider: new age massage-parlor music. Anything else made me physically ill. I had never heard him before that and I've never listened to him since.

Our family was devastated. My brother, Al, left his home in Walla Walla, Washington, where he had gone to escape the nightmare of Los Angeles, to help my father get through the hard times. He moved into the house my mother and father had shared and he lives there still. Life Interrupted. The only time I saw my father smile after my mom's death was upon the birth of my daughter Alexandra on April 30, 1989. She was born at Valley Presbyterian Hospital and her birth changed my life forever. The *new* Howard was going to be faithful to his wife, Susan. He would be monogamous, even if it killed him. There would never be another Emily Situation. I would do everything I could to protect Alex from the drugs and the weirdos and the infidelities that seemed to accompany my chosen profession.

◆ ◆ ◆

In 1989, the hip-hop group De La Soul released an album called *Three Feet High and Rising*, which yielded quite a few R&B hits. As was the custom, famous hit songs of the past were sampled and reworked and released as brand-new product. It was thought to be totally kosher in the record business. That is, until the Turtles came along.

De La Soul had taken our master recording of "You Showed Me" and added new lyrics and an additional rhythm track. And had a huge hit. Somehow, it didn't seem right to us, nor did it sound like a good deal to our lawyer, Martin Cohen. We sued, and it became a famous legal case. No one who had ever been sampled had had the balls to say anything about it, lest they look like they wanted to destroy the new urban music that was coming from the streets. But we didn't care. We had nothing to lose. We were suddenly those fat white guys who were trying to screw rap artists. Many negative articles were written about our bad attitudes in soul publications. But right is right.

We won. And since that famous case, anyone who is sampled for another recording gets paid for it. You can thank us now or send us a check later, but we set the new standard. We've been sampled dozens of times since that court decision and get paid for each use. It's only fair. We were only pointing out the obvious. If you hear yourself on the radio, somebody should be paying you. You're welcome.

❖ ❖ ❖

In the studio with Paul Shaffer, who was producing the new Darlene Love album; we sang with Jefferson Airplane on their reunion album (we'd done Paul Kantner's solo album several years earlier); Roy Thomas Baker enlisted us to sing with Ozzy Osbourne on three songs for *No More Tears*; we contributed to a great album produced by friend Hal Willner for an Irish pop star named Gavin Friday. I loved the session work. I loved our constant weekend working. I loved my daughter. I loved my life. I bought a new Beemer.

Back in L.A., we were now part of the Tim Powers/K. W. Jeter/James Blaylock group of sci-fi and fantasy authors that had come into our lives through Joe's publishing career. We spent many nights in Orange County being regaled with stories of Philip K. Dick, of whom these gents were disciples. We did concerts almost every weekend and lived our lives between shows. Sean Connery asked me about my car at the video store.

On October 6, 1989, we signed a contract to go to New York City for a trial run doing daily radio on the biggest classic rock station in

America, K-Rock. I should have sold my car to Sean Connery. We flew to the city on November 8, had station meetings on the 10th, and met the entire staff. We said hello on Meg Griffin's show and cut promos with Bill Kates and genius voice artist Billy West. The next morning, we did *The Howard Stern Show* and said hello to Tony Pigg's audience. It was a fantastic station with brilliant and nationally known personalities and we were going to get a full week of shows to audition for a permanent afternoon slot.

The week was incredible, largely due to our brilliant producer, Robert Benjamin. Alice phoned in from Amsterdam, Richard Lewis did twenty dynamite minutes of original angst. Alvin Lee came in, as did Graham Nash. We talked to Frank Zappa for an astonishing length of time about everything, and Penn Jillette came in for an hour of chat and oldies. He was amazing and we partied into the night. Stern loved our show and that was all we needed. His gigantic audience had gotten the seal of approval from their leader. Flo and Eddie were good guys who did great radio. And the K-Rock executives took notice.

On December 7, we were scheduled to play two shows in the atrium of the World Trade Center. The first show, at 12:30, went off flawlessly. Then, as we were changing clothes for the second set, a fire broke out on the seventh floor of one of the towers and the second show was canceled. That night, we sat in with the judges of the Miller Lite Comedy Competition and felt very much like New Yorkers.

Needless to say, it was a star-studded year for our holiday shows at the Bottom Line. Comics Chris Rush and Bill Hicks opened for us. Joey Ramone was there, as was Kathleen Turner: both great rockers. I played the weekend and had a few days off to hang with Penn and Tony Visconti, who was now married to May Pang, whom I had known from John Lennon's lost Hollywood years. We signed contracts on January 4, 1990. I called Heidi Berger, my new Realtor friend, and rented a little apartment on East Fifty-Fifth Street, near the station, and flew back to L.A. on the 7th.

❖ ❖ ❖

We only had a couple of weeks. I packed what I could and we actually had a gig at a private Mardi Gras party in New Orleans the day before we flew into New York for the first time as natives. Richard Lewis was on our first show, and already there was trouble in paradise as Stern warned us, on the air, that Richard was *his* guest: Make no bones about it. He didn't care if we had grown up with the man, there was a certain guest etiquette that must be obeyed. At K-Rock, you played by Stern's rules or you didn't play. Still, every time he mentioned our little show on his huge, syndicated program, our audience grew. Also, the management knew that we were Rock Personalities and brought a certain street cred to them that they didn't have with any of their other personalities. On our very first afternoon, we finished at 6 P.M., jumped into a waiting limo, and were driven to interview Aerosmith. They had turned down interviews with every other radio station in town but said yes to K-Rock when Steven and Joe heard that Mark and I would be doing the story.

And so it continued. We did comedy bits with Kates and West, had multiple guest stars daily, hosted local shows, drank at the Friars Club. On Monday nights, I would go solo to this bar called Michael's Pub to see my idol, Woody Allen, play clarinet with his Dixieland band. Sue and Alex arrived on February 8 for a visit. Both Mark and I went on Nutrisystem diets on the air and lost a ton of weight. We broadcast live from the Lone Star Cafe with Jimmy Vivino putting our last-minute bands together and represented our borough in the comedy competitions with our pick, a young kid who sounded like Kermit the Frog, named Ray Romano. He won, by the way.

I went home for the weekend in March. Most other weekends were spent doing shows with our band. Back on the air, we spun the platters and talked to Bowie, Keith Richards, Harry Nilsson, and so many others I can't even remember. Michael McKean was a frequent visitor to my strange little former-cathouse apartment—not for the mirrored purple ambiance, but for the forbidden weed that he wasn't allowed to possess. We all have our secrets.

In April, the Arbitron ratings came out and our show won for its time slot and the station went up more than two points. We were heroes. I celebrated with Dom and weed, a Comedy Channel interview with Allan Havey, and a late movie in Times Square with Penn and Eddie Gorodetsky.

In May, after our Romano experience and Cinco de Mayo at the Lone Star, station manager Mark Chernoff finally gave us our own office. That was a big deal. Only Howard Stern had his own office at K-Rock. And now us!

We were officially renewed on May 24, flew into L.A. for the weekend, recorded interviews for Rhino's *Happy Together* documentary, and had a birthday party for Alex with all of her friends and all of Susan's drinking buddies. The "trends" came out in June and showed that our little show had gone from a 1.9 when we started to over a 3, whatever that means. Everyone was happy. On the 22nd, we took a cab out to Yankee Stadium where our competition, WNEW-FM, was hosting a sold-out Billy Joel concert. Absolutely no interviews were being given, but Billy loved us and we went on air with a great, long, and amazing conversation. NEW was pissed. But we had pulled off an amazing coup and no one else could have done it. We brought friendship to New York radio. By August, our ratings had climbed to a 3.6 and we were officially beating out our competition, Scott Muni, a legend at WNEW.

❖ ❖ ❖

It was time for a new apartment and a new way of thinking. I had a new family and wanted to be with them. Mark had chosen to remain a solitary man, commuting when he could to his wife and kids in L.A., and holding court in an amazing bachelor pad downtown and living the single life. On September 10, I found the apartment of my dreams, on the twenty-eighth floor of RiverTower, at East 54th Street between First Avenue and Sutton Place, near the United Nations. The place featured walls of glass with a wraparound view of the East River and the city skyline. I finally had my Manhattan tower. I moved in on September 28 with little furniture, but I had my weed and I had my city.

We went out to L.A. to do a week of shows from Universal City, where we interviewed hundreds of celebrity walk-throughs on this huge radio junket. Paul McCartney was there and we reminisced as Andy tried to play Beatles songs on his tiny Casio.

Sue and Alex arrived in New York City on November 14 and we rented out our Studio City home to, of all people, the actor Chris Elliott, who was doing a series called *Get a Life!* and needed a rental for his dad, the genius Bob Elliott of Bob and Ray fame. Bob was my childhood comedy hero. I would have let him stay there for nothing.

It snowed at Christmas and I loved it. We did our usual Bottom Line shows, but we finally felt like locals. Howard Stern now considered us buddies and we attended his elaborate birthday party on January 10. Uh-oh. Familiarly breeds contempt, my mother used to say. When they stop talking about you, it's trouble. That's what I say.

THIRTY-FOUR

Happy Together

Flo and Eddie give great radio. My routine was to leave RiverTower about noon to walk to the station for show prep. Then, after briefly checking things over, I would frequently stroll around the corner for an amazing sandwich and an Irish coffee or two. That gave me time to smoke a joint in Central Park before our 2 P.M. broadcast. On special days, we would pretape an interview with, say, George Carlin or do television, such as *The Joan Rivers Show* or Geraldo Rivera. In March 1991, Mark Chernoff announced to the staff that K-Rock was now the number one classic rock station in America.

On April 19, Mark's birthday, we brought Todd Rundgren into the studio with his keyboard and guitar and he performed an hour of brilliance. The phones lit up like a Christmas tree. It was fantastic. Afterward, Chernoff called us into his office—we guessed to congratulate us. Instead, he went on a rampage. We were K-Rock. We were supposed to play *more music*! That's what our slogan said. But, during that hour, WNEW had played a dozen records and we had played three—all Todd's. Yes, Chernoff thought that it was great radio, but that didn't neutralize the station's mission, which was to play more music. Suddenly, we found ourselves limited to two and a half minutes to talk or do bits between songs, all guests would need to be approved, and we were to stick to the playlist from now on. Our show was about to sound just like everybody else's. They were paying us over a half million dollars a year to babysit CDs. It was the beginning of the end. Already.

When CBS bought the station during the summer, during which we had spent every weekend doing concerts, they made sweeping changes, the first of which was to let us go. We were costing the network more than five times the salary of any other DJs, and Stern was about to make a huge syndication deal that would place him in stations all over the country. We were replaced in our drive-time slot by veteran jock Pete Fornatale. On September 13, we were officially unemployed.

❖ ❖ ❖

Susan, Alex, and I moved back into our Studio City home after *Get a Life* was canceled, and it was like we had never left. Wendt was still there, we built a childproof fence around the black-bottomed pool, my bad back was returned to the hands of my favorite chiropractor, and concerts happened every weekend.

But . . . we had played a show for KOOL radio at Denver's Mile High Stadium back in May 1988, and the female disc jockey who had introduced us was fabulous. She was blond and glorious and clad in a pink leather dress. She had the unlikely name of Michelle Dibble. Again, the voice went off in the back of my brain—"I WILL HAVE HER!" But since I was married and therefore monogamous, we began—for the time being—a phone friendship that continued for years. Every time I was in Denver, I would see her for platonic chats and infinite wisdom. When she moved to St. Louis to do morning radio there, we kept up our telephone friendship. During my bad times with Susan, she was literally the only one I could talk to. And I did. For hours on end. Before cell phones, it was costly therapy.

Mark was having an equally difficult time adjusting to his daddy and husband role in the Canyon. His kids were grown-ups now, and he really hadn't been an authority figure in their lives for a couple of years. Dinners around the table weren't the same anymore. During almost each and every warm California afternoon, Susan would get together with Mark's wife Pat and their friends around one of our swimming pools for girl talk and gallons of wine.

When I had first encountered Susan, I had thought nothing of her proclivities toward drunkenness, probably because I was largely drunk myself, or something like it. But now that I had dispatched with the worst of my habits, Sue's daily rituals were becoming beyond annoying. She would pass out nightly after some sort of screaming insanity. This had begun long before my move to New York, but I had thought her new location would remove some of her temptations. Instead, in Manhattan, she had been able to actually order liquor up to the apartment, so she never had to leave the house to get her buzz on. Now, in L.A., it was getting to be intervention time. Today, twenty years later, she counsels individuals with the same affliction.

Meanwhile, I was making up for lost time by spending weekends with my father and brother, both still reeling from the effects of my mother's death, and neither one of them ready to move on. Sid, in particular, wasn't doing so well. Sally's belongings were exactly where she had left them before checking into the hospital, although years had passed. It was starting to look like Baby Jane lived in Westchester.

Sue got a job on Ventura Boulevard selling pricey kids furniture at a store called Bellini and we spent another familiar Thanksgiving with the Powers and the Blaylocks in Orange County. On December 26, we flew back to New York to rehearse for the Bottom Line.

Early in '92, Emily flew down for a visit and it felt like we were such a family. Two kids and my white picket fence. But there really weren't that many concerts that year, just enough to keep us going, and it started to seem like L.A. was closing in around us. Plus, my poor dad never pulled out of his tailspin following my mother's death and, despite my brother's constant attention, was losing ground quickly. He needed to go into a nursing home near me in North Hollywood. I visited frequently, but it was a losing battle.

Mark and I flew to New York in March to sing on the new Ramones album, *Mondo Bizarro*. A couple of the guys filtered in and out, but it was 100 percent Joey's show and I loved that guy. He loved us too and was thrilled to have an element of California on the record. We were part of Joey's original vision as he wrote these songs, and it was an honor to be in the same studio with the guy.

❖ ❖ ❖

One afternoon that spring, Alex and I walked the block and a half to the post office. She clutched me tightly at the sight of a toothless, raggedy bum begging for change at the doorway. The guy actually grabbed me by the arm.

"Howard?"

I was scared. It was my old drummer, John Breadeau, who had played with our opening act in the early Zappa days. His sign read WILL WORK FOR FOOD. We spoke for a while as Alex huddled next to me.

More than ever I needed to get out of there. The three of us took a vacation in Maui at the end of April while the Rodney King trial was taking place in L.A.—the whole city was scared while waiting for the verdict, and it felt good to not be there. I called my Realtor from the hotel and told her to put up a FOR SALE sign on our Studio City lawn. I had had enough. I needed fresh air. I knew where I needed to be: that wonderful stretch of Pacific Coast between L.A. and the Canadian border where the waves crashed against the rocky shoreline and honest people led simpler lives than mine. I started subscribing to *Oregon Coast* magazine and making mental notes.

Pat Volman called to say that Flo was not too thrilled about my moving from L.A. to anywhere—or my escalating pot use. All of a sudden, she was Carrie Nation. Tough shit.

Sue, Alex, and I took a trip to Oregon in the rented car and started driving. The first place we went was a tiny fishing and lumber village just north of the California border called Brookings. From there, we headed north, visiting each and every hamlet along the way. But we couldn't get Brookings out of our heads. It was idyllic. It was perfect. We started shopping for houses. We found one that was fantastic, put in a bid, and waited.

On April 28, the SOLD sign went up in front of our house in Studio City. We had a three-month escrow, so I wasn't panicky. The Brookings house had a lot of restrictions and regulations, and it wasn't the easiest home for which I've ever had to qualify. It was almost like this community didn't particularly take a likin' to us here city folk.

Though it took forever, on June 27, we said farewell to California, packed up my little Nissan Maxima, and drove to our new lives in Oregon. The house was spectacular. It stood by itself on a cliff overlooking the Pacific. It was built like a ship to weather the storms that frequently and dramatically pummeled the coastline. There was a trail down to our own cove where otters and sea lions played. At sunset, I'd pop a Rogue Ale, roll a fatty, and stand on my deck like DiCaprio aboard the Titanic. King of the world, man.

Traveling was impossible, however. That was the biggest drawback. The little Crescent City airport twenty-six miles south only had a few flights each day and was fogged in more often than not, so I had to drive to Eureka, California, about two and a half hours away, to board a commuter flight to San Francisco and fly from there to wherever we were booked. Lots of time to think on those drives. And lots of drives. Too many.

❖ ❖ ❖

Summer was busier than anticipated, and my father passed on August 5, 1992, giving me little time to grieve. This was different than my mother's death, of course, since we had seen it coming and his passing ended his suffering, at least. I had a show in Hartford, Connecticut, the next day. I was numb.

In December, Mark and I went on the radio with Tony Pigg to plug the year-end Bottom Line shows and it felt strange returning to K-Rock as guests. A little bitterness on my end, but by now they had become distressingly corporate and were contemplating a format change. That's what you get when you're penny-wise and pound-foolish.

Time seemed to be moving more quickly in the '90s. On October 16, 1993, Emily got married and the three of us flew up to Seattle, where Alex was the flower girl and I saw my first wife, Melita, for the first time in twenty years. It was slightly surreal, but I knew that Emily would make this marriage work despite all of her childhood influences.

Mark moved out of his Laurel Canyon home and filed for divorce after twenty-eight years of marriage. He moved in with a health food chick and cooked veggie burgers in her Burbank store. She didn't last very long. He also enrolled in community college with an eye on Loyola Marymount in Westchester for his eventual degree. He met his second wife there, too. She graduated with him. She was twenty-four when they got married and, after a brief stint in a home not more than a mile from our high school, they moved to Nashville, where Mark teaches music business at Belmont University when we're not doing shows.

Meanwhile, the arguments with Susan were loud and frequent, and she often just passed out wherever she happened to be. I joined the Elks

Club to fit in with our neighbors in the sleepy little burg we now called home. And I began writing. I did two short stories for different anthologies of horror and they were both published. One book is called *Phantoms of the Night* and the other is called *Forbidden Acts*. I had purchased on old Jeep that I traded for a new giant Lexus 450 and pretended that everything was perfect. But it wasn't.

Everything exploded on Thanksgiving of 1994 when Emily and her husband, Lyle Rothenberg, came to visit. I was already living downstairs in the guest room, but we were trying to act like a family until Susan's wine kicked in. The screaming never stopped. The kids left our house to stay in some motel, *any* motel. And I left too. I spent the next month house-sitting at a fabulous waterfront mansion before I kissed Alex goodbye on Christmas Eve.

Michelle Dibble met me at the airport in Medford, Oregon. I had cried during the entire drive from Brookings. We made the trip across America in the Lexus during hellacious winter storms and got to St. Louis by January 2, 1995. After living briefly in two rental places, we finally bought an amazing and gigantic home in the Clarkson Valley subdivision of Chesterfield, Missouri, just west of the city. I lived in the Midwest for almost seven years, but when Clear Channel bought Y98, the station where Michelle did her show, the entire staff was replaced by interns who didn't demand the six figures formerly paid to air personalities. They got paid 20k a year and prayed for airtime. Time to go.

We threw a dart at a map of the U.S. and decided to move to Seattle; close to both of my kids and somewhere I wouldn't have to shovel snow. We found a lovely home in Bellevue that sits on a lake and backs up to a park.

❖ ❖ ❖

By late 1992, Frank Zappa's cancer was in the news. It's not like I was the first one to know. He was losing weight and speaking hoarsely but the smile never left his face and the danger never left his eyes. Some time after that, he summoned Mark and me up to the purple house in the Canyon and greeted both of us with huge hugs. His wife, Gail, was there and she made us coffee. We talked about the Montreux fire, what it felt like to be onstage together, what he thought he was going to miss the most. It was difficult not to cry, but the man wouldn't have stood for it.

We watched and listened to hours of concert and road recordings that never got released, talked about that *Billy the Mountain* movie that never got made; tons of private jokes punctuated by Frank's dry cough. He drank his black coffee from his thermos mug, as always, chain-smoked his Winstons, as always, and when it was time for lunch, it was his beloved anchovy pizza. Mark and I must have given each other the rolling eye, 'cause Frank caught the look and said, "What? I'm dying here! I'm certainly not going to give up the things that I love *now*!"

Point well taken. It was incredibly sad when he passed away on December 4, 1993, sadder than my own father's death had been. Frank *was* my father figure, and that afternoon I got the closure with Zappa that I had never gotten from my own father, and a validation that I had never received either.

We hugged goodbye. We didn't say it, but it was understood. We would never see each other again.

When Bolan died, I had gone into shock. I had been ready for Frank's death, but it left the same kind of hole in my heart.

The following year I experienced another profound loss. About two months before his death in 1994, Harry Nilsson called me up. This on its own wasn't unusual. We spoke often. Harry knew what his prognosis was and, much like Frank, had chosen to ignore it. He was chain-smoking and eating greasy junk food, same as ever. He picked me up at Andy Cahan's little studio where he was recording the last songs he had written in the hopes that his music would live on. He needn't have worried: Harry is a legend. He wore only his famous blue bathrobe—he never got dressed anymore. Harry had given up.

And we drove. That's all. We drove into the valley, past the shopping centers and the record stores. He needed to stop at In-N-Out Burger and I sure didn't challenge him. The entire time, we listened to Harry's old music. The hits. The masterpieces.

When "The Puppy Song" played, Nilsson's eyes filled with tears. "Dreams are only made of wishes and a wish is just a dream you hope will come true."

"I was a pretty good singer once, wasn't I?"

"You're the best there ever was." I told him, meaning every word. I was tearing up too.

"He took it from me. He stole my voice and I never got it back!"

The "he" that Harry referred to was John Lennon, who famously produced the *Pussy Cats* album for Nilsson in 1974. Harry spoke of the primal screaming contests that John would coerce him into.

"I can scream louder and longer than you!" and John could. But, sweet, gentle Harry couldn't do it. He tried. The competition was fierce, and by the time Lennon returned to London, abandoning May Pang and the lost California years, it was too late; the damage had been done. Harry's vocal cords were abraded beyond repair and the new stuff was scratchy and desperate. Harry cried.

"Once I was a king, Howard. Now look at me. I'm just waiting to die." There was nothing that I could say. He dropped me back at my car and went off into the sunset.

Literally. When Harry ended, that's the day that the music kind of died for me. I started looking at concerts differently. I stopped caring so much about the little things. I began to trust myself more to the flow of the universe. I stopped obsessing and spending sleepless nights on un-solvable problems. I stopped thinking, consciously, about 38 percent of the time. I lost weight and stopped eating any food that was white.

I don't want to die like Harry. No one was there at the end, not in his perception.

He might have pushed them away himself, but Harry died alone.

❖ ❖ ❖

As a result of my conscious decisions, my life changed in many positive ways. Sometime in the '90s, Mark and I were working at the Miss Universe offices and had a lot of free time on our hands. And for us, free time always meant trouble. We were both still heavily into coke, and one after-noon we both found ourselves taking a well-deserved drug break in the lavatory. This drug stuff had now been going on for a great many years, and although we were still lucid and productive, the seductive drug was beginning to take its toll. Both of us were sniffling badly. Like cokeheads do in the movies. And then I started getting a nosebleed. It was funny for a minute, and then, under the sobering fluorescent overhead lights of that scuzzy bathroom, it suddenly wasn't anymore. The smiles left our faces at the same moment.

"What do you think?" I asked.

"Let's do it!" Mark answered, and we each took the large vials out of our pockets and flushed the provocative white powder down the drain.

"No going back!" I reiterated.

"No going back!" came the reply.

And neither of us ever did. Not for one second. Never again. We saved our lives that day.

And by the way, the Abbot drug company stopped making Placidyl in 1999 and I spent a couple of really interesting weeks adjusting to the final rumblings of Dr. Lax's Curse.

❖ ❖ ❖

And I'm still busy in the twenty-first century. I made a solo album in 2003 at Billy Bob Thornton's house in Beverly Hills. It's called *Dust Bunnies* and you can get it on iTunes. I wrote a movie about the draft board and our trip to London. Rhino produced it and I went to L.A. to film *My Dinner with Jimi*, which played festivals and won awards. It's on Netflix if you care to experience it. And I decided to write a book, which you, dear reader, have rewarded me for doing.

In 2006, a New York–based company called Flower Power Concerts put on a national show called Hippiefest and we went out on the road for our first bus tour in forty years. Still hating tour buses, Mark and I followed behind in an Escalade and played shows with our friends from the '60s all over America.

After a couple of years of Hippiefest, the promoters decided to relaunch the Happy Together tour in 2009. That same year, "Happy Together" was predominantly featured in *The Simpsons Movie* and Mark and I were flown into New York to sing with our old pals U2 at Carnegie Hall. The summer tours continue and life looks sweet as the so-called golden years approach.

❖ ❖ ❖

Michelle and I got married on March 24, 2005, and have been together eighteen years in all as of this writing. Alex graduated from the Evergreen State College in 2011 and moved to—where else?—Manhattan, where she has a normal boyfriend and a badass band. Emily, Lyle, and my grandson, Max, moved to Post Falls, Idaho, just across the state, where Em continues her career at Coca-Cola. Max is fourteen as of this writing. Melita made the move with her and lives six houses away. Go figure.

And I'm in hog heaven with my kitties, Leeloo and Dubdie, and my goldendoodle, Poochifer, and seventeen miles of hiking trails behind my house. I still hang with former Mother of Invention Jeff Simmons, who still lives here. We're actually working on an album together as I finish writing this book. I love my wife and I love being in a place where my beloved weed is legal. For medicinal purposes only, you understand. I have a pot card. I'm living the dream.

I'm not sure how much longer I can do this entertainment shit. Everybody tells me that I'll never quit 'cause show business is in my blood. They're probably right, but you already know my fears about giving it up in some sleazy hotel room. When it's all over and the piper plays "Happy Together" one last time, I want to kiss my wife, hug my dog, take a giant toke, and smile my way though the obsidian void.

Now, *that* was a life!

Index